WEB 2.0 AND SOCIAL NETWORKING

Weaver Birds in Information Superhighway

WEB 2.0 AND SOCIAL NETWORKING

Weaver Birds in Information Superhighway

Shiva Sukula

Ess Ess Publications
New Delhi

Web 2.0 and Social Networking

Weaver Birds in Information Superhighway

ISBN: 978-81-7000-677-0

Rs.1075/-

First Published 2012

Published by:
Ess Ess Publications
4831/24, Ansari Road,
Darya Ganj,
New Delhi-110 002.
INDIA
Phones: 23260807, 41563444
Fax: 41563334
E-mail: info@essessreference.com
www.essessreference.com

Cover Design by *Patch Creative Unit*

Printed and bound in India at Salasar Imaging Systems.

CONTENTS

INDIAN INSTITUTE OF TECHNOLOGY, DELHI

Prof. H.C.Gupta
Professor of Physics
IIT Delhi 110 016 INDIA
email:hcgupta@physics.iitd.ernet.in
Phone :91-11-26591345
FAX :91-11-26581114

December 1,2011

FOREWORD

Dr. Shiva Shukla has made a nice timely attempt to write a book entitled "Web 2.0 and Social Networking: Weaver birds in Information Superhighway". The attempt is an ideal balance between libraries and social networking tools in the web. Social networking plays an important role in our lives and hence the book will prove extremely useful to the readers from the discipline of computer science, information technology, software engineering, bloggers and twitters.

The emphasis of the book has been on aspects of Web 2.0, Library 2.0 and Enterprise 2.0. As substantial progress has been made in systematizing and clarifying the conceptual aspects of web of science, there has been a tendency to introduce increasing amounts of this at the library level. The chapters on "Social networking tools and libraries", "Instant messaging and services in library", and "Library 2.0" reflect the flavour of the subject. The discussion also includes details of blog and blogging. In the final analysis, the book is very interesting to the people who interact through web.

H.C.Gupta

PREFACE

In addition to technical skills and access to information technologies, in the knowledge society, it is becoming increasingly important for people to have diversified and supportive social connections. One may not necessarily be aware of their existence, or even have direct access to them. Resources and opportunities may be available, in those cases, knowing people from different backgrounds, grades of expertise, and social levels turn out to be essential. Throughout our lives, we tend to form different kinds of relationships with different people. With people like us, our greatest buddies and closer relatives, we establish strong ties that reinforce our beliefs and provide us with the support required to endure life's challenges. The Literature reflects that it is through them that we become aware of new opportunities and broaden our horizons.

The principles behind web services are stunningly simple, and are nothing new in the world of distributed computing and the Internet. The web service provider defines a format for requests for its service and the response the service will generate, a computer makes a request for the web services across the network and the web service performs some action, and sends the response back. Some studies even demonstrate that, in many ways, the Social aspect of the Computer is more important than the impressive technologies that are available there. With the concept of Social networking on the platform of Web 2.0, the community is powered and it can find people of similar interest and promote themselves as well. More or less, every person is somehow, encouraged to use the Social Web and create a resource for themselves and their community. From Facebook to MySpace, YouTube to Second Life, social software is reshaping the world we live in.

The effect of social networking and web 2.0 technologies has been inevitable in consumer market. Today's social experience is disjointed due to individualistic identities in myriad social networks. A simple set of technologies is required for transforming marketing, eCommerce, CRM, and advertising. The Web will evolve step by step from separate social sites into a shared social experience. Socially connected consumers will strengthen communities and shift power away from brands. Such technologies have triggered changes in a person's social and web contexts. The Social Web has initiated the creation of Social Relationships by connecting people to others and share. Further it brought the Social Functionality. This kind of functionality converted the Social networks into some kind of operating system. Social Colonization came into existence as every experience could be social. The Social Context could hardly resist making personalized and accurate content. The social networking and web 2.0 let the communities define future products and services.

1

WEB 2.0 AND RECENT DEVELOPMENTS

WHAT IS WEB 2.0?

Web 2.0 is a category of new Internet tools and technologies created around the idea that the people who consume media, access the Internet, people use the Web shouldn't passively absorb what's available; rather, (i) they should be active contributors, (ii) helping customize media and technology for their own purposes, as well as those of their communities. In utmost sense, Web 2.0 is a stream of events, people and connections. Web 2.0 is the beginning of a new era in technology. It isn't just the latest set of toys for tech-geeks. This is a set of technologies which promises:

- *to help nonprofits operate more efficiently,*
- *to generate more funding, and*
- *to affect more lives.*

These new tools include:

- *blogs,*
- *social networking applications,*
- *RSS,*
- *social networking tools, and*

- *wikis.*

One of the most exciting areas today is that of Web 2.0. It has to do with a more engaging and personal interactive web.

APPLICATIONS OF WEB 2.0:

Applications are broken down into the following categories:

- *Academic*
- *Audio*
- *Bookmarks*
- *Calendar*
- *Collaboration*
- *Database*
- *Desktop*
- *Documents*
- *Drawing*
- *Feed Reader*
- *File Manager*
- *Forms*
- *Lists*
- *Miscellaneous*
- *News*
- *Organizer*
- *Photos*
- *Polls*
- *Presentation*
- *Project*
- *Spreadsheet*
- *Video*
- *Weblog*

- *Wiki*
- *Word Processor.*

TRANSFORMING INTO WEB 2.0

Web 2.0 offerings weren't seen popping up years ago. The older attributes were significant, but enough to produce viable Web 2.0 products. It has two types of attributes:

(i) Foundation Attributes : Some of the attributes associated with Web 2.0 were introduced and commercialized as early as the mid 1990s. These could be called as Foundation Attributes.

(ii) Experience Attributes : The attributes can be differentiated as significant but not sufficient attributes from the more recent Experience Attributes. Those that create the kind of value that's caused the recent excitement over Web 2.0, are called Experience Attributes. When Experience Attributes are combined with Foundation Attributes for a Web 2.0 offering, the result can be a valuable new service with a fast-growth business model. The Experience attributes captured concisely the capabilities of Web 2.0. Rather than returning to the underlying functional features of Web 2.0 (e.g., tagging, RSS), or overextending into the business impacts (e.g., mash-up ecologies), these attributes outline the capabilities of Web 2.0 independent of specific business concepts. Together, they represent the aspects of Web 2.0 success that user can apply in multiple market spaces.

UNDERSTANDING FOUNDATION ATTRIBUTES

Amazon was taking advantage of the Long Tail before we even had a name for the concept that has since become widespread. Ebay capitalized on the network effect to create a many-to-many marketplace. Early blogs were already embracing the value created from individual users. These attributes — user-contributed value, the Long Tail, and network effect — are all Foundation Attributes of Web 2.0 services. They're a part of many Web-based offerings, including some that we don't call Web 2.0:

- *User-Contributed Value : Users make substantive contributions to enhance the overall value of a service.*
- *The Long Tail : Beating the sales of one or two best-seller products by using the Internet to sell a cumulatively greater amount of the products that have low demand or low sales.*
- *Network Effect : For users, the value of the network substantially increases with the addition of each new user.*

All of these attributes are significant parts of the Web 2.0 economic model, but aren't sufficient to create the new value of Web 2.0 on their own. They enable Web 2.0 offerings to generate and maximize value from many sources, no matter how small they may be.

UNDERSTANDING EXPERIENCE ATTRIBUTES

Flickr, Google Maps, and Wikipedia are all unique services that were undeliverable before Web 2.0. These services use Experience Attributes to generate value. Foundation Attributes then distribute that value across the network and down the Long Tail. Experience Attributes include:

- *Decentralization : Users experience services on their terms, not those of a centralized authority, such as a corporation.*
- *Co-creation : Users participate in the creation and delivery of the primary value of a service.*
- *Remixability : Experiences are created and tailored to user needs by integrating the capabilities of multiple services and organizations.*
- *Emergent Systems : Cumulative actions at the lowest levels of the system drive the form and value of the*

overall system. Users derive value not only from the service itself, but also the overall shape that a service inherits from user behaviors.

These services have pioneered new value streams that can output new types of offerings, harness new efficiencies, and produce higher levels of continuous innovation. Experience Attributes make Web 2.0 offerings fierce competitors in their respective marketplaces.

HOW WEB 2.0 EVOLVED!

The current status has not arrived in a single day

It can be explained in the following sections:

1. The beginning (structured experience): In the initial ten years, a wide range of experiences online, from highly structured to nearly formless were seen. Websites, like blogs, homepages, marketing and communication sites, the big content providers (in one form or another), and search engines were structured experiences. Their form and content are determined mainly by their designers and creators.

2. Moving on to Share (semi-structured experience): Rich, desktop-like applications have migrated to the Web, due to Ajax, Flex, Flash, Laszlo, and whatever else comes along. These have been traditional desktop applications like word processing, spreadsheets, and email. But the more interesting will be Internet-native, those built to take advantage of the strengths of the Internet: collective actions and data, social communities across wide distances, aggregation of many sources of data, near real-time access to timely data (news etc.), and easy publishing of content from one to many (blogs etc.). These experiences are semi-structured.

3. The intermingled finally (unstructured experience): The unstructured experiences are a glut of new services, many of which won't have Websites to visit at all. Loose collections of application parts, content, and data that don't exist anywhere really, yet can be located, used, reused, fixed, and remixed. The content searched for and used might reside on an individual computer, a mobile phone, even traffic sensors along a remote highway. But user probably won't need to know where these loose bits live; the tools will know. These unstructured bits won't be useful without the tools and the knowledge necessary to make sense of them, sort of how an HTML file doesn't make much sense without a browser to view it. Indeed, many of them will be inaccessible or hidden if user don't have the right tools.

NEW TOOLS FOR A NEW(ER) WEB

Current whole toolset will need to adapt and change. Users will be more interested in doing things on the Web than in visiting places on the Web. As Ross Mayfield puts it, "the Web is increasingly less about places and other nouns, but verbs." The tools would be required to find, read, filter, use, mix, remix, and connect users to the Internet will have to be smarter and do a lot more work than the ones we have now. Visual design is moving away from its decentralized locations on websites. Indeed, design is becoming centralized in the tools and methods users use to view and interact with content. Firefox users can already use extensions like Adblock, and to change the look of the Web pages they visit. RSS readers let users customize how they want to view feeds from a variety of sources. This type of customization van be seen happening with bits of functionality as well as content in future.

He varied experiences of Web 2.0 will probably affect browsers most. The current browsers were designed for navigating through a hypertext content space. These are nearly useless for unstructured ones. The browser has not evolved all that much. The basic concept or vision has not changed. Web 2.0 requires new means of using (not just navigating) the Web to take advantage of the full continuum of experiences. It is essential that tools have good design practices baked into them. They will determine what we can do, how we can do it, and how it will feel. The experience with Web 2.0 will largely depend on how good these tools are, in much the same way the first ten years of the Web were shaped by the browsers they have been used to be viewed.

During 2004-2005, around the world many of internet users have never heard of blogs. The first thing to happen was disorientation, but normal eventually. It has taken time for users to acclimate to the semi-structured experiences available on the Web, and even longer to accept the unstructured experiences. Some of the metaphors — sites, bookmarks, pages, and so on were shed by which users were used to orient themselves on the Web. The little Web is growing up.

VARIOUS PLATFORMS/WEBSITES OF WEB 2.0

1. Academic

Chalksite: It's the quickest, simplest route to expanding the classroom onto the internet. Teachers, students and parents have a central point to access grading, assignments and messaging. Chalksite is a total web package designed just for teachers, giving user a personal website and tools user actually need without requiring an IT degree to use them.

elgg : Elgg is a learning environment based around choice, flexibility and openness: a Personal Learning Landscape that places individuals at the centre of their learning.

engrade : Engrade is a free online gradebook that allows teachers to manage their classes online as well as post grades, assignments, attendance, and upcoming homework online for students and parents to see. Engrade is free and easy to use.

SchoolTool: SchoolTool is a project to develop a common global school administration infrastructure that is freely available under an Open Source licence.

Schoopy: It is Classroom Organizer

Windows Live Academic: Windows Live Academic currently indexes content related to computer science, physics, electrical engineering, and related subject areas. Academic search enables user to search for peer reviewed journal articles contained in journal publisher portals and on the web in locations like citeseer.

wink: Wink is a Tutorial and Presentation creation software, primarily aimed at creating tutorials on how to use software (like a tutor for MS-Word/Excel etc). Using Wink user can capture screenshots, add explanations boxes, buttons, titles etc and generate a highly effective tutorial for the users.

2. *Audio*

Odeo : Odeo is a creative way to record and share audio and it's free.

3. Bookmarks

del.icio.us: del.icio.us is a collection of favorites for anyone and everyone else's. people use del.icio.us to keep links to the favorite articles, blogs, music, restaurant reviews, and more on del.icio.us and access them from any computer on the web; user can share favorites with friends, family, and colleagues; and discover new things.

Diigo: By combining social bookmarking, clippings, in situ annotation, tagging, full-text search of everything, easy sharing and interactions, Diigo provides a powerful personal tool and a rich social platform.

Simpy: Simpy is a social bookmarking service. With Simpy, user can save, tag and search the own bookmarks and notes or browse and search other users' links and tags. User can be open and share the links with others, or keep them private.

4. Calendar

30 Boxes: Eighty-Three Degrees, Inc. has released a public beta of their new social calendaring application, 30 Boxes.

Google Calendar: With Google Calendar, it's easy to keep track of all the life's important events such as birthdays, reunions, little league games, doctor's appointments.

kiko: Kiko brings user a great, dead simple calendar user can use right in the web browser.

5. Collaboration

Gabbly: User can chat about any content on the web by adding 'gabbly.com/' in front of any URL.

eSnips: eSnips is the one place where user can share thoughts, photos, files, stuff user find on the web and user control who user share it with and how.

My Web 2.0: My Web 2.0 is a new way to find, save, and share knowledge on the Web. My Web lets user: save favorite web content so user can easily re-find it; connect with others so user can selectively share the sites user save; and benefit from the selected content of a large community of My Web users.

6. Database

Lazybase: Lazybase allows designing, creating and sharing a database of whatever they like.

MyOwnDB: Myowndb is a web application with the goal to let user manage the data easily. User can view it as a database with which user get an interface to enter, modify, delete and search data once user has defined its structure.

7. Desktop (Webtop)

30 Boxes: It is based upon a calendar and it is also a webtop application making use of newer technologies to give it more of a desktop feel.

Netvibes: Netvibes is the personalized page, user can now modify everything: move modules, add new RSS/ ATOM feeds, change the parameters for each module, etc. The modifications are saved in real-time and user will find the page when user gets back on Netvibes.com.

Windows Live: Windows Live brings various items or facilities for example, the friends, the latest information, the e-mails, powerful search and the PC files.

8. Documents

goowy: When user log into goowy, the dashboard is the first view user see. The dashboard gives user a list of all of the applications inside of goowy as well as the most common commands for the applications such as mail, integrated instant messaging, file storage, calendar, minis, contacts and games.

Tagyu: Tagyu is a hosted service that automates the process of creating document metadata by discovering what keywords, tags, and categories are relevant for a document. Instead of relying on machine learning to understand what a document is about, Tagyu uses human intelligence. Tagyu harnesses the collective wisdom that is already present in the documents to categorize the other text.

ThinkFree Office Online: ThinkFree Online service uses Java technology to allow users to leverage the power of ThinkFree Office from any computer connected to the Internet. Users are able to access Write, Show, and Calc.

9. Drawing

ajaxSketch: It is great for diagramming, flow charts, free hand drawing, and more. With a similar look and feel to popular drawing programs, users don't need to learn a new interface. It is a completely web-based program based on Ajax programming techniques, with the quick response of conventional software.

Gliffy: It draws and shares diagrams on the web.

10. FeedReader

Google Reader: Google Reader helps user keep up with it all by organizing and managing all the content user is interested in. Instead of continuously checking the favorite sites for updates, user can let Google Reader do it for user.

NewsAlloy: News Alloy is a free service for discovering, reading, and sharing Internet news and information.

11. FileManager

Backpack : Users do collect the ideas, to-dos, notes, photos, and files online. They can set email and mobile reminders so users don't forget the little things.

Box.net : It is online file storage with space 1GB free.

DropSend: DropSend enables user to send files of up to 1GB.

openomy: Openomy is an online file system. User can store files on Openomy and access them from any computer. Openomy organizes files and users via tags as opposed to folders.

TotoExpress: TotoExpress is a web-based service that changes the way content producers are able to collaborate, share and deliver their work. It provides an efficient, easy to use, and secure method of sending and receiving large files from the clients via the internet.

12. Forms

formspring: It provides the easy way to build, host and process online forms.

13. Lists

iOutliner: iOutliner is a powerful way to manage the tasks, ideas, and projects in structured lists. It is simple to use and customizable to the way user work and best of all its completely free.

Ta-Da List: It is very simple, sharable to-do and other types of lists.

14. Miscellaneous

coComment: coComment is a service to simplify of one of the most painful and ineffective processes on the Web: blog commenting. coComment is free, and will help user keep track of the comments and conversations user and others are making on blogs.

dropcash: dropcash is a simple way to organize a fundraiser. Dropcash lets user set up a page so everyone can follow the progress as user near the goal.

Flock: It is a browser.

GahooYoogle: It facilitates searching Google and Yahoo at the same time.

Orangoo: This little application lets user spell correct from any system or computer that has Internet access.

SuprGlu: SuprGlu is a new way to gather all the content from services like del.icio.us, flickr, blogger, typepad, etc.

Webaroo: It helps searching the web when user is not connected.

Widgetbox: Widgetbox is a service of PostApp, Inc. it facilitates to assemble, share and integrate everything on the web desired by the user.

14. News

Dig : Digg is a technology news website that combines social bookmarking, blogging, RSS, and non-hierarchical editorial control. With digg, users submit stories for review, but rather than allow an editor to decide which stories go on the homepage, the users do.

Rojo: Rojo means "RSS with mojo." That's an ingredient for creating the best RSS feed reader on the web and so user can discover and read news and blogs as efficiently as possible.

tech.memeorandum: tech.memeorandum offers user a window into this new world of news, focusing on technology, particularly tech business news and innovations in computing and the Internet. It auto-generates a news summary every 5 minutes, drawing on experts and pundits, insiders and outsiders, media professionals and amateur bloggers.

Technorati : Technorati is the authority on what's going on in the world of weblogs.

15. Organizer

AirSet: AirSet puts user in control of the complicated life. User can manage family, work, and social group schedules and communications using a web browser or mobile phone.

Zoho Planner: Zoho Planner is an online organizer to plan and organize. User can create the own space on the web; organize himself by creating new tasks and marking completed. User can quickly post the thoughts as blogs, Interact with people.

16. Photos

Flickr : Flickr is almost certainly the best online photo management and sharing application in the world. It helps people make their photos available to the people who matter to them and enabling new ways of organizing photo

riya : Riya is more than photo search. It helps finding every photo of user on the web.

17. Polls

Zoho Polls: People can use Zoho Polls to narrow down the choices and get opinion from others.

18. Presentation

S5: S5 is a slide show format based entirely on XHTML, CSS, and JavaScript. With one file, user can run a complete slide show and have a printer-friendly version as well. The markup used for the slides is very simple, highly semantic, and completely accessible

SlideShare: User can upload the slides, share with a link, embed in a blog, discover interesting slideshows, tag, and comment and have fun.

Thumbstacks: It is a new site for making and sharing presentations on the web.

Vyew: Vyew is a free browser-based conferencing and always-on collaboration platform that provides instant visual communication without the need for client downloads or installations. It is limited to 20 participants.

Zoho Show : Zoho Show is an online tool to create, edit, publish, and show presentations. It's web-based. User needs only a browser (Firefox 1.0 + or IE 6.0+ or Mozilla) and internet connection.

19. Project

BasecampHQ : Basecamp is a unique project collaboration tool. Projects don't fail from a lack of charts, graphs, or reports; they fail from a lack of communication and collaboration. Basecamp makes it simple to communicate and collaborate on projects.

voo2do : It provides an advanced task and priority management for busy, ambitious individuals.

20. Spreadsheet

ajaxXLS viewer: ajaxXLS 0.5 viewer is a web-based viewer application with a look and feel similar to Microsoft Excel. With one click user can easily open any .xls file in just a few seconds. The interactivity and responsiveness provided by AJAX programming allows user to enjoy the power and utility of a spreadsheet.

Num Sum: It facilitates easy, sharable web spreadsheets.

Zoho Sheet : User can create, store, access and manage the spreadsheets online.

21. Video

eyespot : User can easily shoot, mix, and share the Video. It can be used to edit and combine the videos, music and photos online! User can share the video and mixes with the world for Free.

YouTube : YouTube was founded in February 2005, by early commerce pioneers of PayPal, YouTube is a consumer media company for people to watch and share original videos worldwide through a Web experience.

22. Weblog

TypePad : It is a powerful, hosted weblogging service.

WordPress : WordPress.com is an easy and powerful way to start blogging.

23. Wiki

JotSpot : JotSpot was founded in 2004 and it provides an application wiki.

PBwiki : PBwiki is the world's largest consumer wiki farm. Wikis are simple Web pages that let user collaborate with others.

stikipad: StikiPad is a hosted wiki solution and it gives user an easy way to organize the information and share information with others. It runs completely in the browser with no downloads and easy administration. It lets user take the StikiPad wherever user have access to the Internet.

24. Word Processor

ajaxWrite: The look, feel, and functionality of Microsoft Word is available in a completely web-based AJAX platform.

Writeboard: Writeboards are sharable, web-based text documents that let user save every edit, roll back to any version, and easily compare changes. Users can use Writeboard to write solo or collaborate with others.

Writely : It is a Web Word Processor

Zoho Writer: It is an online tool to create a document, edit in the way, and share.

WEB 2.0 TOOLS AND RESOURCES

E-Cover Creator : This eCover software makes creating 3D ebooks, software boxes, DVD's, and CD's amazingly simple and the best part is it's compatible with any graphics editor. This software application makes it "point and click easy" to create incredible eCovers.

Link Directory Submitter : Link Directory Submitter is the perfect solution for sending the sites to a multitude of pre-configured online directories. Link Directory Submitter comes with 2700+ link directories to submit to, more than half ranging from PR4 to PR7.

Automatic Blog Commenter : This application supports in getting Backlinks come from blog comments. With those blog comments, user can get links to his site and it's very useful for increasing his site position in Search Engines such as Google, Yahoo, Bing, etc. by doing so user can increase PR and site traffic.

Virtual Sales Bot : With the help of this application, users have complete control over the exit traffic without spending a fortune on programming costs and market testing. Virtual Sales Bot allows user to offer coupons, discounts, direct the visitors to question and answer pages, or even an affiliate site.

Power Effects : This application is more than animated GIFs, Flash, or Photoshop wizardry. User can create the own animated headlines, subheads, graphics by just "point and click" on the fly and get them to catch the instant attention of the website visitors.

Word To Web Page : WordToWebPage is an easy to use desktop application that allows user to convert any Microsoft Word document into a ready to upload webpage. It requires absolutely no programming experience.

Ultimate Exit Popup : This helps in getting traffic to the site. It makes sense then to take steps to turn as many visitors as possible into prospects.

WEB 3.0

Web 3.0 is a different way of building applications. Web 3.0 will ultimately be seen as applications which are pieced together. There are a number of characteristics: the applications are relatively small, the data is in the cloud, the applications can run on any device, PC or mobile phone, the applications are very fast and they're very customizable. Furthermore, the applications are distributed virally: literally by social networks, by email. You won't go to the store and purchase them. Web 3.0 delivers a very different application model than we've ever seen in computing.

Web 2.0 is well documented and talked about. The power of the Net reached a critical mass, with capabilities that can be done on a network level. We are also seeing richer devices and richer ways of interacting with the network, not only in hardware like game consoles and mobile devices, but also in the software layer. You don't have to be a computer scientist to create a program. We are seeing that manifest in Web 2.0 and 3.0 is a great extension of that, a true communal medium, the distinction between professional, semi-professional and consumers will get blurred, creating a network effect of business and applications. Web 3.0 makes the leap from "display only" to meaningful information by tagging information with descriptors like "mailing address." Further, it allows users to find relationships between tagged information using inference rules and data organizational tools called "ontologies" that provide logic and structure to the information embedded in web pages. As a result, machines can do a lot of the information grunt work currently required of humans. When it comes to a web search, for example, the semantic web makes a reasonable pass at collating, synthesizing, and cross-referencing the results for users. It does this by employing software agents that can locate and combine information from many sources to build meaningful information collages. Ultimately, the goal of Web 3.0 is, in a phrase, data integration. The semantic web understands this concept. It addresses the use of common definitions, inference rules, and ontologies that will turn the web from a series of information containers into an ecosystem in which the parts of the web are interrelated.

WEB 3.0 IN EDUCATION

The implications for education are profound. There are three areas of impact:

- *knowledge construction,*
- *personal learning network maintenance, and*
- *personal educational administration*

1. Knowledge Construction

Currently, Googling the search returns a big number

of hits, many of which link to complex data resources that link to other resources and so on. The presumption of knowledge in this approach to information gathering and evaluation is faulty, if not potentially dangerous in its limitations. One vision of a well-developed semantic web includes a search feature that would return a multimedia report rather than a list of hits. That report would draw from many sources, including websites, articles from scientific repositories, chapters in textbooks, blog dialogue, speeches posted on YouTube, information stored on cell phones, gaming scenarios played out in virtual realities—anything appropriate that is accessible by the rules of Web 3.0. The report would consist of short sections that coalesce around knowledge areas that emerged naturally from your research, with keywords identified and listed conveniently off to one side as links.

The information in the report would be compared, contrasted, and collated in a basic way, presenting points of agreement and disagreement, and perhaps associating these with political positions or contrasting research. The result is that user spends less time searching and sifting and more time absorbing, thinking, and participating.

2. Personal learning networks (PLNs)

Under Web 3.0, PLNs are built primarily around subjects, not services. Personal learning agents identify relevant information from any source that is semantically accessible and provide an information synthesis tailored to personal learning objective. The result is similar to the one described in the "global warming" search example, but applied to an educational goal. Again, the objective is to spend less time searching for information and more time trying to understand, critically assess, and creatively expand it. The semantic web makes it possible for the web to become an effective and focused information resource that can be tailored for specific content area objectives. User sits at the hub of a personal learning network (PLN) that connects user to his/her interests. Unfortunately, much of the time is spent finding useful information rather than interacting with it and thinking about it. User troll blogs, search the web, wade through long podcasts, and converse with friends in the hopes of finding something we can use. Some services, like iGoogle, make a modest attempt to streamline this process by allowing to automatically log into web services, like news services or various podcasting sources. But user still needs to pick through that day's offerings to determine whether they contain anything relevant to interests.

3. Personal educational administration

The Semantic Web is historically unique in that for the first time society can see a foundational shift in technology well in advance of its arrival. For the past 25 years we have been in reactive mode, as one wave of technological revolution after another caught us unawares. The Semantic Web being both inevitable and slow to develop. In fact, the Semantic Web is far enough into the future that developers can actually help shape it. Educators would do themselves, students, and the world a tremendous favor by jumping into the discussion now and helping Web 3.0 developers realize a vision that recognizes education and promotes the public good as top priorities.

REFERENCES

1. *Evaluating various sites: http://www.judybrown.com/tools.html*
2. *http://tinyurl.com/d7f7k*
3. *http://tinyurl.com/dk3xq*
4. *http://tinyurl.com/a32cq*
5. *http://ross.typepad.com/blog/2005/08/web_of_verbs.html*
6. *http://www.wired.com/wired/archive/13.09/start.html?pg=7*
7. *http://www.wired.com/wired/archive/13.09/start.html?pg=7*
8. *Wired http://www.wired.com/news/technology/*

0,1282,68823,00.html

9. Flock browser http://www.flock.com/home/

10. http://en.wikipedia.org/wiki/Daemon_%28computer_software%29

11. Paul Miller, "Sir Tim Berners-Lee: Semantic Web Is Open for Business," The Semantic Web, posted February 26, 2008, http://blogs.zdnet.com/semantic-web/?p=105.

12. Michael Dertouzos, The Unfinished Revolution: Human-Centered Computers and What They Can Do for Us (New York: HarperCollins, 2001).

13. William Gibson, http://en.wikipedia.org/wiki/William_Gibson_%28novelist%29

14. Chalksite. http://www.chalksite.com/

15. http://elgg.org/

16. engrade http://www.engrade.com/

17. SchoolTool http://www.schooltool.org/

18. Schoopy http://www.schoopy.com/

19. Windows Live Academic http://academic.live.com/

20. wink http://www.debugmode.com/wink/

21. Diigo http://www.diigo.com/

22. Simpy http://simpy.com/

23. 30 Boxes http://30boxes.com/

24. Google Calendar http://calendar.google.com/

25. My Web 2.0 http://myweb2.search.yahoo.com/

26. Lazybase http://lazybase.com/

27. MyOwnDB http://www.myowndb.com/info/presentation/home

28. Netvibes http://www.netvibes.com/

29. Windows Live http://www.live.com/

30. goowy http://www1.goowy.com/

31. Tagyu http://tagyu.com/

32. ThinkFree Office Online http://online.thinkfree.com/

33. ajaxSketch http://www.ajaxsketch.com/

34. Gliffy http://www.gliffy.com/

35. NewsAlloy http://www.newsalloy.com/

36. Box.net http://www.box.net/

37. *DropSend http://www.dropsend.com/openomy*
38. *TotoExpress http://www.totoexpress.com/*
39. *Ta-Da Lists http://www.tadalist.com/*
40. *dropcash http://www.dropcash.com/*
41. *Flock http://www.flock.com/*
42. *GahooYoogle http://www.gahooyoogle.com/*
43. *Orangoo http://orangoo.com/spell/*
44. *SuprGlu http://suprglu.com/*
45. *Webaroo http://www.webaroo.com/*
46. *Widgetbox http://beta.widgetbox.com/*
47. *digg http://www.digg.com/*
48. *Rojo http://www.rojo.com/today/*
49. *tech.memeorandum http://tech.memeorandum.com/*
50. *Technorati http://technorati.com/*
51. *AirSet http://www.airset.com/*
52. *Zoho Planner http://www.zohoplanner.com/organizer/login.do*
53. *flickr http://www.flickr.com/*
54. *riya http://www.riya.com/*
55. *S5 http://www.meyerweb.com/eric/tools/s5/*
56. *SlideShare http://slideshare.net/login*
57. *Thumbstacks http://www.thumbstacks.com/*
58. *Vyew http://vyew.com/content*
59. *BasecampHQ http://www.basecamphq.com/*
60. *voo2do http://voo2do.com/*
61. *ajaxXLS viewer http://www.ajaxxls.com/*
62. *Num Sum http://numsum.com/*
63. *Zoho Sheet http://www.zohosheet.com/*
64. *eyespot http://www.eyespot.com/*
65. *YouTube http://youtube.com/*
66. *TypePad http://www.typepad.com/*
67. *WordPress http://www.wordpress.com/*
68. *JotSpot http://www.jotspot.com/*
69. *PBwiki http://www.pbwiki.com/*
70. *stikipad http://www.stikipad.com/*
71. *ajaxWrite http://www.ajaxwrite.com/*

72. *Writeboard writely http://www.writely.com/*
73. *Zoho Writer http://www.zohowriter.com/Home.do*
74. *http://www.w2point.com/category/softwares/*
75. *http://www.w2point.com/author/W2POINT/*
76. *http://www.w2point.com/ecover-creator/*
77. *http://www.w2point.com/link-directory-submitter/*
78. *http://www.w2point.com/virtual-sales-bot/*
79. *http://www.w2point.com/power-effects/*
80. *http://www.w2point.com/word-to-web-page/*
81. *http://www.w2point.com/ultimate-exit-pop-up/*
82. *http://www.w2point.com/auto-blog-commenter/*

2

Online Social Communication and Innovations

ONLINE COMMUNICATION

Social software applications include communication tools and interactive tools. Communication tools typically handle the capturing, storing and presentation of communication, usually written but including audio and video as well. Interactive tools handle mediated interactions between a pair or group of users. They focus on establishing and maintaining a connection among users. These software applications facilitate the mechanics of conversation and talk. Online communication includes following services:

1. Text chat: Internet Relay Chat (IRC) and other online chat technologies allow users to join chat rooms and communicate with many people at once. It happens publicly. Depending on choice, users may join a pre-existing chat room or create a new one about any topic. Once inside, user may type messages that everyone else in the room can read, as well as respond to messages from others.

2. Instant Messaging: An instant messaging

application or client allows one to communicate with another person over a network in real time. It happens in relative privacy. Popular consumer-oriented clients include AOL Instant Messenger, Google Talk, ICQ, Meebo, MSN Messenger, Skype and Yahoo! Messenger. Instant messaging software have been designed for use in business also. There includes IBM Lotus Sametime, XMPP and Microsoft Messenger. One can add friends to a contact or "buddy" list by entering the person's email address or messenger ID. If the person is online, the name will be listed as available for chat. Clicking on their name will activate a chat window with space to write to the other person, as well as read their reply. Instant messaging facilitates both one-to-one (communication) and many-to-many interaction.

3. Wikis: It is web page whose content can be edited by its visitors. Examples of wikis include Wikipedia, Wiktionary, MeatballWiki, CommunityWiki and Wikisource.

4. Internet forums: Internet forms were originally modeled after the real-world paradigm of electronic bulletin boards of the world before internet was born. Internet forums allow users to post a "topic" for others to review. On Internet forms other users can view the topic and post their own comments in a linear fashion. Most forums are public, allowing anybody to sign up at any time. A few Internet forms are private, (gated communities) where new members must pay a small fee to join.

Forums can contain many different categories in a hierarchy according to topics and subtopics. Other features include:

- *(i) The ability to post images or files or to quote another user's post with special formatting in one's own post.*
- *(ii) Forums often grow in popularity until they can boast several thousand members posting replies to tens of thousands of topics continuously.*

Current successful services have combined new tools with the older newsgroup and mailing list paradigm to produce hybrids like Yahoo! Groups and Google Groups. For example, wiki user pages have become social portals for individual users and may be used in place of other portal applications.

5. Collaborative real-time editors: Simultaneous editing of a text or media file by different participants on a network was first demonstrated on research systems. It was initiated during 1970s, but is now practical on a global network. SubEthaEdit, SynchroEdit, ACE and Moonedit are examples of this type of social software. Google Docs, Spreadsheets and Zoho allow joint editing; few other users will only see changes after saving. Etherpad has been open sourced.

6. Blogs: Blogs (short for web logs) are like online journals for a particular person. The owner will post a message periodically, allowing others to comment. Topics often subjects important to them. Blogs mean many things to different people, ranging from "online journal" to "easily updated personal website." Beyond being a simple homepage or an online diary, some blogs allow comments on the entries, thereby creating a discussion forum. They also have blogrolls (i.e. links to other blogs which the owner reads or admires). Pingback and trackback allow one blog to notify another blog, creating an inter-blog conversation. Blogs engage readers. It has capacity to build a virtual community around a particular person or interest. Examples include Slashdot, LiveJournal, and BlogSpot.

7. Social network services : Social network services allow people to come together online. The factors are; around shared interests, hobbies or causes. For example, some services enable business networking (Ryze, XING and LinkedIn) and social event meetups (Meetup). Some large wikis have effectively become social network services by encouraging user pages and portals. Anyone can create their own social networking service using hosted offerings on flexible, installable software like Elgg, BuddyPress, phpFox or Concursive's ConcourseConnect.

SOCIAL NETWORK SEARCH ENGINES

Social network search engines are a class of search engines that use social networks:

(i) *to organize,*

(ii) *prioritize or*

(iii) *filter search results.*

There are two subclasses of social network search engines:

Explicit social network search engines : There allow people to find each other according to explicitly stated social relationships such as XFN social relationships. XHTML Friends Network allows people to share their relationships on their own sites. It forms a decentralized/distributed online social network.

Implicit social network search engines : There allow people to filter search results based upon classes of social networks they trust, such as a shared political viewpoint. This was called an epistemic filter in the 1993 "State of the Future Report" from the American Committee for the United Nations University. It was predicted that this would become the dominant means of search for most users. This type of social network search engine mines the web to infer the topology of online social networks. For example, the NewsTrove search engine infers social networks from content - sites, blogs, pods and feeds by examining, among other things, subject matter, link relationships and grammatical features to infer social networks.

TYPES OF SOCIAL NETWORKS

Various types of social networks are available due to priorities of users:

1. Deliberative social networks : Deliberative social networks are webs of discussion and debate for decision-making purposes. They rely upon informed opinion and advice that is given with a clear expectation of outcomes.

2. Commercial social networks : Commercial social networks are designed to support business transaction. These tend to build a trust between an individual and a brand, which relies on opinion of product, ideas to make the product better. It enables customers to participate with the brands in promoting development, service delivery and a better customer experience. An example of these networks is Dell IdeaStorm.

3. Social guides : A social guide recommending places to visit or contains information about places in the real world such as coffee shops, restaurants and wifi hotspots, etc. One such application is wikitravel.

Other applications of Social Networking websites

1. Social libraries: This applications allows visitors to keep track of their collectibles, books, records and DVDs. Users can share their collections. Some sites offer a buddy system, as well as virtual "check outs" of items for borrowing among friends. Folksonomy or tagging is implemented on most of these sites. Examples include discogs.com, imdb.com and LibraryThing.

2. Social online storage: Social online storage applications allow their users to collaboratively create file archives containing files of any type. Files can either be edited online or from a local computer which has access to the storage system. Such systems can be built upon existing server infrastructure (e.g. GDrive) or leverage idle resources by applying P2P technology (e.g. Wuala). Such systems allow public file distribution and direct file sharing with friends.

3. Virtual worlds: Virtual Worlds are services where it is possible to meet and interact with other people in a virtual environment reminiscent of the real world.

4. Massively Multiplayer Online Games (MMOGs): MMOGs are virtual worlds (also known as virtual environments) that add various sorts of point systems, levels, competition and winners and losers to virtual world simulation. Commercial MMOGs include Everquest and World of Warcraft. The Dotsoul Cyberpark is one of the more innovative non-commercial worlds, with the look and feel of Second Life and Active Worlds. It is an adamantly anti-corporate stance. Other open-source and experimental examples include Croquet project, VOS and Solipsis.

CONCEPT OF COMMUNICATION AND INTERACTIVE TOOLS

Communication tools are generally asynchronous. By contrast, interactive tools are generally synchronous, allowing users to communicate in real time (phone, net phone, video chat) or near-synchronous (IM, text chat).

- *(i) Communication involves the content of talk, speech or writing. In other words, a communication tool may want to make access and searching of text both simple and powerful.*
- *(ii) Interaction involves the interest users establish in one another as individuals. An interactive tool may want to present as much of a user's expression, performance and presence as possible. The organization of texts and providing access to archived contributions differs from the facilitation of interpersonal interactions between contributors enough to warrant the distinction in media.*

DESIGN CHOICES

Social software may be better understood as a set of debates or design choices, rather than any particular list of tools. Broadly conceived, there are many older media such as mailing lists and Usenet fora that qualify as "social". Recent software genres such as blogs and wikis are followed by most users. Social software not refers to a single type of software, but rather to the use of two or more modes of computer-mediated communication that result in "community formation." In this view, people form online communities by combining:

(i) *one-to-one (e.g. email and instant messaging),*

(ii) *one-to-many (Web pages and blogs) and*

(iii) *many-to-many (wikis) communication modes. Some groups schedule real life meetings and so become "real" communities of people that share physical lives.*

Features

(i) *Most definers of social software agree that they seem to facilitate "bottom-up" community development.*

(ii) *The system is classless and promotes those with abilities.*

(iii) *Membership is voluntary, reputations are earned by winning the trust of other members and the community's missions and governance are defined by the members themselves.*

FORMATION OF COMMUNITIES

Communities formed by "bottom-up" processes are often contrasted to the less vibrant collectivities formed by "top-down" software, in which users' roles are determined by an external authority and circumscribed by rigidly conceived software mechanisms (such as access rights). Given small differences in policies, the same type of software can produce radically different social outcomes. For instance, TikiWiki CMS/Groupware has a fine-grained permission system of detailed access control so the site administrator can, on a page-by-page basis, determine which groups can view, edit or view the history. By contrast, mediawiki avoids per-user controls, to keep most pages editable by most users and puts more information about users currently editing in its recent changes pages. The result is that TikiWiki can be used both by community groups who embrace the social paradigm of mediawiki and by groups who prefer to have more content control.

TRAITS DEPEND ON DESIGN. HOW?

By design, social software reflects the traits of social networks and is designed very consciously to let social network analysis work with a very compatible database. All social software systems create links between users, as persistent as the identity those users choose. Through these persistent links, a permanent community can be formed out of a formerly epistemic community. The ownership and control of these links (who is linked and who isn't) is in the hands of the user. Thus, these links are asymmetrical, no matter a user related to another and vice versa. These links are functional, not decorative. User can choose not to receive any content from people he is not connected to, for example.

LITERACY AND SOCIAL NETWORKING

Social networking tools give users meaningful ways to use and improve reading and writing skills. All social networking software requires users to read and write. When a user:

- *Creates a profile on a social networking site,*
- *Posts or comments on a blog*
- *Adds or edits content on a wiki*
- *Searches for social content*

- *Consults peers online as a part of research*

Since reading and writing skills are required, these technologies are often referred to as the read/write web.

AUGMENTATION CAPABILITIES

The augmentation capabilities of social software were demonstrated in early internet applications for communication such as e-mail, newsgroups, groupware, virtual communities etc. These collaborative tools add a capability "that aggregates the actions of networked users." This indicates to a powerful dynamic that distinguishes social software from other group collaboration tools and as a component of Web 2.0 technology. Capabilities for content and behavior aggregation and redistribution present some of the more important potentials of this media. Further academic experiments, Social Constructivism and the open source software movement are expected to be notable influences.

Systems of this kind could support software for public critical discussion, collaborative development, group commitment, and collaborative filtering of content based on voting and rating. Social technologies (or conversational technologies) is a term used by organizations. It describes the technology that allows the storage and creation of knowledge through collaborative writing.

Back in times, prototyped in 1983, the first version of Computer Supported Intentional Learning Environments (CSILE) was installed in 1986 on a small network of Cemcorp ICON computers, at an elementary school in Toronto, Canada. CSILE included text and graphical notes authored by different user levels (students, teachers, others) with attributes such as comments and thinking types which reflect the role of the note in the author's thinking. Thinking types included "my theory", "new information", and "I need to understand." CSILE later evolved into Knowledge Forum.

In 1989, Tim Berners-Lee circulated a proposal for an in-house online document sharing system which he described as a "web of notes with links" later on called as the World Wide Web.

In the beginning of last decade, Adrian Scott founded Ryze, a free social networking website designed to link business professionals, particularly new entrepreneurs. In February 2002, the suvi.org Addressbook started its service. It was the first service that connected people together. The idea was simply to have an up to date Addressbook and not to loose contact with friends. Other people on the globe had the same idea. friendster, faceboook and many other services where successors to this. In April 2002, Friendster came in picture. In 2003, Hi5, LinkedIn, MySpace, and XING were launched. In February 2004, Facebook was launched. In 2004, Levin acknowledged that many of characteristics of social software (hyperlinks, weblog conversation discovery and standards-based aggregation) "build on older forms." Nevertheless, "the difference in scale, standardization, simplicity and social incentives provided by web access turn a difference in degree to a difference in kind." Key technological factors underlying this difference in kind in the computer, network and information technologies are: filtered hypertext, ubiquitous web/computing, continuous internet connectivity, cheap, efficient and small electronics, content syndication strategies (RSS) and others. Additionally, the convergence of several major information technology systems for voice, data and video into a single system makes for expansive computing environments with far reaching effects. In October 2005, Ning, an online platform was founded where users can create their own social websites and networks. Ning is now running more than 275,000 networks. Ning is part of "white label social networking providers". Due to its services it is often compared to rSitez and Flux and few other similar platforms. Later on in the last five years, ultimate progress in social communication has been discerned. The virtual worlds are created and established their niche.

HOW ONLINE SOCIAL NETWORKING FACILITATES LEARNING IN SCHOOLS & LIBRARIES

What are social networking technologies? They are software that enables people to connect, collaborate and form virtual communities via the computer and/or Internet. Social networking web sites are those that provide this opportunity to interact. Sites that allow visitors to send emails, post comments, build web content and/or take part in live chats are all considered to be social networking sites. Social networking technologies have many positive uses in schools and libraries. They are an ideal environment for teens to share what they are learning or to build something together online. The nature of the medium allows teens to receive feedback from librarians, teachers, peers, parents, and others. Social networking technologies create a sense of community (as do the physical library and school) and in this way are already aligned with the services and programs at the library and/or school.

Schools and libraries are working to integrate positive uses of social networking into their classrooms, programs, and services. By integrating social networking technologies into educational environments, teens have the opportunity to learn from adults how to be safe and smart when participating in online social networks. They also learn a valuable life skill, as these social networking technologies are tools for communication that are widely used in colleges and in the workplace. A school can use blogging software to publish its newspaper. The blog format allows for timely publication and the ability to make updates easily. This format also allows for comments from readers and easy navigation to archived stories. Publication costs are minimal (no color print costs!) and there is no limit to the length of the paper, allowing for more student participation. For example, an author creates a blog as a way to reflect on the reading and writing experience. Teens who enjoy the author's work keep up on what the author is writing and thinking through the blog. The author blog is used as a research source and as a way to communicate with the author about books, reading, and writing. A public library can create a My Space site as a way to connect with teens in the community. The space includes quick and easy access to the library catalog and other research tools. It can also include information on programs and services at the library in which teens can take part.

SOCIAL NETWORKING SITES

del.icio.us : (www.del.icio.us) Combines bookmarking and tagging. Allows users to network with others in order to keep track of what is being bookmarked by those with similar interests.

Flickr : (www.flickr.ooml/) A photo-sharing site that allows users to tag images.

My Space : (www.myspace.com) Users build their space on the web and then invite others to be their friends.

Technorati : (www.technorati.coml/) A searchable database of blogs that gives bloggers the ability to tag content for easy access by others.

Wikipedia : (www.wikipedia.orgl/) A wiki encyclopedia that gives anyone the ability to add to and change entries.

SOCIAL NETWORKING IN A WORK ENVIRONMENT

In a sense, social networking at work is similar to a large ongoing group meeting. Sometimes excellent results occur, but other times major amounts of time are wasted. Sometimes output benefits from everyone's input and ongoing consultation, other times, individual work without constant obligation to check in and gain consensus may be more productive. The output of a "committee" is sometimes worse than that of an individual or small team. As information supply increases, the average time spent evaluating individual content has to decrease. Eventually, much communication is summarily ignored - based on very arbitrary and rapid heuristics that will filter out the information for example by category. Bad information crowds out the good - much the way SPAM often crowds out potentially useful unsolicited communications.

EDUCATING THE COMMUNITY ABOUT ONLINE SOCIAL NETWORKING

1. *In the media there are many examples of how social networking has played a dangerous role in teen lives. Librarians should play an active role in educating parents, teachers, and other members of the community about the positive benefits of social networking in teen lives. The following examples of how library can educate its community provide a starting point.*
2. *Library can create and distribute brochures and post information online about what the library is already doing to ensure that children and teens are safe online. Library can include information about Internet filters and Internet Acceptable Use Policies that the library has.*
3. *Library can invite parents and educators to a workshop where they can learn about My Space and other social networking tools. In the workshop have librarians and teachers discuss how My Space is being used in the classroom and library. Library can have law enforcement officials talk about how to help teens stay safe while participating in social networking online. Library can have users with well-designed MySpace*

spaces demonstrate the positive ways they use social networking tools.

4. *Library can create an online demo or class that gives adults the chance to test out and discuss social networking technologies at their leisure and in a somewhat anonymous setting. Library can make the demo available from the library's web site.*
5. *Library can use social networking technologies as an access point for the library's services. Library can set up a blog where adults and teens read about what's going on in the library and can add comments about programs, materials, and so on.*
6. *Library can develop a booklist wiki where adults and teens can add titles of books on specific themes.*
7. *Library can inform community members about how social networking tools allow for schools and libraries to integrate technology in meaningful ways with and for teens at low (or no) cost. With free blogging software a school librarian or teacher can create a website without learning how to code and can update and maintain that website with no extra training.*
8. *Library can produce a podcast for teachers, administrators, parents, and community members that focuses on the positive aspects of social networking technologies.*

FREE DOWNLOADABLE OPEN SOURCE SOCIAL NETWORKING SOFTWARE

Following list is of best free, downloadable, open source social networking software.

spree: Spree is an expert search engine where users ask questions to find other participating users, who are knowledgeable in that area and willing to help.

iSocial: iSocial is a free social networking CMS software that allows creating own Friendster and Orkut like sites. Use bookmarks, dating and create groups with just one mouse click.

Mahara: Mahara is fully featured electronic portfolio, weblog, resume builder, and social networking system for connecting users and creating online communities.

Yogurt: This is a Social Network module for xoops CMS.

VMukti: VMukti is a Unified Social Collaborative conferencing engine. It allows access through personalized, mashable web-interface. Core features are Video conferencing, Audio conferencing, IP Telephony, Desktop sharing, Chat, Whiteboard, Presentation and More.

The PeopleAggregator: The PeopleAggregator is a next-generation social networking system that goes beyond the idea of social networks as mating games, and attempts to use open standards, network inter-connectivity and massive flexibility.

Appleseed:Appleseed is (augmented) social networking software, ie Friendster, only distributed. Sites running Appleseed will interoperate, and form the 'Appleseed Social Network.' Development is focused on privacy and security, as well as ease of configuration.

Mugshot Project: The Mugshot site lets user track what the friends are doing online across a variety of popular web sites ? music, photos, blog posts, and more.

GetBoo: Web 2.0 bookmarking system, both social (with tags) and private (with folders). Import and export the bookmarks from Firefox, IE, Mozilla, Netscape. Admin management section, translations, groups, bookmarklets, Firefox extension, RSS feeds, and more!

Akarru: Akarru is a social bookmarking engine, is used to build social bookmarkings sites, like www.blogmemes.com. Users posts links and promote links to front page using voting system.

Scuttle: Web-based social bookmarking system. Allows multiple users to store, share and tag their favourite links online.

SemanticScuttle: SemanticScuttle is a social bookmarking tool (based on Scuttle) experimenting new features as hierarchical tags, collaborative descriptions or OpenID authentification.

AROUNDMe: Create collaborative social websites (like Ning, Myspace, Yahoo or Google groups). Each group can create a multiple web pages. They get a drop in guestbook, blog, forum and wiki. Each group is fully customizable using xHTML, CSS, Javascript and PHP.

Clonesumating: Clonesumating is the open source version of the code that runs CONSUMATING.COM. It features many state of the art social networking functions including user profiles, user tagging, matching and discovery based on quirky tag combinations, group activities such as weekly photo contests and blog questions, an event calendar, RSS feeds for everything, etc. It is written primarily in mod_perl.

BeWelcome Rox: Get to know the global village and other cultures, share the place. BW Rox is the platform driving www.bewelcome.org and other social networks, aiming to bring people together in real life. Organize the travel or stay abroad, travelblog, meetings.

ICEcore: ICEcore open team collaboration software uses social networking to unify team workspaces w/ real-time web conferencing. Collaboration for knowledge networking, program management, communities-of-practice, telework.

Memephage: Memephage is an automated web log (blog). It passively gathers and summarizes links from various places. Currently: IRC, social MUDs, e-mail, and web browsers. Uses the POE multitasking and networking framework for Perl.

InteractOLE: A platform for the delivery and support of online learning. It differs from many other elearning platforms in that its aim is to concentrate on the social/ interactive aspects of teaching and learning rather than the delivery of content to students.

Elgg: Elgg is an open source social networking platform developed for LAMP (Linux, Apache, MySQL, PHP) which encompasses weblogging, file storage, RSS aggregation, personal profiles, FOAF functionality and more.

CommunityNews: CommunityNews uses social bookmarking and bayesian techinques to provide periodic postings to blogs. Users can vote for or against RSS sources. It increases the chances that the source is used again. Spam filtering (bayesian) is provided by spam bayes.

OpenPNE: OpenPNE is a Social Networking Service Engine written in PHP. It has many features(friend control,friend invitation,diary,blog feeds,message box,etc).

MonkeyChow: Feed Aggregator Reader (branched from FeedOnFeeds) with Social Bookmarks (del.icio.us, Blogger, Newsvine, Technorati, mailto), Article Starring, Feed Tagging, OPML, Article Search, Reblogging and Refeeding, Aging, and Edit feed attributes.

NewsCloud: NewsCloud is an open source media platform for citizen journalism and the social news network hosted at NewsCloud.com.

Feed Me Links: Feed Me Links stores the bookmarks online so user can get to them anywhere. Import the favorites and share the links with friends. It adds tags to organize the links.

WorldSpace: WorldSpace is a user-extensible shared

virtual environment, aimed at being a next-generation social networking system.

Social Networking POC: A networking site on the lines of Orkut.

Zoints: Zoints is intimately aware that online communities are the most important aspect of the internet. The free software solutions are designed to help solve the three major problems forum owners face: Member acquisition, Member retention and Profitability.

earth-life-simulation: A simulation of the world, there will be a global map representation and players can choose a country or civilization and develop it's social, political and military existence.

PHPizabi: PHPizabi is one of the most powerful social networking platforms on the planet. With literally thousands of websites powered by PHPizabi including everything from simple friends sites to the most complex networking super sites out there.

Ozcode: Ozcode is the source code behind Ozmozr.com, a microformat-aware RSS aggregator, social networking, resource sharing, identity aggregation and presentation site.

TallStreet: TallStreet.com is a new search engine concept where users make investments, with fictional money, in their favourite websites and the rankings are determined entirely by the users.

Jamss: Jamss is a social news site based off of Digg.com. Jamss allows for peer submission and review of web articles and can be adapted to fit a variety of themes. Jamss runs on PHP/MySQL.

Dolphin: Dolphin is open-source and free, although there is a cost associated with removing the company?s links from the site.

Ospo: Ospo is an opensource social portal project. It use standard function (add, remove friends, top10), forums integration, music module (artists directory with albums, songs), shoutcast integration, blog (add, delete, modify, view) and so on.

AstroSPACES: AstroSPACES is the world's first open source social networking solution. Coded from scratch, it is highly efficient and very easy to use.

FlightFeather: FlightFeather's goal is "social networking for everyone".

SNOSS: Social Networking Open Source Software, an open source social networking framework, written in PHP, Javascript and MySQL with an AJAX UI.

OpenSocialNetwork: OpenSocialNetwork is a social network of open source.

S3B: S3B - Social Semantic Search and Browsing - is a middleware that delivers a set of search and browsing components that can be used in J2EE web applications to deliver user-oriented features based on semantic descriptions and social networking.

Facelift: Facelift is visualization and analysis software for online social networking services. It displays a given community as a node-link diagram and provides several search / filtering functions as well as cluster analysis features.

LIFE 2.0 AND COMMUNICATION

Life 2.0 is a new digital lifestyle. It is changing the culture and challenging the way people think about themselves and the world. It mixes the physical world with the digital world. It uses a combination of digital tools—PDA, MP3, laptop, cell phone, camera, PC, GPS. Through this, people are connected to one another and to the Web. Life 2.0 increasingly impacts as faster travel, more channels, better communications, and more convenience. The Life 2.0 characteristics are directly related to the "digital-ness" of media. These are easy; perfect copying and nearly free storage and transmission. The effect is that their use has become fundamentally different for consumers. The flow of information about digital objects is more important to many groups—advertisers, governments, authors, and than the content. And when people interact with a digital object, they add to its content. Librarians are habitual of dealing with volumes of metadata as a matter of course. Most people, though, don't think of their lives as being cataloged beyond facts such as phone number, address, social security number, etc. Now, however, users create a wealth of both content and information about themselves; some private, much of it public.

REFERENCES

1. *www.searchinstitute. org*
2. *ImaginOn Library Loft, www.myspace.com/libraryloft Hennepin County Library, www.myspace.com/hennepincountylibrary*
3. *Rachel Cohn, www.myspace.com/rachel_cohn*
4. *http://pc4sw06.blogspot.com/*
5. *www.uni.uiuc.edu/gargoyle/*
6. *www.sparksflyup.com/weblog.php*
7. *Vivalogo Resources. http://www.vivalogo.com/vl-resources/ index.htm*
8. *"Jumper 2.0 Tags the Enterprise". John Udell, Web 2.0 News. 17 April 2009. http://www.amazines.com/article_detail.cfm? articleid=869844.*
9. *http://sourceforge.net/projects/communitynews/*
10. *http://sourceforge.net/projects/opennetwork/*
11. *Forrester Report, "Vendor Product Catalog of Community Platforms For The Interactive Marketer "*
12. *CMS Watch, "Enterprise Social Software Vendor List"*
13. *Sheizaf Rafaeli & Noy, A. (2002), Online auctions, messaging, communication and social facilitation: a simulation and experimental evidence, European Journal of Information Systems, September 2002, vol. 11, no. 3, pp. 196-207.*

14. *http://project.askspree.de/*

15. *http://sourceforge.net/projects/socialnetwork/*

16. *http://www.mahara.org/*

17. *http://sourceforge.net/projects/galeriayogurt/*

18. *Stowe Boyd, "Are You Ready for Social Software?" http://www.stoweboyd.com/message/2006/10/are_you_ready_f.html*

19. *Clay Shirky, "A Group is Its Own Worst Enemy" http://www.shirky.com/writings/group_enemy.html*

20. *Matt Webb, "On Social Software" http://interconnected.org/home/2004/04/28/on_social_software*

21. *Trustlet, Definition of trust network http://www.trustlet.org/wiki/Trust_network*

22. *CMS Watch, "A Scenario-based Approach to Evaluating Social Software" http://www.cmswatch.com/Feature/187-Social-Software*

23. *http://sourceforge.net/projects/vmukti/*

24. *http://www.broadbandmechanics.com/*

25. *http://s3b.sourceforge.net/*

26. *http://www.patrick-opitz.com/projects/facelift/*

27. *Sheizaf Rafaeli and Noy, A. (2005). "Social Presence: Influence on Bidders in Internet Auctions". EM-Electronic Markets, 15(2), 158-176.Helen Hasan & Charmaine C Pfaff. 2006. "The Wiki: an environment to revolutionise employees' interaction with corporate knowledge" ACM International Conference Proceeding Series; Vol. 206, pp.377-380.*

28. *Helen Hasan & Charmaine C Pfaff. 2006. "Emergent Conversational technologies that are Democratizing Information Systems in Organizations: the case of the corporate Wiki" Proceedings of the Information Systems Foundations (ISF): Theory, Representation and Reality Conference, Australian National University, Canberra, 27-28 September 2006.*

29. *http://sourceforge.net/projects/akarru/*

30. *http://sourceforge.net/projects/scuttle/*

31. *http://www.bevolunteer.org/trac/*

32. *http://www.interactole.org/spaces/space.php?space_key=1*

33. *http://sourceforge.net/projects/astrospaces/*

34. *Allen, Christopher (2004). http://www.lifewithalacrity.com/2004/10/tracing_the_evo.html*

35. *Bush, Vannevar (July 1945). "As We May Think". The Atlantic*

Monthly. http://www.theatlantic.com/doc/194507/bush.

36. *Hegland, Frode; Klijnsma, Fleur; Engelbart, Doug. "The Invisible Revolution". http://www.invisiblerevolution.net/.*
37. *"Previous Recipients of the Draper Prize". National Academy of Engineering. http://www.nae.edu/nae/awardscom.nsf/weblinks/NAEW-4NHMN6?OpenDocument.*
38. *http://elgg.org/*
39. *http://www.boonex.com/products/dolphin/*
40. *Illich, Ivan (1971). Deschooling Society. New York, Harper & Row ISBN 0-06-012139-4*
41. *Bates, Tony & Helm, Croom, eds. (1984). The Role of Technology in Distance Education. Retrieved on 15 August 2006.*
42. *Computer Assisted Learning or Communications:Which Way for Information Technology in Distance Education?*
43. *http://www-personal.umich.edu/~jaylemke/courses/ED750/CSILE_KF_illus.pdf CSILE/Knowledge Forum Scardamalia, M.*
44. *http://www.shokk.com/blog/articles/category/monkeychow/*
45. *http://sourceforge.net/projects/newscloud/*
46. *http://www.nytimes.com/2006/10/15/business/yourmoney/15friend.html?_r=2 Wallflower at the Web Party, NY Times*
47. *http://developer.mugshot.org/wiki/Mugshot_Project*
48. *http://sourceforge.net/projects/ospo/*
49. *The Story Behind the Ning Name, by Gina Bianchini, Ning Blog, April 11, 2007*
50. *TechCrunch: Nine Ways to Build Your Own Social Network - July 24, 2007*
51. *Allen, Christopher (13 October 2004). "Tracing the Evolution of Social Software". http://www.lifewithalacrity.com/2004/10/tracing_the_evo.html.*
52. *http://feedmelinks.com/portal*
53. *Prensky, Marc. Adopt and Adapt. Edutopia, 2005. Available at: www.edutopia.org/magazine/ed1article.php?id=Art_1423&issue=dec_05#*
54. *http://sourceforge.net/projects/worldspace/*
55. *http://www.caslon.com.au/iponote.htm Lists theglobe.com's gain as 866%*
56. *Prensky, Marc. Engage Me or Enrage Me: What Today's Learners Demand. Educause, September/October 2005. Available at: www.educause.edu/ir/library/pdf/erm0553.pdf*

57. *Richardson, Will. Blogs, Wikis, Podcasts and Other Powerful Web Tools for the Classroom. Corwin Press, 2006.*
58. *http://sourceforge.net/projects/astrospaces/*
59. *The Gateway to Educational Materials www.thegateway.org*
60. *The Internet & Teens: Social Networking Safety, by Bill Erbes www.opal-online.org/archivelis.htm*
61. *http://www.thealarmclock.com/mt/archives/2004/08/linkedin_hq_mou.html Linked-In profile*
62. *Internet Safety www.ala.org/ala/washoff/WOissues/techinttele/internetsafety/internetsafety.htm*
63. *http://sourceforge.net/projects/openpne/*
64. *Social Networks: www.lii.org/pub/subtopic/4679*
65. *Internet Safety: www.lii.org/pub/subtopic/948*
66. *Teens Content Creators and Consumers www.pewinternet.org/PPF/r/166/report_display.asp*
67. *Weblogg-ed www.weblogg-ed.com/*

3

SOCIAL NETWORKING TOOLS AND LIBRARIES

INTRODUCTION

Social networks are perhaps the most promising and embracing technology. They enable messaging, blogging, streaming media, and tagging. MySpace, FaceBook, Del.icio.us, Frappr, and Flickr are networks that have enjoyed massive popularity in Web 2.0. While MySpace and FaceBook enable users to share themselves with one another (detailed profiles of users' lives and personalities). For example, Del.icio.us enables users to share Web resources and Flickr enables the sharing of pictures. Frappr is a bit of a blended network, using maps, chat rooms, and pictures to connect individuals. Social software encompasses a range of software systems that allow users to interact and share data. It is a computer-mediated communication and it has become very popular with social sites like MySpace and Facebook. The media sites like Flickr and YouTube as well as commercial sites like Amazon.com have reached to an extent of utmost popularity. These applications share characteristics like open APIs, service-oriented design and the ability to upload data and media.

Applications that allow people to build their social networks and make connections centered on the profile articulate their extended social network (friends of friends) are known as social networking. This amalgamation of technologies is being used for making friends in a specific area, as it is easier to trust friends of friends and helping the business. A social network service focuses on building and reflecting of social networks or social relations among people. It depends upon similar interests and/or activities. A social network service essentially consists of:

(i) a representation of each user (in the form of a profile),

(ii) his/her social links, and

(iii) a variety of additional services.

Most social network services are internet based. These provide means for users to interact, such as e-mail and instant messaging. There is a slight difference between social networking and online community. Social network service usually means an individual-centered service whereas online community services are group-centered. Social networking websites allow users to share ideas, activities, events, and interests within their individual networks.

SOCIAL NETWORKING DEFINED

The following definitions of social networking tools could be helpful in understanding what it is all about.

Blog: It is a web page where someone can write journal entries, reviews, articles, and more. Blog authors can allow readers to post their own comments. No web design knowledge is needed to create a blog.

Podcasts: These are audio files that are available for download. They are usually available for free via subscription so that user can automatically download it to a computer or MP3 player (like an iPOD).

RSS: It is a way for subscribers to automatically receive

information from blogs, newspapers, and podcasts.

Social Networking: In the online world, social networking refers to the ability to connect with people through websites and other technologies, like discussion boards.

Tagging: Tagging refers to the ability to add subject-headings to content in order to organize information in a meaningful way and to connect to others that tag similar content in the same way.

Wiki: It is a collaborative space for developing web content. No web design knowledge is needed to create a wiki.

The main types of social networking services are that which contain category places, means to connect with friends and a recommendation system linked to trust. Popular methods now combine many of these, with Facebook, Bebo, Twitter, MySpace, LinkedIn, Nexopia; Bebo, Hi5, Hyves, StudiVZ, iWiW, Tuenti, Decayenne, Tagged, XING, Badoo, Skyrock; Orkut, Hi5, Friendster, Mixi, Multiply, Orkut, Wretch, renren, Cyworld, Orkut and Facebook.

HISTORY OF SOCIAL NETWORKING

(i) In the 1990s : Early social networking on the World Wide Web began in the form of generalized online communities such as Theglobe.com (1994), Geocities (1994) and Tripod.com (1995). Many of these early communities focused and encouraged users to share personal information and ideas via personal webpages by providing easy-to-use publishing tools and free or inexpensive webspace. Some communities (e.g. Classmates.com) took a different approach by simply having people link to each other via email addresses. Later on user profiles became a central feature of social networking sites, allowing users to compile lists of "friends" and search for other users with similar interests.

(ii) In the last decade : By the end of the 1990s, many

sites began to develop more advanced features for users to find and manage friends. This newer generation of social networking sites began to flourish with the emergence of Friendster in 2002. Friendster was followed by MySpace and LinkedIn a year later, and finally, Bebo. Facebook , launched in 2004, has since become the largest social networking site in the world. There are now over 200 active sites using a wide variety of social networking models.

APPROACHES IN SOCIAL NETWORKS

As the increase in popularity of social networking is on a constant rise,new uses for the technology are constantly being observed. In social networking sites following concept are significant:

1. *Real time*
2. *Location*

1. Real Time Based Services : Real time allows users to contribute content, which is then broadcasted as it is being uploaded (similar to live television broadcasts). Twitter set the trend for "real time" services, broadcast within a 140 character limit. Facebook followed suit with their "Live Feed". Twitter focuses on words, and Clixtr focuses on group photo sharing where users can update their photo streams with photos while at an event.

2. Location based Services : In the location based social networking space, Foursquare gained popularity as it allowed for users to "check-in" to places that they are frequenting at that moment. Gowalla is another such service leveraging the GPS in phones to create a location based user experience. Clixtr, though in the real time space, is also a location based social networking site since events created by users are automatically geotagged, and users can view events occurring nearby through the Clixtr iPhone app. Yelp is also the location based social networking space through check-ins with their mobile app.

HOSTING SOCIAL NETWORK SERVICE

It is a web hosting service that specifically hosts the user creation of web-based social networking services. Such services are also known as vertical social networks due to the creation of SNSes. These cater to specific user interests and niches.

1. Business and corporate world : One popular use for this new technology is social networking between businesses. Companies have found that social networking sites such as Facebook and Twitter are great ways to build their brand image. There are five major uses for businesses and social media:

a. *to create brand awareness,*

b. *as an online reputation management tool,*

c. *for recruiting,*

d. *to learn about new technologies and competitors, and*

e. *as a lead gen tool to intercept potential prospects.*

These companies are able to drive traffic to their own online sites while encouraging their consumers and clients to have discussions on how to improve or change products or services. Social networks connect people at low cost; this can be beneficial for entrepreneurs and small businesses. These networks often act as a customer relationship management tool for companies selling products and services for advertising in the form of banners and text ads. Social networks can make it easier to keep in touch with contacts around the world. LinkedIn.com aims to interconnect professionals. Hub Culture is an invitation only social network for entrepreneurs. It is the idea a brand can build its consumer relationship by connecting their consumers to the brand image on a platform. Brand networking is a new way to capitalize on social trends as a marketing tool.

2. Science and Technology : One other use that is being

discussed is the use of Social Networks in the Science communities. Social networking can allow scientific groups to expand their knowledge base and share ideas, and without these new means of communicating their theories might become "isolated and irrelevant".

3. Academics : Social networks are also being used by teachers and students as a communication tool. Teachers and professors are doing everything from creating chat-room forums and groups to extend classroom discussion to posting assignments, tests and quizzes, to assisting with homework outside of the classroom setting. Social networks are also being used to foster teacher-parent communication. These sites make it possible and more convenient for parents to ask questions and voice concerns without having to meet face-to-face. Social networks focused on supporting relationships between teachers and between teachers and their students are now used for learning, educator professional development, and content sharing.

4. Social Activism and Government Sector : Social networks are being used by activists as a means of low-cost grassroots organizing. Social networking is more recently being used by various government agencies. Social networking tools serve as a quick and easy way for the government to get the opinion of the public and to keep the public updated on their activity. For example, NASA has taken advantage of a few social networking tools, including Twitter and Flickr.

5. Medical applications : Social networks are beginning to be adopted by healthcare professionals as a means to manage institutional knowledge, disseminate peer to peer knowledge and to highlight individual physicians and institutions. The advantage of using a dedicated medical social networking site is that all the members are screened against the state licensing board list of practitioners. A new trend is emerging with social networks created to help its members with various physical and mental ailments. It is found that PatientsLikeMe offers its members the chance to connect with others dealing with similar issues and research patient data related to their condition. For example, SoberCircle gives people in recovery the ability to communicate with one another. DailyStrength offers support groups for a wide array of topics and conditions.

6. Libraries and Information Centers : The use of online social networks by libraries is also an increasingly prevalant and growing tool that is being used to communicate with more potential library users, as well as extending the services provided by individual libraries.

PRESENCE IN LIBRARY

The tremendous popularity of social networking sites presents libraries with unique opportunities for reaching students. Social networking software is a new approach in some academic and public libraries today in order to make libraries not only "cool" in the public's eyes, but also as a third space in which potential library users can participate in an collaborative exchange with their libraries. It also may allow users to build relationships with the library staff and other library users. It is interesting to know how do the students really use various social networking sites, and what part can the library play in this social environment? Sometimes students are uncertain about the library and librarians using Facebook, but are willing to consider accessing the library through this platform in the right circumstances. By listening to students' concerns and identifying standards for interaction, the library's initiatives can be given shape. Libraries can educate patrons about putting content online, conduct market research and decide building presence (library profiles). Examples of the few libraries are as following:

- *Bennington College on Facebook*

- *Denver Public Library on MySpace*
- *UIUC Undergraduate Library on MySpace*
- *Brooklyn College Library on MySpace*
- *Memorial Library on MySpace*

The Web enabled online communication to transition from a strictly textual format to the visual, facilitating the development of the user friendly media sharing sites, wikis, blogs and other types of social software that we are familiar with today. These sites allow users to create pages in which others (potential library users) can view and provide feedback. Some academic and public libraries have created MySpace or Facebook pages in an attempt to promote and extend their library services such as reader's advisory, and third party applications can add increasing usability to pages. In the field of library and information services, the social networking site LibraryThing enables users to catalog their books and view what other users share those books. The implications of this site on how librarians recommend reading to users are apparent. LibraryThing enables users, thousands of them potentially, to recommend books to one another simply by viewing one another's collections. It also enables them to communicate asynchronously, blog, and "tag" their books. Requirements to begin seeing a library as a social network:

1. *Libraries' role is still considered as a communal gathering place, one of shared identity, communication, and action.*
2. *Social networking could enable librarians and patrons to interact*
3. *It enables to share and change resources dynamically in an electronic medium.*
4. *Users can create accounts with the library network and findout what other users have in common to their information needs.*

Social software enables people to con-nect with one another online, is a well-established phenomenon that has continued to grow and develop since the inception of the Internet. Related to social software is the idea of "Library 2.0;" or enhancing library resources and services using social software, to reach users outside the walls of the traditional li-brary. In the last few years the use of social software has grown enormously in society. While a growing number of librar-ies have adopted social software as a way to further interacts with library patrons and library staff, many things are unclear about the use of social software in libraries.

USEFUL SOCIAL NETWORKING TOOLS IN LIBRARIES

1. Organization: Helps in keeping the information handy and accessible with:

- I. *aNobii : This site for book lovers is a place to share reviews and recommendations.*
- II. *Del.icio.us : With this social bookmarking tool, you can create a custom directory for library patrons.*
- III. *Netvibes : In Netvibes' new Ginger beta, library can create a public page that can be viewed by anyone. It is helpful to help guide patrons to helpful Internet sources, news feeds, and more. It can be integrated with many of the tools like Flickr and library blogs.*
- IV. *Connotea : Connotea is a great reference tool, allowing you to save and organize reference links and share them with others.*
- V. *LibraryThing : This social cataloging network is great for librarians, and library can catalog along with Amazon, the Library of Congress, and more than 200 other libraries around the world.*
- VI. *lib.rario.us : Another social cataloging site, library can put media such as books, CDs, and journals on display for easy access and tracking.*

2. Communication: Supportive to keep in touch with staff, and patronswith these tools:

(i) MySpace: Reaching to the students, one of the best places to find them is MySpace. Other libraries have taken advantage of this site's calendar and blog features to improve their presence. With a little help libraries can also include custom catalog search tools.

(ii) Facebook: Another social media site where there is a group just for librarian-centric Facebook apps, a JSTOR search, and much more can be found.

(iii) Ning: This networking toolcan be used to get connected with students, library associations, and more.

(iv) Blog: By creating a blog, library can be able to disseminate information to lots of people at one time. Whether library is updating students on new collections, or just conversing with library staff, blogs are a powerful tool, especially when combined with RSS.

(v) Meebo: Library can network and assist students on Meebo independent of IM client. Library can even embed a chat screen on any webpage using tutorial available on web.

(vi) Twitter: Library can use Twitter, a microblogging application, to keep staff and patrons updated on daily activities, like frequently updated collections, or even just scheduling.

3. Distribution : The following tools make it easy to share information from anywhere:

(i) Flickr : Librarian can create image sets with metadata, as well as take advantage of the many plugins available for Flickr users. It can also help to gather missing information about images.

(ii) YouTube: It can be used to spread the word about

library events, share citizen journalism, and more on YouTube. Iyoutubeandlibrarieswik is a good example for this.

(iii) TeacherTube: This presents an excellent opportunity for instructor-librarian collaboration.

(iv) Second Life: This platform can be used to create a virtual library with streamed media, discussions, classes, and more.

(v) PBwiki: PBwiki is the world's largest provider of hosted business and educational wikis.

(vi) Footnote: On Footnote, original historical documents can be found. Personal anecdotes and experiences are found.

(vii) Digg : Digg's blog function information can be disseminated in an effective way.

(viii) StumbleUpon: StumbleUpon provides great content to find useful content, research tools, and more.

Examples of libraries using social networking technologies to connect with teens:

1. Blogs

- *Alachua County Library District's "Teen Scene" (FL)*
- *Allen County Public Library "ACPLTeens" (IN)*
- *Anderson Public Library "APL Teen Scene" (IN)*
- *Ann Arbor District Library, MI "Axis"*
- *Carnegie Library of Pittsburgh - blog for teens*
- *Chiddix Junior High (IL) library blogs "Mission Read" and "Charger uys Read"*
- *Coshocton Public Library (OH) "Teen News Blog"*
- *Evanston Public Library "The Virtual Loft" (IL)*
- *Fullerton Public Library "Teen E-dition" (CA)*
- *Goshen Public Library blog for teens*

- *Hillsdale Public Library (NJ) "Teen Speak"*
- *Homer Township Public Library, Homer Glen, IL "Teen Events"*
- *Homer Township Public Library, Homer Glen, IL "Teen Reviews"*
- *Lindenhurst Memorial Library (NY), "YA Weblog"*
- *Natrona County Public Library "Teen Zone" (Casper, WY)*
- *Northfield Mount Hernon (MA) school library blog, the "NMH ibrary Reading Room"*
- *Orange County Library System "Techno Teens Blog" (Orlando, FL)*
- *Orange Public Libraries - Orange, MA blog*
- *Osceola Library System (FL) -"Teen Blog"*
- *Pawtucket Public Library "In the Teen Zone"*
- *Pleasanton Public Library (CA) - "Teen Services"*
- *Prince George's County Memorial Library System (MD) "TeenSpace"*
- *Public Library of Mount Vernon and Knox County Branches (Knox*
- *ounty, OH) "YA Library News"*
- *Renton Public Library "RPL Teen Corner" (IN)*
- *Skokie Public Library (IL) "TeenTalk"*

2. *MySpace*

- *Allen County Public Library (KY)*
- *Anderson Public Library's Teen Scene (IN)*
- *Austin Public Library (TX)*
- *Baxter Memorial Library, (Gorham, ME)*
- *Brazoria County Library System (TX)*
- *Chesapeake Central Library (VA)*

- *Dakota County Public Library(MN)*
- *East Lansing Public Library (MI)*
- *Goshen Public Library (Goshen, NY)*
- *Grand Prairie Public Libraries (TX)*
- *Cleveland Heights-University Heights Public Library*
- *Johnston Public Library (IA)*
- *Leesburg Public Library (FL)*
- *Missouri River Regional Library (MO)*
- *Moon Public Library (PA)*
- *Morgan Hill Library, Santa Clara County Library (CA)*
- *Nashua Public Library (NH)*
- *Nelson County Public Library (KY)*
- *Northport-East Northport Public Library (NY)*
- *Niagara Falls Public Library (Ontario)*
- *Orange County Library System (Orlando, FL)*
- *Osceola Library System (FL)*
- *Oliver Wendell Holmes Library, Phillips Academy (Andover, MA)*
- *Pawtucket Public Library (RI)*
- *Prince George's County Memorial Library System (MD)*
- *Plano Public Library System (TX)*
- *Plattekill Public Library (NY)*
- *Science Technology Library (Queens, NY)*
- *Trails Teens Library (Independence, MO)*
- *Woburn Public Library (MA)*
- *Alachua County Library District's Teen Scene (FL)*
- *Augusta Library Teen Scene (GA)*
- *Austin Public Library Teen Services (TX)*
- *Brookfield Public Library Young Adults (IL)*

- *Carnegie Library of Pittsburgh Teen space*
- *Carnegie Library of Pittsburgh, Carrick Branch Teen space*
- *Clark County Public Library (Springfield, OH) Information Place*
- *Contra Costa County Library "Bringing teens and ideas together" (CA)*
- *Cook Memorial Public Library (IL) Teens*
- *Cornelius Public Library (NC) Teen Talk*
- *Coshocton Public Library (OH) Teen Animanga Club*
- *Dakota County Public Library Teen Tech 101*
- *Dearborn Heights City Libraries Teen Advisory Board (MI)*
- *Evanston Public Library Teen Virtual Loft (IL)*
- *Freedom Regional Library (NC) Freedom Teen Zone*
- *Fullerton Public Library YA MySpace page*
- *Glenview Public Library Teen Corner (IL)*
- *Greenwood Public Library (IN) [1]*
- *Haverhill Public Library (MA) Teen Department*
- *Kanawha County Public Library (WV)*
- *London Public Library Teen Annex (ON, CAN)*
- *Mountain Island (NC) Teen Corner*
- *Otis Library (Norwich, CN) YA librarian space Pasadena Public Library's Teen Central (CA)*
- *Peabody Institute Library (Peabody, MA) Wally the YA Wizard*
- *Pleasanton Public Library (CA) PTown Teen Lib*
- *Port Orchard Branch Library's Teen Isle (Kitsap Regional Library, WA)*
- *Public and academic libraries on MySpace*
- *Public Library of Charlotte and Mecklenburg County*

ImaginOn

- *Public Library of Mount Vernon and Knox County TeenSpace (OH)*
- *Seattle Public Library's Teen Center (page managed by the Teen Center Advisors)*
- *Steele Creek (NC) Teen Library*
- *Topeka & Shawnee County Public Library Graffiti (KS)*
- *Wadsworth Public Library Library Teen Loft (OH)*

3. Facebook

- *Arapahoe Library District*
- *DeKalb County Public Library*
- *Evanston Public Library Teen Loft (IL)*
- *Fayetteville Public Library (AR)*
- *Fullerton Public Library (CA)*
- *East Lansing Public Library (MI)*
- *Grand Prairie Public Libraries (TX)*
- *Hennepin County Library*
- *The Houston Public Library*
- *Livermore Public Library*
- *Nelson County Public Library (KY)*
- *Manchester Library and Information Service (UK)*
- *National Library of Scotland*
- *UMASS Boston Healey Library*
- *Worcester Polytechnic Institute Gordon Library*
- *Worthington Libraries*

4. Flickr

- *London Public Library (ON, CAN)*
- *Clark County Public Library (Springfield, OH)*
- *Mesa County Libraries (Grand Junction, CO)*

- *Lindenhurst Memorial Library (NY)*
- *Austin Public Library (TX)*
- *Bloomington Public Library*
- *Faribault's Buckham Memorial Library*
- *Carnegie Library of Homestead (PA)*
- *Central Massachusetts Regional Library System*
- *Hillsdale Public Library (NJ)*
- *Homer Township Public Library*
- *Leesburg Public Library (FL)*
- *Public Library of Charlotte and Mecklenburg County*
- *Osceola Library System (FL)*
- *Oliver Wendell Holmes Library, Phillips Academy (Andover, MA)*
- *Skokie Public Library*
- *Wright Memorial Public Library (OH)*
- *Topeka & Shawnee County Public Library (KS)*
- *Evanston Public Library (IL)*
- *Nelson County Public Library (KY)*
- *Homer Township Public Library's Cicada Project*

5. *Podcasts*

- *"Lindenhurst Memorial Library Podcasts" (NY)*
- *Public Library of Charlotte and Mecklenburg County (NC)*
- *Orange County Library System (Orlando, FL)*
- *Homer Township Public Library (IL) teen audio reviews*
- *Peabody Institute Library "And That's Our Show"*

6. *Del.icio.us*

- *aplteens' bookmarks Austin Public Library (TX)*

- *bfya's bookmarks - Brookfield Public Library Young Adults (IL)*
- *homrteens' bookmarks - Homer Township Public Library, Homer Glen, IL*
- *Teen BookmarksLeesburg Public Library (FL)*
- *Osceola Reference bookmarks - Osceola Library System (FL)*

7. *The Ning*

- *Anderson Public Library's Teen Scene (IN)*

SOCIAL NETWORKING IN LIBRARIES TRENDS

Social software has, however, become much more accessible to the casual computer user since the development of the World Wide Web in 1994. Whilc many libraries had been experimenting with social software prior to 2005, this philosophy of extending services and communication beyond traditional models became very prominent in the literature and practice after this date. The current trends are as following:

- *An increase in the use of mobile applications for library services.*
- *Even more ebook readers and the popularity of the ones that already exist.*
- *The usage of more niche social networking sites for the public at large and this will spill over into libraries.*
- *An increase in the amount and usage of Google Applications such as Google Wave and other similar applications.*
- *Library websites will become more socialized and customized. Patrons will be able to interact more directly with the library's website.*
- *Libraries will use more open source software and more social networking sites to educate their patrons and*

for library literacy in order to save money.

- *More libraries will use podcasting and itunes U to communicate with patrons and to offer value.*
- *Social networking in libraries will be viewed more as a must and as a way to save money than as a fun thing to play with or to use to market the library.*

Libraries have awakened to the previously geek-dominated territory of social networking. The marketing and patron interaction possibilities ached to show their colleagues the new world. Not all librarians, however, have had the desire to leave the familiar surroundings of programs, catalogs, and websites. Social networking has the potential of connecting all three of those pillars and take patron interaction to a new dimension. Here are a few of the key points how social media for libraries is changing how libraries do business:

1. *Social Media has changed how patrons interact with the library.*
2. *Social Media has given libraries new options for marketing their services.*
3. *Social Media can be used as an avenue for change for libraries.*
4. *Social Media can be used very effectively to advocate for libraries.*

Libraries can leverage social media to get more attendance at public classes and other events. Many people simply misunderstand the concept. The social web, however, is much richer than a single social networking platform alone. It represents a cultural shift towards expression, collaboration, and interaction. Increasingly, Internet users are not satisfied with simply reading web pages. It is found that sharing photography on Flickr, reading interests on LibraryThing, or thoughts on Blogger delight to the social networking savvy people. Social sites for various interests are available such as genealogists, cat owners, music lovers, vloggers, crafters, and collectors. Some of library users invest time in the social web. Social web education can lead to a greater understanding and acceptance of this new global phenomenon.

REACHING TO USERS

Most libraries are not really using social media in the best ways possible and librarians. For example, most facebook fan pages for libraries do not get great results. Reason may be that most of the patrons are not on facebook to stay in touch with the library. Library can initiate few other activities such as using the facebook fan page and twitter account for promotion. Library can encourage users to install and use database and library related mobile applications. For example, The University of North Carolina has a great library mobile website. For example, Google Voice as a Google application could be used by a library to offer text messaging for the library. Here are the steps to implement it:

1. *Create a Google email account for the library.*
2. *Create a Google Voice account for the same email.*
3. *Create labels inside the account for each library employee and for each major category that people may contact us about. These include things such as reference questions, library catalog, recommendations, item requests, database and computer problems, etc.*
4. *Develop a work flow procedure for determining who answers the texts library receives and when.*

IMPACT OF ONLINE SOCIAL NETWORKING ON LEARNING

Social networking technologies are software that enables people to connect, collaborate and form virtual communities via the computer and/or Internet. Social networking web sites are those that provide this opportunity to interact. For understanding, sites that allow visitors to send emails, post comments, build web content and/or take part in live chats are all considered to be social networking sites. Social networking technologies have many positive uses among students. The nature of the medium allows them to receive feedback from librarians, teachers, peers, parents, and others. Social networking technologies create a sense of community. Colleges and libraries are working to integrate positive uses of social networking. By integrating social networking technologies into educational environments, students have the opportunity to learn from adults how to be safe and smart when participating in online social networks.

DEVELOPMENTAL ASSETS & SOCIAL NETWORKING

When colleges and libraries help students use social networking tools safely and smartly, they also help students meet their developmental assets as defined by the Search Institute. For example when students can:

- *Learn how to use blogs, wikis, and MySpace sites within an educational context they learn about boundaries and expectations.*
- *Are able to use social networking tools in learning they have a commitment to learning.*
- *Have the opportunity to communicate with peers, experts, authors, etc. via online social networking they develop social & cultural competence.*
- *Work with adults and peers on developing social network sites and teaching how to use these sites they are empowered.*
- *Have a voice in the future of the school or the library they gain a sense of personal identity and value.*
- *See how librarians and teachers use social networks*

they are presented with role models.

FLUCTUATIONS OF SOCIAL NETWORKING IN LIBRARY ENVIRONMENT

OCLC's latest report, "Sharing, Privacy and Trust in Our Networked World" examines web user practices and preferences on their favorite social sites; user attitudes about sharing and receiving information on social spaces, commercial sites and library sites; and information privacy. It also focuses on US librarians to look at social networking practices and preferences; their views on privacy, policy and social networks for libraries. Top reasons provided by general-public respondents for why the library should not build a social networking site included:

1. *'Library is for learning/information',*
2. *'Not the role of the library' and*
3. *'Library is not for socialising'.*
4. *Of the US library directors, few believed that social networking is a role for libraries – only a slightly higher percentage than the general public.*

The top reasons that these library directors provided for why the library should not build a social networking site included:

1. *'Not the role of the library',*
2. *'Enough social networking sites exist already',*
3. *'Library is for learning/information' and*
4. *'No time/resources'.*

Both the total general public respondents and library directors indicated that hosting book clubs was the top social networking service that libraries should consider if they were to build social networking sites. A small number of the total general public respondents also indicated that homework help, support groups, sharing interests and education services could be useful social networking library services. The report suggests that to engage library users on social sites, librarians not only have to participate more, but they will also have to challenge the traditional approaches to protecting users' information privacy. It also points out that the library brand must go from institutional to personal. As web users become both the consumers and the creators of the social web, the implications and possibilities for libraries are significant.

LIFE 2.0 AND LIBRARIES

Library would treat a new neighborhood or academic department in the perspective of Life 2.0. Librarians would come together on how to serve with the help of new tools and technologies and venturing into new areas. The digital lifestyle brings new challenges altogether before a librarian. People are dwelling in Second Life, in mobile devices, in Facebook or Twitter. Following examples of libraries give a picture of actively working to engage and serve people in Life 2.0.

Helsinki City Library : The music branch of this library has a performance stage and digital suites where users rent instruments and record, edit and mix performances—and deposit the result in the library collection. The branch is a vibrant part of the digital music community. The library began with the clientele and what they could do to serve them.

Cornell University Library : LibeCast features audio and video recordings (podcasts and vodcasts) about Cornell University Library and its exhibitions, events, lectures, services and history, offering the world a glimpse of life inside one of the nation's best research libraries. Their 90-second YouTube videos, Research Minutes that explain citations and searching are well-done, thoughtful, and thorough.

Alliance Library System : This library system was among the first to set up a 'library island' in Second Life, a virtual world that has more than 10 million users. The library island serves the Second Life community and has a number of monthly discussion groups, talks by authors and exhibits based on the information needs of residents.

With Life 2.0, librarians need to expand the vision beyond the physical library. Libraries really do have to be somewhere and everywhere, as every library should be. It's the concept, the idea of the library leaking out of the building. Libraries really are trying to figure out this Life 2.0 generation and modify their systems and services to appeal to them. Generation which has grown up with the Web is unique, and librarians understand that this is a real change. One feature that will attract the Google generation into digital libraries is GPS. It is easy to determine the coordinates of anything and to mash that up with Google Maps. Libraries will be able to link information geographically the way we now do topically. People are embracing digital presences differently and at different levels and paces, but it's more and more part of who they are. This is no longer a choice about how to consume media. It is a new way of living, most obvious in younger generation, but slowly expanding to encompass all of the consumers. Notion is that we are all leading steadily increasingly digital lives.

REFERENCES

1. *Yadav, Sid. "Facebook – The Complete Biography." Mashable: Social Networking News. August 25, 2008. http://mashable.com/2006/08/25/facebook-profile/*
2. *http://socialnetworkinglibrarian.com/*
3. *Ronan, Jana. 2003. Chat Reference. Libraries Unlimited, p. 2.*
4. *The WELL. 2008 Salon Media Group Inc. 101 Spear Street, Suite 203, San Francisco, CA 94105*
5. *http://www.well.com/aboutwell.html*
6. *"Social Networking Timeline." Searcher 15 no. 7 (July 2007): 38.*

7. *http://www.collegedegree.com/library/financial-aid*
8. *http://hdl.handle.net/1961/4533*
9. *Alemán, Ana M. Martínez; Wartman, Katherine Lynk, "Online social networking on campus: understanding what matters in student culture", New York and London : Routledge, 1st edition, 2009. ISBN 0-415-99019-X*
10. *Baron, Naomi S., Always on : language in an online and mobile world, Oxford ; New York : Oxford University Press, 2008. ISBN 978-0-19-531305-5*
11. *Cockrell, Cathy, "Plumbing the mysterious practices of 'digital youth': In first public report from a 'seminal' study, UC Berkeley scholars shed light on kids' use of Web 2.0 tools", UC Berkeley News, University of California, Berkeley, NewsCenter, 28 April 2008*
12. *Donald Carrington Davis, "MySpace Isn't Your Space: Expanding the Fair Credit Reporting Act to Ensure Accountability and Fairness in Employer Searches of Online Social Networking Services", 16 Kan. J.L. & Pub. Pol'y 237 (2007).*
13. *Else, Liz, and Turkle, Sherry. "Living online: I'll have to ask my friends", New Scientist, issue 2569, 20 September 2006. (interview)*
14. *Glaser, Mark, Your Guide to Social Networking Online," PBS MediaShift, August 2007*
15. *"Social Nets Engage in Global Struggle" - 66% of MySpace and Facebook users come from North America: Adweek website.*
16. *Nexopia stats on Alexa.com*
17. *Bebo - most popular of its kind in UK,(August 2007): TechCrunch website.*
18. *German Xing Plans Invasion of LinkedIn Turf: article from the MarketingVox website. http://www.marketingvox.com/german-xing-plans-invasion-of-linkedin-turf-030727/*
19. *Elevator Pitch: Why Badoo wants to be the next word in social networking, Mark Sweney , The Guardian, December 24, 2007.*
20. *Hi5 popular in Europe: article from the PBS MediaShift website.*
21. *"Why Users Love Orkut" - 55% of users are Brazilian: About.com website.*
22. *The Network Nation by S. Roxanne Hiltz and Murray Turoff (Addison-Wesley, 1978, 1993)*
23. *Cotriss, David (2008-05-29). "Where are they now: TheGlobe.com". The Industry Standard. http://www.thestandard.com/news/*

2008/05/29/where-are-they-now-theglobe-com.

24. *Romm-Livermore, C. & Setzekorn, K. (2008). Social Networking Communities and E-Dating Services: Concepts and Implicationsý. IGI Global. p.271*
25. *Knapp, E. (2006). A Parent's Guide to Myspaceý. DayDream Publishers. ISBN 1-4196-4146-8*
26. *Steve Rosenbush (2005). News Corp.'s Place in MySpace, BusinessWeek, July 19, 2005. (MySpace Page Views figures)*
27. *"Social graph-iti": Facebook's social network graphing: article from The Economist's website.*
28. *Over 200 social networking sites: InfoJuice website.*
29. *Gross, R and Acquisti, A (2005). Information Revelation and Privacy in Online Social Networks (The Facebook case). Pre-proceedings version. ACM Workshop on Privacy in the Electronic Society (WPES)*
30. *Danah boyd, (2007), Why Youth (Heart) Social Network Sites, MacArthur Foundation Series on Digital Learning - Youth, Identity, and Digital Media Volume (ed. David Buckingham). MIT Press*
31. *A New Generation Reinvents Philanthropy, Wall Street Journal website.*
32. *Search for "e-commerce, social networking". Google Trends.*
33. *Yelp Enables Check-Ins On Its iPhone App; Foursquare, Gowalla Ousted As Mayors*
34. *Nimetz, Jody. "Jody Nimetz on Emerging Trends in B2B Social Networking". Marketing Jive, November 18, 2007.*
35. *Liebeskind, Julia Porter, et al. "Social Networks, Learning, and Flexibility: Sourcing Scientific Knowledge in New Biotechnology Firms". Organization Science, Vol. 7, No. 4 (July-August 1996), pp. 428–443.*
36. *Carlson, Ben (April 28, 2010). "March 2.0: Success of the National Equality March relied on social media tools". Media Bullseye. http://www.mediabullseye.com/mb/2010/04/march-2-0-success-of-the-national-equality-march-relied-on-social-media-tools.html#idc-container. Retrieved 2010-04-29.*
37. *Arabie, Phipps, and Yoram Wind. "Marketing and Social Networks". In Stanley Wasserman and Joseph Galaskiewicz, Advances in Social Network Analysis: Research in the Social and Behavioral Sciences. Thousand Oaks, Calif.: Sage Publications, 1994, pp. 254–273. ISBN 0-8039-4302-4*

38. Chambers, Clem. "Murdoch Will Earn a Payday from MySpace". Forbes, March 30, 2006.

39. Tynan, Dan. "As Applications Blossom, Facebook Is Open for Business" Wired, July 30, 2007.

40. Flor, Nick V. (2000). Web Business Engineering: Using Offline Activities to Drive Internet Strategies. Reading, Mass.: Addison-Wesley. ISBN 0-201-60468-X; Flor, Nick V. "Week 1: The Business Model Approach to Web Site Design". InformIT, March 2, 2001. Description of the autonomous business model used in social network services.

41. Social network launches worldwide spam campaign E-consultancy.com.

42. Moreno MA, Fost NC, Christakis DA (2008). "Research ethics in the MySpace era". Pediatrics 121 (1): 157–61. doi:10.1542/peds.2007-3015. PMID 18166570.

43. David Rosenblum (2007). "What Anyone Can Know: The Privacy Risks of Social Networking Sites". http://www.computer.org/portal/web/csdl/doi/10.1109/MSP.2007.75.

44. Henry Jenkins and Danah Boyd (2006-05-24). "Discussion: MySpace and Deleting Online Predators Act (DOPA)". http://www.danah.org/papers/MySpaceDOPA.html.

45. Susan B. Barnes (2006-09-04). "A privacy paradox: Social networking in the United States". http://firstmonday.org/htbin/cgiwrap/bin/ojs/index.php/fm/article/viewArticle/1394/1312.

46. BBC (2009-03-25). "Social Network Sites 'Monitored'". http://news.bbc.co.uk/1/hi/uk_politics/7962631.stm

47. http://www.facebook.com/policy.php?ref=pf

48. Boyd, danah. "Why Youth (Heart) Social Network Sites: The Role of Networked Publics in Teenage Social Life"

49. Fatal MySpace internet hoax mother is charged, Herald Sun, 17 May 2008

50. Banned for keeps on Facebook for odd name, Sydney Morning Herald, 24 September 2008

51. Enhancing Child Safety and Online Technologies. Internet Safety Technical Task Force, Final Report of the Internet Safety Technical Task Force to the Multi-State Working Group on Social Networking of State Attorneys General of the United States. 2008 (published 31 December 2008). http://cyber.law.harvard.edu/pubrelease/isttf/ ; Mangu-Ward, Katherine (May 2009). "MySpace = Safe Space". Reason 41 (1): 16.

52. *Wilson, Charles (May 27, 2010), Child porn 'social networking site' busted by feds, Associated Press, http://www.washingtonpost.com/wp-dyn/content/article/2010/05/27/AR2010052700559.html*
53. *Computer Science Illuminated*
54. *Boyd, Danah. "Why Youth (Heart) Social Networking Sites: The Role of Networked Publics in Teenage Social Life." Dokutech Eres. Web. <http://eres.ucsc.edu/eres/coursepage.aspx?cid=3840&page=docs#>.*
55. *http://www.dailymail.co.uk/news/article-1153583/Social-websites-harm-childrens-brains-Chilling-warning-parents-neuroscientist.html*
56. *http://blogs.forbes.com/docket/2010/06/17/amazon-secures-patent-for-social-networking-system/*
57. *US Patent and Trademark Office Patent number 7,739,139*
58. *Network World*
59. *"MySpace exposes sex predators", use of its content in the courtroom: Herald and Weekly Times (Australia) website.*
60. *"Getting booked by Facebook", courtesy of campus police: Milwaukee Journal Sentinel website.*
61. *"Police use Facebook to identify weapon carriers" The Journal (England) website.*
62. *Government Agencies Establishing Presence on Social-Networking Sites*
63. *OSTP Press Release Announcing Review (pdf, 50k)*
64. *Latest LinkedIn Facts*
65. *MySpace, Facebook Add Opportunity for Love, Trouble to Online Dating, FOXNews.com website.*
66. *MySpace Adds a Security Monitor, NPR.com website.*
67. *Online Dating: Can Social Networks Cut In?, internetnews.com website.*
68. *Online Dating vs. Social Networking – Which Will Emerge as Premier Matchmaker?, WRAL.com website.*
69. *Social networks vs. dating sites Commentary: Fragmenting may save online dating sites, marketwatch.com website.*
70. *Seeking Love Around The Web , Forbes.com website.*
71. *learncentral.org*

72. *Social Networking: Now Professionally Ready, PrimaryPsychiatry.com website.*

73. *Social Networks Impact the Drugs Physicians Prescribe According to Stanford Business School Research, Pharmalive.com website.*

74. *Comprehensive listing of medical applications using social networking via Dose of Digital*

75. *http://opensource.appleseedproject.org/*

76. *http://onesocialweb.org/*

77. *How Libraries Can Really Use Social Media to Make a Difference and Reach Their Patrons*

78. *March 20, 2011 by • 1 Comment*

Filed under: Social Networking for Libraries

79. *Share http://www.facebook.com/sharer.php?u=http%3A%2F%2Fsocialnetworkinglibrarian.com%2F2011%2F03%2F20%2Fhow-libraries-can-really-use-social-media-to-make-a-difference-and-reach-their-patrons%2F&src=sp*

80. *"http://wikis.ala.org/yalsa/index.php/Examples_of_libraries_using_social_networking_technologies_to_connect_with_teens"*

81. *http://feeds.feedburner.com/blogspot/Friends*

82. *http://bennington.facebook.com/profile.php?id=69000469*

83. *http://www.myspace.com/denver_evolver*

84. *http://profile.myspace.com/index.cfm?fuseaction=user.viewprofile&friendid=55463981*

85. *http://profile.myspace.com/index.cfm?fuseaction=user.viewprofile&friendid=42712933*

86. *http://profile.myspace.com/index.cfm?fuseaction=user.viewprofile&friendid=66100981*

87. *http://wikis.ala.org/yalsa/index.php/Special:Whatlinkshere/Examples_of_libraries_using_social_networking_technologies_to_connect_with_teens*

88. *http://acldteenscene.wordpress.com/*

89. *http://acplteens.wordpress.com/*

90. *http://andersonya.blogspot.com/*

91. *http://www.aadl.org/services/axis*

92. *http://clpteens.blogspot.com/*

93. *http://cjhsimc.edublogs.org/*

94. *http://guysread.edublogs.org/*

95. *http://yablog.coshoctonlib.org/teenblog.html*
96. *http://eplteen.wordpress.com/*
97. *http://www.fullertonlibrary.org/yablog/*
98. *http://teens.goshenpubliclibrary.org/*
99. *http://hillsdale.bccls.org/teens/index.html*
100. *http://www.homerlibrary.org/teenevents.asp*
101. *http://www.homerlibrary.org/teenreviews.asp*
102. *http://lindenhurstmemoriallibrary.wordpress.com/*
103. *http://ncplteenzone.blogspot.com/*
104. *http://nmhlibrary.typepad.com/the_reading_room/*
105. *http://blog.ocls.info/teens/*
106. *http://orangelibraries.blogspot.com/*
107. *http://osceolateens.blogspot.com/*
108. *http://teenlibrarianreads.blogspot.com/*
109. *http://www.ptownteenlib.blogspot.com/*
110. *http://pgteenspace.wordpress.com/*
111. *http://yalibrarynews.blogspot.com/*
112. *http://yalibrarynews.blogspot.com/*
113. *http://rentonteens.blogspot.com/*
114. *http://skokietalk.info/teentalk*
115. *http://www.myspace.com/allencountypubliclibrary*
116. *http://www.myspace.com/andersonlibrary*
117. *http://www.myspace.com/austinpubliclibrary*
118. *http://www.myspace.com/baxterlibrary*
119. *http://www.myspace.com/chesapeake_library_teens*
120. *http://www.myspace.com/dakotacountylibrary*
121. *http://www.myspace.com/goshenpubliclibrary*
122. *http://www.myspace.com/gp_libraries*
123. *http://www.myspace.com/leesburgpubliclibrary*
124. *http://www.myspace.com/ocls*
125. *http://www.myspace.com/nenplteenspace*
126. *http://www.myspace.com/plattekill_library*
127. *http://www.myspace.com/trailswest*
128. *http://www.myspace.com/owhlibrary*
129. *http://www.myspace.com/science_tech_library*

130. *http://www.myspace.com/woburnpubliclibrary*
131. *http://www.myspace.com/acld_teenscene*
132. *http://www.myspace.com/augustateenscene*
133. *http://www.myspace.com/aplteens*
134. *http://www.myspace.com/bfya*
135. *http://www.myspace.com/ourlibrary*
136. *http://www.myspace.com/teentech101*
137. *http://www.myspace.com/evanstonteenloft*
138. *http://www.myspace.com/kcplteenzone*
139. *http://groups.myspace.com/myspacelibraries*
140. *http://socialnetworkinglibrarian.com/2011/03/20/how-libraries-can-really-use-social-media-to-make-a-difference-and-reach-their-patrons/*
141. *How Libraries Can Really Use Social Media to Make a Difference and Reach Their Patrons. http://www.ncsu.edu/featured-stories/innovation-discovery/nov-2009/mlib/index.php*
142. *Using Google Voice to Offer Text Reference. http://socialnetworkinglibrarian.com/2011/02/16/use-google-voice-to-offer-text-reference/*
143. *www.searchinstitute. Org*
144. *Joe Janes. The impact of Life 2.0 on libraries. http://www.ischool.washington.edu/people/facdirectory.aspx?id=3122*
145. *http://www.lib.hel.fi/*
146. *http://www.library.cornell.edu/*
147. *http://www.alliancelibrarysystem.com/*
148. *http://secondlife.com/*

4

INSTANT MESSAGING AND SERVICES IN LIBRARY

INTRODUCTION

Instant messaging (IM) is a form of real-time direct text-based communication between two or more people using personal computers or other devices. It includes shared software clients. The user's text is conveyed over a network, such as the Internet. More advanced instant messaging software clients also allow enhanced modes of communication, such as live voice or video calling. IM falls under the umbrella term online chat, as it is a real-time text-based networked communication system, but is distinct in that it is based on clients that facilitate connections between specified known users (often using "Buddy List", "Friend List" or "Contact List"), whereas online 'chat' also includes web-based applications that allow communication between (often anonymous) users in a multi-user environment.

In addition to e-mail and the World Wide Web, instant messaging is one of the most popular services on the Internet. In its simplest form, instant messaging allows users to have instant, live, text-based "chats" with others over the Internet. Unlike e-mail, in which one sends a message that is stored in the recipient's electronic mailbox until he or she logs on to read it, when using an IM service both sender and recipient are online simultaneously; the moment one sends a message, the other sees it on his or her screen. Instant messaging allows online communication between two or more people using typed text sent via computers in real time. The use of instant messaging in libraries to provide a virtual reference service increases the availability of services to clients at no cost to the library offers an alternative method of communication to users and brings the library to the community. Basically, instant messaging is a collection of technologies used for real-time text-based communication between two or more participants over the Internet, or other types of networks. Online chat and instant messaging differs from other technologies such as e-mail due to the perceived synchronicity of the communications by the users –chat happens in real-time. Some systems permit messages to be sent to people not currently 'logged on' (offline messages), thus removing some of the differences between IM and e-mail (often done by sending the message to the associated e-mail account). IM allows effective and efficient communication. It allows immediate receipt of acknowledgment or reply. In many cases instant messaging includes additional features which can make it even more popular. Instant messaging may be a controversial topic for libraries and reference work, but that many years ago libraries also debated telephone reference.

EXAMPLES OF LIBRARIES USING INSTANT MESSAGING

Homer Township : Public Library in the US offers instant messaging homerlibrary.org/.

St. Joseph County : Public Library, also in the US, has user names for AIM, Yahoo! and MSN Messenger.

BACKGROUND

Instant messaging predates the Internet, first appearing on multi-user operating systems like Control time-Sharing System (CTSS) and Multics in the mid-1960s. With the development so networks developed, the protocols spread with the networks. Some of these used a peer-to-peer protocol (e.g. talk, ntalk and ytalk), while others required peers to connect to a server (as talker and IRC). During the Bulletin board system (BBS) phenomenon that peaked during the 1980s, some systems incorporated chat features which were similar to instant messaging; Freelancin' Roundtable was one prime example.

In the last half of the 1980s and into the early 1990s, the Quantum Link online service for Commodore 64 computers offered user-to-user messages between currently connected customers which they called "On-Line Messages" (or OLM for short). Quantum Link later became America Online and made AOL Instant Messenger (AIM). It could be considered a sort of GUI, albeit much more primitive than the later Unix, Windows and Macintosh based GUI IM programs. OLMs were what Q-Link called "Plus Services" meaning they charged an extra per-minute fee on top of the monthly Q-Link access costs.

Modern, Internet-wide, GUI-based messaging clients began to take off in the mid 1990s with PowWow, ICQ, and AOL Instant Messenger. Similar functionality was offered by CU-SeeMe in 1992; though primarily an audio/video chat link, users could also type messages to each other. AOL later acquired Mirabilis, the creators of ICQ; a few years later ICQ (now owned by AOL) was awarded two patents for instant messaging by the U.S. patent office. Meanwhile, other companies developed their own applications (Excite, MSN, Ubique, and Yahoo), each with its own proprietary protocol and client; users therefore had to run multiple client applications if they wished to use more than one of these networks. In 2000, an open source application and open standards-based protocol called Jabber was launched. The protocol was standardized under the name Extensible Messaging and Presence Protocol" (XMPP). XMPP servers could act as gateways to other IM protocols. Multi-protocol clients can use any of the popular IM protocols by using additional local libraries for each protocol. IBM Lotus Sametime's November 2007 release added IBM Lotus Sametime Gateway support for XMPP. In the current era, social networking providers often offer IM capabilities. Many instant messaging services offer video calling features, Voice Over IP (VoIP) and web conferencing services. Web conferencing services can integrate both video calling and instant messaging capabilities. Some instant messaging companies are also offering desktop sharing, IP radio, and IPTV to the voice and video features.

Before the Internet became popular, a lot of people were already online. The major online services, such as America Online (AOL), Prodigy and CompuServe, were the main way that ordinary people could connect and communicate with each other online. Online services provide the actual interface that you use when you're connected to the service, which creates a targeted experience for users. Instant messaging really exploded on the Internet scene in November 1996. That's when Mirabilis introduced ICQ, a free instant-messaging utility that anyone could use. ICQ (I seek you), uses a software application, called a client, that resides on user's computer. The client communicates with an ICQ server whenever he is online and the client is running. In June 1998, AOL acquired Mirabilis and ICQ. The ICQ model is the basis for most instant-messaging utilities on the market today.

Instant messaging, or IM in Internet slang, consists of sending real time messages to another Internet user. Instant messaging is a bit more private than a typical chat room, and it is a much faster and simpler way to communicate than using email. Since instant messaging allows users to communicate in real time, users can respond quickly to questions or comments. Instant messaging is a great way to stay in touch with family members and friends while saving money on the long distance phone bills. Predators have been known to use instant messaging as well as chat rooms to seek out victims, so while IM may seem safer, it is not without risks. It is also possible to obtain viruses, worms, and Trojan horses through messaging, so care should be taken when accepting any files. Instant messaging is a great way to communicate. Like anything else, it should be used with care.

USING INSTANT MESSAGING

The following steps explain how to install an instant-messaging service.

1. *User goes to the download page and gets a copy of the free software client for the computer.*
2. *He installs the software and opens the client.*
3. *The client tries to connect to the server. It uses a proprietary protocol for communication.*
4. *Once the client is connected to the server, user can enter his name and password to log in to the server. If this is his first time on, he can sign up for an account and immediately begin using it. When the server verifies his name and password, he is logged in.*
5. *The client sends the server the connection information (IP address and number of the port assigned to the client) of the computer user is using. It also provides the user with the names of everyone in the contacts list.*
6. *The server creates a temporary file that has the connection information for user and the list of his contacts. It then checks to see if any of the users in his contact list are currently logged in.*

7. *If the server finds any of user's contacts logged in, it sends a message back to the client on his computer with the connection information for that user. The server also sends his connection information to the people in his contact list that are signed on.*
8. *When his client gets the connection information for a person in the contact list, it changes the status of that person to "online." User clicks on the name of a person in his contact list who is online, and a window opens that he can enter text into. User enters a message and clicks "send" or hit return to communicate with that person.*
9. *Because his client has the IP address and port number for the computer of the person that user sent the message to, his message is sent directly to the client on that person's computer. In other words, the server is not involved at this point. All communication is directly between the two clients.*
10. *The other person gets user's instant message and responds. The window that each of user sees on his respective computers expands to include a scrolling dialog of the conversation. Each person's instant messages appear in this window on both computers.*
11. *When the conversation is complete, user closes the message window. Eventually, he goes offline and exit. When this happens, the client sends a message to the server to terminate the session. The server sends a message to the client of each person on his contact list who is currently online to indicate that user has logged off. Finally, the server deletes the temporary file that contained the connection information for his client. In the clients of his contacts that are online, user's name moves to the offline status section.*

HOW INSTANT MESSAGING WORKS

The Internet has revolutionized the way of communication. E-mail has been the most rapidly adopted form of communication ever known. Less than two decades ago, not many people had heard of it. Now, many of us e-mail instead of writing letters or even calling people on the phone. People around the world send out billions of e-mail messages every day. But sometimes even e-mail isn't fast enough. This is why instant messaging has become so popular. Most IM programs provide these features:

- *Instant messages : Send notes back and forth with a friend who is online*
- *Chat : Create a chat room with friends or co-workers*
- *Web links : Share links to the favorite Web sites*
- *Video : Send and view videos, and chat face to face with friends*
- *Images : Look at an image stored on user's friend's computer*
- *Sounds : Play sounds for the friends*
- *Files : Share files by sending them directly to the friends*
- *Talk : Use the Internet instead of a phone to actually talk with friends*
- *Streaming content : Real-time or near-real-time stock quotes and news*
- *Mobile capabilities : Send instant messages from the cell phone*

MOBILE INSTANT MESSAGING

Mobile Instant Messaging (MIM) is the technology that allows Instant Messaging services to be accessed from a mobile/cellular device, ranging from a standard cell phone to an iPhone, to a Blackberry, to an Android-based device. It is done two ways:

- *Embedded Clients : There are tailored IM client for every specific device.*
- *Clientless Platform : It is a browser-based application that does not require downloading any software to the handset, and which enables all users and all devices from any network to connect to their Internet IM service– ideally. In practice, browser capabilities can pose problems.*

CONCERNED STAFF

For staff, library must train staff. This is the keystone to success and it need not be expensive. Training can be hands on, lecture style or it can be a virtual online tutorial using inexpensive web conferencing technology. In March 2005 the State Library of Queensland's Opal training project introduced a new course for Queensland public library staff. Emerging technology is a one day hands on course exposing the participants to blogs, wikis, RSS feeds, podcasts, screencasts/flash tutorials, and WiFi. The past years have seen a steady growth in the use of these technologies in world wide libraries. Librarians have introduced some of these new technologies to assist in the delivery of services.

For example:

- *Screencast tutorials can be created using the software product CaptureCamPro.*
- *Services Unit created a password protected wiki for its staff. The wiki is a project to create a complete, up to date and reliable source for various ICTS documents.*
- *The Public Library Services Unit has also developed a wiki for the Country Lending Service libraries of Queensland. Library staff throughout Queensland are encouraged to share their ideas, seek advice and support each other the Opal training project has been successfully using the Opal-Online and Talking*

Communities web conferencing software to deliver virtual online tutorials to library staff throughout Queensland.

INSTANT MESSAGING PROVIDERS

Not long after AOL bought ICQ, AOL Instant Messenger (AIM) became the IM leader. In the past few years, though, a number of services have cut into AIM's audience. Windows Live Messenger (formerly MSN Messenger) and Yahoo! Messenger, in particular, have become widely used around the globe. Google recently introduced its IM system, Google Talk. Proprietary multiprotocol applications like Trillian and Pidgin, which allow users to IM on several services at once, are also rapidly gaining in popularity. According to a 2006 study by comScore, which measures Internet usage, about half of the online population uses IM. The major IM utilities use a proprietary protocol that is not understood by other instant-messaging services, so users of one service are usually blocked from contacting members of another. A key reason for AIM's initial popularity is that it allowed AOL subscribers to communicate with nonmembers. One of the provisions of the AOL-Time Warner merger in 2001 was that AOL would allow access to the AOL community and AIM protocol, but since then other instant-messaging utilities have provided more accessibility. Microsoft and Yahoo! joined forces in 2006 to allow their users to communicate with each other on one service. It is important to note that instant messaging is not considered a secure way to communicate. Messages and connection information are maintained on servers controlled by the provider of the IM utility. Most utilities do provide a certain level of encryption, but they are not so secure that user should send any confidential information through the system. There have been reported cases of IM user logs being captured and used by nefarious sorts, and hackers have been known to instant-message virus-infected files. Voice Over Internet Protocol is thought to be more vulnerable to infiltration than text-based instant-messaging.

To address the information needs of clients and especially future users, libraries must understand and adopt the new and inexpensive tools and present conventional library services using these tools to connect with the community. As Helling observes 'Any effort we make to integrate technology into our library to address basic challenges can lead to new services that satisfy both our staff and clients'. These emerging technologies should be used to resolve problems, broaden the library service, ensure the viability of a service whilst increasing effectiveness and saving money. It is important to research the technologies now available and use them creatively to better serve the needs of library users—by providing simple access to what they want, when they want it and how they want it.

APPLICATIONS

Instant messaging has proven to be similar to personal computers, e-mail, and the World Wide Web, in that its adoption for use as a business communications medium was driven primarily by individual employees using consumer software at work, rather than by formal mandate or provisioning by corporate information technology departments. Tens of millions of the consumer IM accounts in use are being used for business purposes by employees of companies and other organizations. The adoption of IM across corporate networks outside of the control of IT organizations creates risks and liabilities for companies who do not effectively manage and support IM use. Companies implement specialized IM archiving and security products and services to mitigate these risks and provide safe, secure, productive instant messaging capabilities to their employees. The applications can be summarized as below:

- *It allows a user interact synchronously over the internet with anyone in the world*
- *Growth of distance learning*
- *It's free*
- *Easy to learn how to use and get up and running*

IN LIBRARIES

This technology has already been embraced quite rapidly by the library community. More widely instant messaging allows real-time text communication between individuals. Libraries have begun employing it to provide "chat reference" services, where patrons can synchronously communicate with librarians much as they would in a face-to-face reference context. Many might consider IM a Web 1.0 technology, as its inception predates the technology market crash and it often requires the downloading of software, whereas most 2.0 applications are wholly web-based. It is consistent with the tenets of Library 2.0: it allows a user presence within the library web-presence; it allows collaboration between patrons and librarians; and it allows a more dynamic experience than the fundamentally static, created-then-consume nature of 1.0 services. It is also considered 2.0 as it is becoming a more web-based application, and the software used by chat reference services is usually much more robust that the simplistic IM applications that are so popular (they often allow co-browsing, file-sharing, screen-capturing, and data sharing and mining of previous transcripts).

The future of these technologies in the library arena is interesting. By providing this interactive Web service, libraries have positioned themselves to adopt its successors quickly and expertly. Already the text-based nature of IM applications is changing into a more multi-media experience, where audio and video messaging is becoming more common. Even as they provide more multi-sensory experiences, they will become ubiquitous, available throughout the library's web-presence. Already libraries are placing links to their chat reference services within resources themselves, such as at the article level in subscription databases. Much as a patron in a physical library is almost by definition never far from a librarian, chat reference becoming more pervasive could provide a similar circumstance in the world of the Web. The time is perhaps not far away when chat reference can take place within the framework of the library network, providing a more seamless experience.

Further, it is conceivable that should a user allow such a service, these chat reference services can be prompted when certain user seeking behaviors are detected. For instance, as a user browses through certain resources, repeating steps and moving cyclically through a classification scheme or series of resources, a synchronous messaging service could be prompted to offer assistance. The physical counterpart to this is of course a patron wandering in book stacks, and a librarian, sensing their aimlessness, offering help. Library 2.0 will know when users are lost, and will offer immediate, real-time assistance. Libraries may do well to continue adopting this technology as it evolves, as it allows reference services in an online media to closely approximate the more traditional services of the physical library. The time will almost certainly soon come when Web reference is nearly indistinguishable from face-to-face reference; librarians and patrons will see and hear each other, and will share screens and files. In addition, the transcripts these sessions already provide will serve library science in ways that face-to-face reference never did. For the first time in the history of libraries, there will be a continuously collected transcription of the reference transaction, always awaiting evaluation, analysis, cataloging, and retrieval for future reference.

How libraries can set up IM based reference service

The library can follow the following steps to initiate the IM based reference service. It includes various activities such as installation of IM software to staff training as well.

1. *Register accounts*
   - *One popular service like AIM or multiple (MSN, Yahoo, AIM, GTalk, etc.) can be used.*
2. *Choose software (it's free)*
   - *Popular options: GAIM, Trillian, AOL Instant Messenger, Meebo*
3. *Determining the hours of service*
4. *Development of policies*
5. *Training to the staff*
6. *Market service to students*

INSTANT MESSAGING SERVER

Instant Messaging Server integrates easily with other suite products. Key features of it include:

- *Based on Java and XMPP*
- *Comprehensive IM features including presence, multi-user chat, alerts, file transfer, polls and avatar*
- *Client-to-client voice chat with Jingle protocol extension*
- *SMS gateway that delivers chats and alerts to offline users via SMS*
- *IMPS gateway that enables mobile instant messaging and presence service*

Benefits

Real-time collaboration : Enables instant messaging or chat, persistent conferences, moderated conferences, alerts, news, polls, file transfers, and calendar reminders for improved enterprise productivity and efficiency, enhanced service provider offerings, and building blocks for other real-time applications

XMPP support : Facilitates integration of instant messaging and presence functionality with a wide array of third-party and open-source clients, components, and other applications

Gateways to public networks : Can aggregate contacts across XMPP-based servers and public networks; provides out-of-the-box interoperability with AIM, MSN and Yahoo Messenger networks through co-packaged gateways that are included with the product

Presence awareness and management : Automatically updates users' availability as indicated by online activity and enables users to control access to their own presence, including the ability to be "invisible" while online

Enhanced security and privacy : Enables secure access via any browser inside or outside a corporate firewall using SSL

Virtual domain support : Allows service providers to host services for multiple organizations or corporate IT to host multiple departments within the enterprise on a single server, reducing the number of servers needed, facilitating management of large deployments, and lowering TCO

Scalability and availability : Provides organizations the ability to easily scale their deployments according to the size of the organization without having to re-architect their deployment

Voice and mobile support : Enables organizations to extend instant messaging capabilities to mobile phone users or give users the option of turning a chat session into a live voice call over the Internet

APIs and modular architecture : Protects infrastructure investments by enabling products to be easily extended and customized to meet specific or changing business requirements.

NEW INSTANT MESSAGING INNOVATIONS

IM capabilities have greatly expanded in recent years. Most services offer file-sharing, and AOL, Yahoo!, Google and MSN have integrated IM service with e-mail service, so users can receive e-mail notifications while instant messaging. Many providers also allow users to IM and file-share from their cell phones and mobile devices, allowing access to their services any place, any time. For example:

(i) A Google Talk user can archive IM conversations and also drag files and folders directly onto the chat window, with photos showing up instantly in their friend's chat window.

(ii) Windows Live Messenger allows instant-messaging between Xbox 360 gamers.

Most IM programs, including Windows Live Messenger and Google Talk, allow users to talk just as user would over a telephone, and some offer video-chat capabilities. Several free utilities combine various services. For example, Trillian provides a centralized location for AIM, ICQ, Windows Live, Yahoo! Messenger and IRC contacts. All contacts are shown in the same window, with different-colored circles representing each service. Trillian's "metacontact" feature displays one entry in the contact list for people with multiple IM memberships, and it's the only multiservice client that offers video-chat capabilities on nominal fees. It is for understanding that users of Pidgin can IM, transfer files and share photos with contacts in AIM, ICQ, IRC, Google Talk, Windows Live Messenger and Yahoo! Messenger. Its "Buddy Pounce" feature sends notifications when selected contacts change their online status or send IMs. Universal IM providers Meebo and eBuddy are Web-based, meaning they don't require a software download. eBuddy also offers a version of its service for cell phones. Friends IMing on Qnext, which works with all the major IM providers, can listen to each other's music files without having to download them.

IM technology is constantly changing. New features are rolled out so frequently that a roundup like this is almost obsolete before it's posted! MySpace is developing an IM service, which could have a considerable impact on the IM world. The next big thing could also be location-aware IMing, in which services pinpoint users' locations and allow them to communicate with people who are IMing in their areas. AOL has introduced a plug-in for IM users who have WiFi capabilities. Users can open a map to find out where people on their buddy lists are. Meetro is a multiservice IM service that encourages users in the same area to chat and view each others' profiles and pictures. This technology isn't yet available for cell phones and mobile devices.

Shibbolised Jabber Instant Messaging : Shibboleth Jabber Instant Messaging agent (Open Source Software for IM) utilizes Jabber IM with out-of-band Shibboleth authentication for secure anonymous chat (e.g. between an authenticated library user and a librarian), with programmable behaviour.

SOFTWIN is the first company in the world to foresee the explosion of Instant Messaging applications and the need to close the security loopholes left by these applications in the IT environment. SOFTWIN is the world leader in the protection of Instant Messaging Software (IMS) communications. Libraries can download freeware products and use them to protect their IMS communications.

RAKIM is an in-house system for live, online, chat-based reference. RAKIM stands for 'RAKIM: A Knowledge Instant Messenger'. The software can be downloaded here: http://styro.lib.muohio.edu/rakim/

Features are listed here:

- *Unlimited number of operators/librarian*
- *Librarian-patron chat*

- *Page-push*
- *Shared queue of patrons*
- *Ability to refer patrons to other librarians (personal queue)*
- *Shared/personal bookmarks*
- *Email transcripts to patrons*
- *Audible alert to librarian when new patron arrives*
- *Audible alert to patron when their call is answered*
- *Editable preferences for librarian*
- *Browser-based - no plugins (except to play alerts, and this can be turned off)*
- *Needs frames/javascript/css; right now, this means Netscape 4.X and IE, but support for Mozilla (and its offspring), Opera, Konqueror, and others is planned (clean up some javascript code)*
- *Relational database backend, using PHP's database abstraction layer provided by PEAR; in English, any relational database that PHP can connect to can be used to run the software...PHP runs on Unix-es and Win32, so the server platform is quite flexible.*
- *Currently, the only databases supported are MySQL and PostgreSQL; this will change in the near future*

EXPERIENCES AT LIBRARIES

The use of instant messaging (IM) technology for providing online reference services is increasing by leaps and bounds. There can be differences arising from the medium itself, differences in the categories of reference questions received, using several different categorization schemes, and differences in factors affecting willingness to return, to determine strengths and weaknesses of this medium. Since many libraries are considering implementing such a service, it is like for staff to provide reference service this way. The

IM can suggest ways of addressing some of the challenges of this new medium. Various studies reflect the increasing popularity of instant messaging (text messaging), once the domain of Internet enthusiasts and teenagers, for communication within and without companies. The advantages of the technique:

(i) immediacy of the telephone with the power of written words,

(ii) ease of use,

(iii) useful for collaborating on projects and sharing applications, and

(iv) the use of less storage than electronic mail and a much reduced archiving problem, whilst content is still held at server level.

Any specific software should include following aspects as well:

- *Finish administrative/reporting features*
- *Scripted interactions (automated-walkthrus)*
- *Exit surveys*
- *Librarian-to-librarian messages*
- *Voice over ip, if there is a Free, cross-platform solution*
- *More configurability*

VIRTUAL REFERENCES AND INSTANT MESSAGING:

The one activity where libraries have incorporated instant messaging is virtual reference (VR) services. The VR services that have become widely deployed in the last few years have often served as a librarian's first exposure to the world of instant messaging. The software for a typical virtual reference environment includes a chat window for communicating with the person who's posing the question, along with features that allow the librarian to push the appropriate Web page, or lead the customer through a session on a Web-based information resource. The chat component of most VR environments tames and domesticates the media, providing session logs, macros, and e-mail escape hatches. These features are not unlike the enhancements in other business-class instant messaging systems. Librarians may start using IM for its own sake because they have become aware that other types of organizations find it an attractive medium for certain kinds of exchanges.

Few considerations:

(i) *The success of chat-based reference at least partially depends on the level of comfort that the librarian at the keyboard has with conventions of instant messaging and the informal and terse slang that comes with the territory. Again, IM seems to be just as much about the style of communication as about the software that carries it.*

(ii) *Maybe other libraries have different patterns, but most of the libraries don't see much use of instant messaging among their staffs. Would the library staff be more comfortable with using chat-based VR to "talk" with patrons who have much more experience with IM?*

How it takes place!

Instant messaging isn't the only technology that gets my vote as "hip." Gigabit Ethernet gives us the ability to build networks that outpace the demand for bandwidth. The 802.11a and g flavors of Wi-Fi deliver wireless networks that offer more than-decent performance. RFID (radio frequency ID) chips can revolutionize the way libraries circulate and inventory their collections. OpenURL-based reference linking helps liberate libraries from the futile exercise of hard-coding links to electronic resources in their catalogs and provides an infrastructure where library users easily click through from a citation to the full text it describes. Metasearch technologies enable users to more easily find information within the myriad of electronic resources to which libraries subscribe. Web Services provide an infrastructure that supports the sharing of resources among diverse Web-based applications. Long apart of the e-commerce infrastructure, library applications are just beginning to latch on to this important Web architecture. There is a great promise of making a positive difference in the way librarians deliver services to their users. Although today finds each technology early in its life cycle, it is assumed each as stable enough to warrant serious attention. It's important, though, to distinguish solid, forward-looking "hip" technologies from those that are only "hype" technologies.

For example, University of Nevada, Las Vegas offers Instant Messaging Reference Service. There, the users are advised to use their favorite Instant Messenger to chat live with a UNLV librarian! Just add their screen name to their contact list to start chatting. Their services are as following:

	Service	*Screen Name*	*Web Login*
	AOL Instant Messenger (AIM)	*unlvlibrarian*	*AIM Express*
	Yahoo! Messenger	*unlvlibrarian*	*Yahoo! Web Messenger*
	iChat	*unlvlibrarian add as an AIM contact*	*Not available*
	MSN Messenger	*unlvlibrarian@ hotmail.com*	*MSN Web Messenger*
	Google Talk	*unlvlibrarian@ gmail.com*	*Not available*

Many individuals-mostly from the younger generation-prefer instant messaging to e-mail and other forms of electronic communication. In educational and business environments, instant messaging stands as the most popular means of communication. Instant messaging sometimes even displaces the telephone. Instant messaging isn't just about chatting with text. Some IM services let user enrich his instant messaging experience with live video. Instant messaging isn't limited to computers. It thrives on all sorts of mobile devices. PDAs and cell phones include text messaging capabilities. These represent a huge amount of communications. One of the recent developments involves interoperability in the instant messaging services, between providers such as AOL and cellular telephone text-messaging systems from companies like Cingular.

CREATING A USEFUL LIBRARY CATALOG

Libraries can discern the benefits of using IM or chat in the library catalog. Questions about using the library catalog are probably the second most frequent interaction at the reference desk. Students could chat with a reference librarian while they were having difficulties in the catalog. Staff can help the students at the point of need, helping their research. The users need not to come down to the reference desk to ask a question. For this purpose, example of the Meebo widget could be a great solution.

INSTANT MESSAGING AT WORKPLACE

Instant messaging increasingly finds use in the workplace-usually informally. It cannot happen without institutional support. In the same way that IM facilitates interactive person-to-person communication for personal relations, it serves as a natural medium for conversing with co-workers. Instant messaging emulates the hallway conversations-where the best exchange of ideas often takes place-much better than e-mail. Communicating in real time among a geographically dispersed group of co-workers fuels a level of collaboration.Yet several of the qualities of instant messaging that make it attractive for individual communications might cause problems when used at work.

Consumer oriented IM systems lack authentication, security, and accountability features essential in many business environments.

Instant messaging lends a sense of privacy. In a business environment, that lack of accountability and permanency can be a real problem. Instant messaging often finds its way into official business transactions such as confirming prices and availability of products, placing orders, answering questions asked by customers, assigning work tasks, and the like. In some industries, regulatory mandates exist that require that all such communications be documented and retained. In an evaporative medium such as instant messaging, compliance with these mandates presents a challenge. In acknowledgment of IM's benefits as a communications genre, a number of enterprise or business-class instant messaging systems have emerged. Palo Alto Networks, a company specializing in enterprise network products, summarized application traffic assessments for 20 large organizations — representing the behavior of over 350,000 users, and came to some interesting conclusions. It appears that enterprises have largely given up on controlling the use of IM, and existing policies, if any, are largely ignored.

Organizations of all types must protect themselves from the liability of their employees' inappropriate use of IM. The informal, immediate, and ostensibly anonymous nature of instant messaging makes it a candidate for abuse in the workplace. In most countries, corporations have a legal responsibility to ensure harassment-free work environment for employees. The use of corporate-owned computers, networks, and software to harass an individual or spread inappropriate jokes or language creates a liability for not only the offender but also the employer. Companies now include instant messaging as an integral component of their policies on appropriate use of the World Wide Web, e-mail, and other corporate assets.

In the last decade, a new class of IT security provider emerged to provide remedies for the risks and liabilities faced by corporations who chose to use IM for business communications. The IM security providers created new products to be installed in corporate networks for the purpose of archiving, content-scanning, and security-scanning IM traffic moving in and out of the corporation. Similar to the e-mail filtering vendors, the IM security providers focus on the risks and liabilities. With rapid adoption of IM in the workplace, demand for IM security products began to grow in the mid-2000s. During last quarter of previous decade, the preferred platform for the purchase of security software had become the "computer appliance", according to IDC.

Instant Messaging software solutions Companies/ Software

- *Lotus Sametime : As the leader in real-time collaboration for e-business, Sametime can make working with the extended team easier than ever before. It's not only about instant messaging, it's about using the Web to improve customer service, reduce travel costs, and create communities among the employees, customers, partners, and suppliers.*
- *Tech Instant Messenger : Tech Instant Messenger (TIM) is a simple messaging utility designed for local area networks. Modeled after AOL, Yahoo, and MSN Instant Messengers, TIM has the essential functionalities but not ads or fancy but useless features. The server is a light-weight program that can run on any Windows system. Any user on the local network or over the Internet can get on TIM if given the server's computer name or IP address. Communication in a household or business building no longer requires active Internet connection.*
- *NetLert : It is globally recognized Authority in Real-Time Communication. It facilitates Live, Reliable,*

Timely Support. No costly hardware upgrades are required. Custom Solutions for the organization and it is Platform Independent.

- *Network Assistant : Network Assistant is a multiple-mode user-friendly network communication utility, including real-time chat, shared whiteboard, and instant messaging. It is intended to be used in small office or home office (SOHO) local networks.*
- *Jabber : Jabber Communications Platform (JCP) is a robust software platform for instant messaging and presence-enabled applications and services. The platform has been designed to meet the rigorous demands of large-scale deployments, where requirements mandate superior server scalability, security, performance, reliability, and network integration.*
- *Odigo : Instant Messaging Solution. Odigo offers the most robust, interoperable and customized Instant Messaging & Presence Solutions available. Our suite of products and services include: Open IM Server - Odigo's highly scaleable, robust, reliable, and fault tolerant IM server is available for licensing or hosting by Odigo. Custom IM Clients - including fully customized Windows, Macintosh, Java, WAP, SMS, I-Mode and HTML clients, as well as additional community products and opportunities.*
- *People Link : PeopleLink Instant Messaging delivers the power of one-to-one and one-to-many real time text messaging to the business. Instant Messaging enables the employees, customers, and partners to quickly and easily communicate and share documents over the Web site, intranet, and extranet.*
- *VyPRESS : Founded in 1997, VyPRESS Research is a leading provider of instant messaging solutions for*

LANs/WANs and customized instant messaging systems for business. The Company's products are currently licensed in more than 60 countries. VyPRESS's clientele includes large corporations, government education entities and individual users worldwide.

- *12Planet : 12Planet Instant Messaging Server software offers a powerful solution for private business instant communication and collaborative work. 12Planet Instant Messaging Server enables the quick deployment of a powerful, dynamic, easy-to-use, reliable and cost-efficient instant messaging network allowing companies to offer either MSN, AIM, ICQ, Yahoo compatible public IM services or totally secure and private intranet or extranet instant messaging. The software is very easy to install and there is no need for client-side software.*

CHAT

Chat is a client/server solution that permits numerous users to conduct live public or private communications sessions via the Internet or corporate intranet. Users are required to install chat software on their machines. Many of the chat products offer Java-based client software, which requires a Java-enabled browser. Few others offer an HTML client that works in any Web browser or native clients, such as plug-ins for Netscape Navigator or Internet Explorer. Chat can be an important component of a business' CRM strategy, since it can help electronic business sites maintain a persistent customer base, cultivate customer loyalty, and build brand awareness by encouraging visitors to remain on a site longer and then consistently return to it. Chat can make a Web site less static and more dynamic.

- *Businesses should use chat. First, it allows customer support to communicate with consumers in a one-on-*

one conversation, answer their questions in real time, and moderate product demonstrations.

- *Chat can build customer communities increasing a customer's sense of ownership and compelling them to return. Scheduled chats, for example, have the potential to attract prospective customers who can discuss their experiences and share opinions.*
- *Chat sessions can also be held on a corporate intranet to improve communications and collaboration.*
- *Several risks that businesses may experience with the use of chat software to reach consumers. The most damaging is customer resentment.*

COMPARISON OF INSTANT MESSAGING CLIENTS

Basic general information about the real time communication services: creator/company, license/price, amongst others is given here:

Name	Author/ Creator	First public release	Type	License
Adium	Adam Iser, Evan Schoenberg	2001	Multi-protocol	GPL v2
AOL Instant Messenger (AIM)	AOL	1997	Single protocol	Clickwrap license
aMSN	The aMSN team	2002	Single protocol	GPL
Ayttm	Colin Leroy and Philip Tellis	2003	Multi-protocol	GPL
BitWise IM	BitWise Communi-cations, LLC	2002	Single protocol/ Encrypted	Clickwrap license
BitlBee	Wilmer van der Gaast	2002	IRC Gateway, Multi-protocol	GPL
Brosix	D-Bross	2006	Single protocol/ Encrypted	Clickwrap license

Name	*Author/ Creator*	*First public release*	*Type*	*License*
Centericq	*Konstantin Klyagin*	*1999*	*Multi-protocol*	*GPL*
climm	*Mattew D. Smith (up to ICQv5); Rüdiger Kuhlmann*	*1997; 2001*	*Dual protocol*	*GPL v2*
Coccinella	*Mats Bengtsson*	*1999*	*Single protocol*	*GPL v3*
Cspace	*Tachyon Technologies*	*2008*	*Single protocol*	*GPL*
Digsby	*Steven Shapiro*	*2008*	*Multi-protocol*	*Clickwrap license*
eBuddy	*Paulo Taylor*	*2003*	*Multi protocol*	*Clickwrap license*
eM Client	*E&S Software Ltd.*	*2006*	*Single protocol*	*Free*
EQO	*EQO Communications*	*2006*	*Multi-protocol*	*Clickwrap license*
emesene	*Luis Mariano Guerra*	*2006*	*Single protocol*	*GPL*
Empathy	*GNOME*	*2007*	*Multi-protocol*	*GPL*
Exodus	*Peter Millard*	*2002*	*Single protocol*	*GPL*
Fire	*Eric Peyton*	*1999*	*Multi-protocol*	*GPL*
Gabtastik	*Mesa Dynamics, LLC*	*2008*	*HTTP*	*Clickwrap license*
Gadu-Gadu	*Aukasz Foltyn*	*2000*	*Single protocol*	*Clickwrap license*
Gajim	*Yann Le Boulanger*	*2004*	*Single protocol*	*GPL*
GCN	*Jason K. Resch*	*2000*	*Single protocol*	*Clickwrap license*
GOIM	*Herbert Poul*	*2005*	*Single protocol*	*GPL*
Goofey	*Tim Mackenzie*	*1990s (Early 1990s)*	*Single protocol*	*Clickwrap license*

Name	Author/ Creator	First public release	Type	License
Google Talk	Google, Inc.	2005	Dual protocol	Clickwrap license
Gyachi		2006	Single protocol	GPL
iChat	Apple Inc.	2002	Multi-protocol	Clickwrap license
IBM Lotus Sametime	IBM, Ubique	1998	Multi-protocol-proprietary T.120, SIP, XMPP	Clickwrap license
ICQ	Mirabilis (AOL)	1996	Single protocol	Clickwrap license
IM+	SHAPE Services	2002	Multi-protocol	Clickwrap license
IMVU	Will Harveyfq	2001	Single protocol	Clickwrap license
InSpeak Commun-icator	Mark Jaafar GLobal Unicom, LLC	2004	Multi-protocol	Clickwrap license
Instantbird	Florian Quèze and Quentin Castier	2007	Multi-protocol	GPL v2
Jabbin	Jabbin Team	2005	Single protocol	GPL v2
Kadu	Kadu Team	2001	Single protocol	GPL v2
KMess	The KMess team	2002	Single protocol	GPL v2
Konnekt	Stamina	2002	Multi-protocol	Clickwrap license
Kopete	Kopete Team	2002	Multi-protocol	GPL
Licq	Graham Roff (up to v1.0) Jon Keating	1998	Multi-protocol	GPL
Mail.ru Agent	Mail.ru	2003	Single protocol	Clickwrap license
MCabber	Mikael Berthe	2005	Single protocol	GPL
meebo	Meebo, Inc.	2005	Multi-protocol, web-based	Clickwrap license

Name	*Author/ Creator*	*First public release*	*Type*	*License*
Meetro	*Paul Bragiel & Samuel Stauffer*	*2005*	*Multi-protocol*	*Clickwrap license*
Mercury Messenger	*Danny*	*2003*	*Single protocol*	*Clickwrap license*
MindSpring	*EarthLink*	*2006*	*Multi-protocol*	*Clickwrap license*
Miranda IM	*Miranda IM project*	*2000*	*Multi-protocol*	*GPL*
MySpaceIM	*MySpace*	*2006*	*Single protocol*	*Clickwrap license*
Naim	*Daniel Reed*	*1998*	*Multi-protocol*	*GPL*
Ometheus	*Ometheus*	*2007*	*Multi-protocol, web-based*	*Commer-cial license*
Omegler	*Flamefusion*	*2009*	*Single protocol*	*N / A*
Pandion	*Dries Staelens, Sebastiaan Deckers*	*2002*	*Single protocol*	*GPL*
Palringo	*Palringo Ltd*	*2006*	*Multi-protocol*	*Clickwrap license*
Paltalk	*Jason Katz*	*1998*	*Multi-protocol*	*Clickwrap license*
Pidgin (formerly Gaim)	*Mark Spencer*	*1998*	*Multi-protocol*	*GPL*
PopNote	*Mike Raymond*	*2004*	*Single Protocol*	*GPL v2*
pork	*Ryan McCabe*	*2002*	*AIM, IRC Gateway*	*GPL v2*
Proteus	*Justin Wood, et al.*	*2001*	*Multi-protocol*	*GPL*
Psi	*Justin Karneges*	*2001*	*Single protocol*	*GPL*
psyced	*psyced.org Project*	*1997*	*IRC+XMPP+ PSYC Gateway, Multi-protocol*	*GPL*

Name	*Author/ Creator*	*First public release*	*Type*	*License*
QIP	*Ilgam Zyulkorneev*	2004	*Multi-protocol*	*Clickwrap license*
Qnext	*Qnext Corp.*	2004	*Multi-protocol*	*Clickwrap license*
QuteCom	*QuteCom*	2004	*Multi-protocol*	*GPL*
qutIM	*Rustam Chakin, Ruslan Nigmatullin*	2008	*Multi-protocol*	*GPL*
Tencent QQ	*Tencent*	1999	*Single protocol*	*Clickwrap license*
RealTime Query	*realtimequery .com*	2005-2007	*Single protocol*	*Clickwrap license*
Scrapboy	*Scrapboy Digital Media Corporation*	2006	*Single protocol*	*N / A*
Skype	*Niklas Zennström and Janus Friis*	2003	*Single protocol*	*Clickwrap license*
talk	*Kipp Hickman*	1982	*Single protocol*	*BSD*
Tkabber	*Alexey Shchepin*	2002	*Single protocol*	*GPL*
Trillian	*Cerulean Studios*	2000	*Multi-protocol*	*Clickwrap license*
Trillian Pro	*Cerulean Studios*	2002	*Multi-protocol*	*Clickwrap license*
VZOchat	*Visicron Systems*	2005	*Single protocol*	*Clickwrap license*
Windows Live Messenger (formerly MSN Messenger)	*Microsoft Corporation*	1999	*Dual protocol*	*Clickwrap license*
Windows Messenger	*Microsoft Corporation*	2001	*Multi-protocol*	*Clickwrap license*

Name	Author/ Creator	First public release	Type	License
Microsoft Office Communicator	Microsoft Corporation	2005	Single protocol	Clickwrap license
Xfire	Xfire Inc.	2004	Dual protocol	Clickwrap license
Yahoo! Messenger	Yahoo!	1999	Dual protocol	Clickwrap license
Zephyr	Project Athena	1987	Single protocol	MIT
Sococo	Social Communi-cations Company	2008	Multi protocol	Clickwrap license

Features available to certain services are listed in table:

Client	Handwriting mode	Doc-kable	Multi-account	Spell check	User-Defined Graphical Smileys	Animations
Adium	No	Yes	Yes	Yes	Partial	Partial
AIM	No	Yes	No	No	?	Partial
aMSN	Yes	Yes	Yes	Yes	Yes	Yes
Ayttm	No	No	Yes	Yes	Yes	No
Brosix	?	?	?	?	Yes	Yes
Coccinella	?	Yes	Yes	Yes	?	?
Digsby	No	Yes	Yes	Yes	No	No
eM Client	No	Yes	Yes	Yes	No	No
Empathy	No	Yes	Yes	Yes	Yes	?
EQO	n/a	n/a	Yes	No	No	No
Gajim	?	Yes	Yes	?	Yes	Yes
Google Talk (standalone)	No	Yes	No	No	No	No
Google Talk (Gmail)	No	?	?	No	No	Yes
Gyachi	No	Yes	No	No	No	Yes

Client	Handwriting mode	Doc-kable	Multi-account	Spell check	User-Defined Graphical Smileys	Animations
iChat	No	?	Yes	Yes	?	?
ICQ	No	Yes	No	Yes	No	Yes: tZer
InSpeak Commu-nicator	Yes	No	Yes	No	Yes	Yes
Kadu	?	Yes	?	Yes	Partial	Yes: smileys
KMess	Yes	Yes	Yes	Yes	Yes	Yes
Kopete	No	Yes	Yes	Yes	Yes	Yes: smileys
Mercury Messenger	Yes	Yes	Yes	No	?	?
Miranda IM	No	Yes	Yes	Yes	Yes	Yes
Microsoft Messenger for Mac	No	?	?	No	Yes	Partial
Nimbuzz	No	No	No	No	No	No
QuteCom	?	?	Yes	?	?	?
Pandion	No	No	No	No	Yes	Yes
Pidgin formerly Gaim	No	Yes	Yes	Yes	Yes	Yes: smileys and user icons
PopNote	Yes	No	Yes	No	No	No
Psi	No	?	Yes	Yes	?	?
psyced	No	No	No	No	?	?
QIP	Yes	Yes	Yes	Yes	Yes	Yes: smileys
QQ	No	Yes	Yes	No	Yes	Yes
qutIM	No	Yes	Yes	No	Yes	Yes: Animated emoticons
Sim-IM	?	Yes	Yes	Yes	Yes	No
Skype	No	No	No	No	?	Yes:

Client	Handwriting mode	Doc-kable	Multi-account	Spell check	User-Defined Graphical Smileys	Animations
						Animated emoticons
Trillian	Yes	Yes	Yes	No	No	Yes: Animated emoticons
Trillian Pro	Yes	Yes	Yes	Yes	?	Yes: Animated emoticons
Trillian Astra	Yes	Yes	Yes	Yes	Partial	Yes: Animated emoticons
VoxOx	No	No	Yes	Yes	No	No
VZOchat	No	No	No	No	No	Yes: Animated user icons
Windows Live Messenger	Yes	No	Yes	No	Yes	Yes: Animated emoticons, winks
Windows Messenger	No	No	No	No	?	?
Yahoo! Messenger	?	?	?	No	?	?

MULTIPROTOCOL INSTANT MESSAGING APPLICATION

A multiprotocol instant messaging application is client software composed of an IM application which may connect to multiple IM networks. The networks supported include: AOL Instant Messenger, ICQ, XMPP (including Google Talk, Gizmo5, and other XMPP-based networks), MSN Messenger, QQ, Yahoo! Messenger, as well as specialized networks such as Novell GroupWise and Zephyr. Some provide an IM *interface to IRC. The major IM networks have moved to block multi-protocol clients. At one stage, the Trillian developers made new releases every few days to restore access, as AOL attempted to discourage use of the third-party clients. XMPP itself provides an alternative to directly managing each IM account through the multi-protocol client: IM gateways, or transports. Using transports, connections to the closed IM networks are handled by a gateway on the users XMPP server, while XMPP users talk to each other directly. This seems to function well for users running a private XMPP server, but large public XMPP servers sometimes become the subject of IP blocks from the large networks, or are not able to handle the high load. On the other hand, using a XMPP transport brings several advantages, both for the end user and the programmer of the client:*

(i) *less complexity on the client level,*
(ii) *possibility to log in with multiple clients (e.g. mobile phone and computer) to the same account,*
(iii) *lower chance for security and privacy risks for the end user thanks to the use of only one connection that can be secured to the Internet and thanks to the fact that people will not know your IP,*
(iv) *possibility to archive messages on the XMPP server (as easy as normal XMPP messages) to comply with regulations such as the Sarbanes-Oxley Act, amongst others.*

Few examples are given as below:

- *Adium, Fire, iChat, and Proteus (for Mac)*
- *Miranda IM, Trillian and Digsby (for Windows)*
- *Kopete (for Linux and other operating systems running KDE)*
- *Empathy (for Linux and other operating systems running GNOME)*

- *Pidgin, Qnext and SIM[1] (multi-platform)*
- *IM+[2] (mobile multi-platform)*

Risks and liabilities

Although instant messaging delivers many benefits, it also carries with it certain risks and liabilities, particularly when used in workplaces. Among these risks and liabilities are:

- *Security risks (e.g. IM used to infect computers with spyware, viruses, trojans, worms)*
- *Compliance risks*
- *Inappropriate use*
- *Trade secret leakage*

Crackers (malicious "hacker" or black hat hacker) have consistently used IM networks as vectors for delivering phishing attempts, "poison URLs", and virus-laden file attachments from 2004 to the present. Hackers use two methods of delivering malicious code through IM. Viruses, computer worms, and trojans typically propagate by sending themselves rapidly through the infected user's buddy list. An effective attack using a poisoned URL may reach tens of thousands of people in a short period when each person's buddy list receives messages appearing to be from a trusted friend. The recipients click on the web address, and the entire cycle starts again. Infections may range from nuisance to criminal, and are becoming more sophisticated each year. IM client software often requires the user to expose open UDP ports to the world, increasing the threat posed by potential security vulnerabilities.

REFERENCES

1. *Homer Township: Public Library in the US offers instant messaging homerlibrary.org/.*
2. *St. Joseph County: Public Library, also in the US, has user names for AIM, Yahoo! and MSN Messenger. libraryforlife.org/asksjcpl/*

asksjcpl.html.

3. *Using Instant Messenger Services By Jeffrey Branzburghttp://www.techlearning.com/db_area/archives/TL/2002/11/inservice.html)*
4. *http://communication.howstuffworks.com/ip-telephony.htm*
5. *http://www.aim.com/*
6. *http://messenger.msn.com/*
7. *http://www.google.com/talk/*
8. *http://gaim.sourceforge.net/*
9. *http://www.ceruleanstudios.com/*
10. *http://www.aim.com/*
11. *http://www16.meebo.com/*
12. *http://communication.howstuffworks.com/file-sharing.htm*
13. *http://shibjim.sourceforge.net/*
14. *Instant messaging reference: how does it compare? by : Christina M Desai The Electronic Library V. 21 No: 1 Page: 21-30 2003*
15. *Instant benefits (instant messaging) Author: K. Cushing | Computer Weekly (UK) 18 Jul 2002: p. 24*
16. *http://styro.lib.muohio.edu/rakim/*
17. *http://www.unlv.edu/*
18. *http://www.aim.com/aimexpress.adp*
19. *http://people.live.com/*
20. *www.bitdefender.com/html/freeware_products.php*
21. *An example of Creating a useful library catalog. http://socialnetlibraries.wordpress.com/2007/12/11/creating-a-useful-library-catalog/*
22. *www.meebo.com*
23. *http://www.paloaltonetworks.com/literature/aur_registration.html*
24. *Lotus Sametime http://www.lotus.com/products/lotussametime.nsf/wdocs/homepage*
25. *www.kingofmath.com/Freeware/tim/*
26. *www.kingofmath.com/Freeware/tim/*
27. *NetLert. http://www.netlert.com/*
28. *http://www.gracebyte.com/nassi/*
29. *Jabber. http://www.jabber.com/products/index.shtml*

30. *Odigo. http://corp.odigo.com/products/index.html*
31. *People Link. http://www.peoplelink.com/genome/os_apps_im.html*
32. *VyPRESS. http://www.vypress.com/about.asp*
33. *12Planet. http://www.12planet.com/en/software/messenger/*
34. *Instant messaging corporate applications http://www.tek-tips.com/gthreadminder.cfm/lev2/67/lev3/73/pid/611*
35. *www.BitDefender.com*
36. *www.bitdefender.com/html/freeware_products.php*
37. *http://www.librarysupportstaff.com/Issues%20in%20Science%20and%20Technology%20Librarianship*
38. *http://www.techrepublic.com/article.jhtml?src=search&id=r00520001006ggr01.htm*
39. *http://netforbeginners.about.com/od/blogchatinstantmessaging/f/email_vs_im.htm*
40. *Instant Messaging on CTSS and Multics*
41. *Screenshot of a Quantum Link OLM*
42. *Summary of final decisions issued by the trademark trial and appeal board, January 16-20, 2006*
43. *"Important and Long Delayed News", Announcement of Gaim renaming (to Pidgin), April 6, 2007*
44. *http://news.bbc.co.uk/2/hi/uk_news/magazine/8698174.stm*
45. *Instant Messaging, NetworkDictionary.com.*
46. *"Oracle Buzzes with Updates for its Beehive Collaboration Platform". CMSWire. http://www.cmswire.com/cms/enterprise-20/oracle-buzzes-with-updates-for-its-beehive-collaboration-platform-004538.php.*
47. *http://im.about.com/od/imforbusiness/a/topbizims.htm*
48. *http://im.about.com/b/2008/03/15/reader-questions-im-privacy-at-work.htm*
49. *"IM Security Center". http://www.imsecuritycenter.com/.*
50. *"Why just say no to IM at work". blog.anta.net. 2009-10-29. ISSN 1797-1993. http://blog.anta.net/2009/10/28/why-just-say-no-to-im-at-work/.*
51. *"ESG compliance report excerpt, Part 1: Introduction". http://searchstorage.techtarget.com/tip/0,289483,sid5_gci906152,00.html.*

52. *FINRA, Regulatory Notice 07-59, Supervision of Electronic Communications, December 2007*

53. *"Akonix Warns Corporations of Risqué Employee IM Behavior". http://www.akonix.com/press/releases-details.asp?id=130.*

54. *Chris Christiansen and Rose Ryan, International Data Corp., "IDC Telebriefing: Threat Management Security Appliance Review and Forecast"*

55. *http://tencent.com/en-us/content/ir/news/2009/attachments/20090812.pdf*

56. *XMPP Software: Clients*

57. *Coccinella | Instant Messaging Program with Whiteboard*

58. *Stephens, M Weblogs and libraries Sirsi. Dynix Institute Video 2006 www.sirsidynixinstitute. com/viewvideo.php?vid=20060215*

59. *Blood, R The weblog handbook: practical advice on creating and maintaining your blog Cambridge MA, Perseus Publishing 2002*

60. *Clyde, L Weblogs and libraries Oxford, Chandos Publishing 2004*

61. *Watson, K and Harper, C Blogs, wikis and reference services: discovering the Australian library context 2006 Unpublished*

62. *Cohen, S Keeping current: advanced internet strategies to meet librarian and patron needs Chicago IL, American Library Association2003*

63. *Schwartz, G Blogs for libraries Webjunction 2005 webjunction.org/do/DisplayContent?id =767*

64. *Rainie, L and Madden. M Podcasting Pew internet and American life project 2005 www.pewinternet.org*

65. *Wikipedia Vodcast. en.wikipedia.org/wiki/ Vodcast*

66. *Peters, T. Auditory options Library journal 15 April 2004 www.libraryjournal.com/article/ CA406013.html*

67. *Shiu, E and Lenhart, A Instant messaging Pew internet and American life project 2004 www.pewinternet.org*

68. *Schmidt, A and Stephens, M IM me Library journal 1 April 2005 www.libraryjournal.com/ article/CA512192.html*

69. *Helling, B New library, new technologies, new services Presentation to Computers in libraries 2006 www.cdpl.lib.in.us/CIL2006/cil2006 helling.html*

70. *http://socialnetlibraries.wordpress.com/2007/12/11/creating-a-useful-library-catalog/*

71. *Instant Messaging Reference Service http://library.nevada.edu/*

72. *http://library.nevada.edu/ask/index.html*

73. *Instant messaging corporate applications*

74. *http://www.tekips.com/gthreadminder.cfm/lev2/67/lev3/73/pid/611*

75. *Download these FREE Tools for Instant Messaging applications from BitDefender.com*

76. *Information excerpt quoted from website www.bitdefender.com/html/freeware_products.php*

77. *Libraries of the 21st Century http://library.tamu.edu/21stcentury/*

78. *Chat in the Special Library Association's Chat Rooms http://www.sla.org/content/interactive/chat/index.cfm*

79. *The Chat Reference Experience at Carnegie Mellon University http://www.contrib.andrew.cmu.edu/~matthewm/ALA_2001_chat.html*

80. *ARL Bimonthly Report 219 , December 2001, Chat Reference: An Exciting New Facet of Digital Reference Services, by Jana Ronan, Interactive Reference Coordinator, George A. Smathers Libraries, University of Florida, Gainesville http://www.arl.org/newsltr/219/chat.html*

81. *The Teaching Librarian, Index of Chat Reference Services http://pages.prodigy.net/tabo1/chatindex.htm*

82. *Providing Chat Reference Service: A Survey of Current Practices, Matt Marsteller and Paul Neuhaus, Carnegie Mellon University Libraries http://www.contrib.andrew.cmu.edu/~matthewm/survey.html*

83. *Breeding, Marshall. (Instant messaging: it's not just for kids anymore. Computers in Libraries Publication Info: Volume 23 Number 10 Issue: November / December 2003 Page(s): 38 http://www.librarytechnology.org/ltg-displaytext.pl?RC=10779*

84. *http://www.oracle.com/us/industries/consumer/index.html*

85. *http://www.oracle.com/us/industries/communications/oracle-communications-suite-066166.html*

5

LIBRARY 2.0

INTRODUCTION

Libraries are especially important now when the whole idea of education is stressing more and more independent learning. Readers must be able to find and use information. Without there are access points to material and it is chaotic. Library 2.0 may offer:

(i) many access points and

(ii) organization for an easy access to information.

Like the purpose of libraries is to preserve and disseminate information, library 2.0 has the same purpose. Like many technologies, Library 2.0 is part of a natural evolution of library services. The term Library 2.0 (L2) has been co-opted by a growing group of libraries, librarians, and particularly vendors to push an agenda of "change" that deflects attention from some very real issues and concerns without really changing anything. The true pursuit of Library 2.0 involves a thorough recalibration of process, policy, physical spaces, staffing, and technology so that any hand-offs in the patron's library experience are truly seamless. Librarians are learning a lot about collaboration and individual empowerment from Web 2.0, Library 2.0 is a transformation in the way library services are delivered to library users. It provides new tools to make the library space (both virtual and physical) more interactive, collaborative and driven by community needs. It encourages collaborative two-way social interactions between library staff and library customers. Library 2.0 requires as well as provides a platform for user participation and feedback in the development and maintenance of library services.

FROM WEB 2.0 TO LIBRARY 2.0

The most common definition of Web 2.0 is given by Tim O'Reilly. Companies that survived the collapse of the technological sector during the 1990s had in common particular methods, concepts and technologies that allowed and offered assessments of their products and services online. Customers used them to write personal comments and suggestions. It created a network of information that was then used by the same company to improve their products and services. The request for new methods of communication online capable of satisfying the various needs of users have facilitated the development of Web 2.0 technologies like:

- *(i) the folksonomie, keywords that are created by those who organizes the information available online;*
- *(ii) the AJAX, that allow an interactive and dynamic use of Web applications; and*
- *(iii) feeds that make interoperable content of different applications or platforms. Summarizing, we can say that Web 2.0 is an assortment of technologies that offer a distinct level of interaction with the user. The concept of allowing people to exchange information freely online is part of the dynamic of the Internet.*

How did we move from Web 2.0 to the Library 2.0? The two terms have created confusion because it was not clear what they were. It was thought that Library 2.0, like Web 2.0, was a new type of technology, while it referred to the applications of Web 2.0 tools within the library field. Library 2.0 can be defined as a set of innovative technologies and services that are integrate with the library, facilitating the use of library resources and services, allowing library user to participate and keeping the librarians updated in their field. Library 2.0 is being an evolution and not a revolution. It is a refinement of what libraries have always done (i.e., provided an information service and attracted users to this service). For this reason, the role of libraries has not changed, but the nature of the service being offered has. Participants noted that library 2.0 has heralded a change in the tools employed in libraries and used by both librarians and users.

THE BEGINNING

The 'Library 2.0' phrase was coined by Michael Casey in his blog, LibraryCrunch, in 2005, although the concepts that collectively make up "Library 2.0" existed well before then. The term was a spinoff of "Web 2.0" which had been coined by O'Reilly Media. Personal web-pages were evolving into blogs, encyclopedias into Wikipedia, text-based tutorials into streaming media applications, taxonomies into "folksonomies," and question-answer/email customer support infrastructures into instant messaging (IM) services. The application of Web 2.0 thinking and technologies to library services and collections has been widely framed as "Library 2.0".

"Library 2.0": the application of interactive, collaborative, and multi-media web-based technologies to web-based library services and collections.

Much of what libraries adopted in the first Web revolution are static. For example, online public access catalogs (OPACs) require users to search for information, and though many are beginning to incorporate Web 2.0 techniques by gathering data regarding a user (checked-out items, preferred searches, search alerts), they do not respond with recommendations, as does Amazon.com, a more dynamic, Web 2.0 service. For example, the first generation of online library instruction was provided via text-based tutorials that are static. These, however, have begun evolving into more interactive, media-rich tutorials, using animation programming and more sophisticated database quizzes. Libraries are already moving into Web 2.0, but the move has only just begun. Other blogging librarians have begun conceptually exploring what Library 2.0 might mean, and because of this disparate discussion with very wide parameters, there is some controversy over the definition and relative importance of the term. The literature provides a very thorough account of the ambiguity and confusion surrounding the term, partially suggesting that there is nothing inherently novel about the idea.

Key principles of Library 2.0:

- *Browser + Web 2.0 Applications + Connectivity = Full-featured OPAC*
- *It harness the library user in both design and implementation of services*
- *Library users should be able to craft and modify library provided services*
- *It harvests and integrates ideas and products from peripheral fields into library service models*
- *It continues to examine and improve services and be willing to replace them at any time with newer and better services.*

Some concerns about Library 2.0 relate to access to technology, privacy and security. Library 2.0 can be considered as a continuing conversation about the future of libraries, and it makes sense to try to round up some voices that challenge Library 2.0 conventional wisdom."

THE LIBRARY 2.0 ONLINE PUBLIC ACCESS CATALOG

Library 2.0 is a new way of providing library service through new Internet technologies, with emphasis on "user-

centered" change and interaction. Like Web 2.0, a full-featured Library 2.0 OPAC gets better the more that users are involved in the process of interacting with the catalog and sharing content.

Librarians have been working to retool library catalogs in order to make them more useful for patrons to find, organize, and interact with information in a way that has infinite potential for user customization. In the past the information flow was mostly one way, from library to user. With new web tools information can be released to flow in following direction:

- *(i) library to user,*
- *(ii) user to library,*
- *(iii) library to library, and*
- *(iv) user to user.*

The valuable attributes desired by users in their OPAC are:

- *(i) flexibility,*
- *(ii) customizability and*
- *(iii) plain language approach. Librarians should take account of these issues so that planning for improvement can begin.*

ELEMENTS OF LIBRARY 2.0

The application of Library 2.0 theory to aspects of librarianship reaching beyond Web 2.0 technology has created its niche. Indeed, the recurrence of similar ideas throughout library history and landmark discussion of this user-centered philosophy external to web-services has been found. There is simply no need to use the term "Library 2.0" in these environments. It is a much more useful theory if it is focused on web-services, much as it has been defined. A theory for Library 2.0 could be understood to have these four essential elements:

It is user-centered : Users participate in the creation of the content and services they view within the library's web-presence, OPAC, etc. The consumption and creation of content is dynamic, and thus the roles of librarian and user are not always clear.

It provides a multi-media experience : Both the collections and services of Library 2.0 contain video and audio components.

It is socially rich : The library's web-presence includes users' presences. There are both synchronous (e.g. IM) and asynchronous (e.g. wikis) ways for users to communicate with one another and with librarians.

It is communally innovative : This is perhaps the single most important aspect of Library 2.0. It rests on the foundation of libraries as a community service, but understands that as communities change, libraries must not only change with them, they must allow users to change the library. It seeks to continually change its services, to find new ways to allow communities, not just individuals to seek, find, and utilize information.

Sometimes technologies are being employed before people figure out which problems they might solve. Whether it is owing to a lack of time, a desire to quickly implement new technologies, or allowing bandwagon mentality to rule, rarely do most of us allow sufficient time to carefully design a strategy for technology innovation. Not only do librarians likely fail to conduct an analysis to first determine the feasibility of a new technology application, but rarely take the time to adequately determine if the users would value the new service. In a nutshell, the approach is to identify a solution before they fully understand the problem.

This will be the biggest challenge set out for librarian by the major changes in information culture happening all around them. But maybe this is a two-way street. In other words, maybe the slow build-up of new technologies and new physical environments in a library can have an effect on that library's culture. There are bits and pieces of recalibration going on, and these things are happening due to a variety of forces, some of them external to the library. Ideas are percolating, and initiatives emerging. The movement will find the ideal criteria for advancement.

It is important to understand that librarians can't expect students to envision how every new technology in the library might benefit them. The OCLC report 'Sharing, Privacy and Trust in our Networked World' recognized this by showing, for example, that only a small sample of college students surveyed think libraries should build social networking sites. These networks were defined by a number of different features. It may sound the end of the road for social networking in academic libraries? It requires some thought provoking exercise. This particular response would mean that academic librarians will play no visionary, groundbreaking role in the evolution of social scholarship. This alone is enough to think that libraries need to look beyond student feedback and think more about leadership. Librarians can devise an action plan for a 2.0 Library. Any plan is not meant to be universally relevant, but potentially relevant to a particular library. Librarians can take a few steps into the 2.0 world.

IMPORTANCE OF LIBRARY 2.0

Library 2.0 is a user-centered virtual community. It is a socially rich, often egalitarian electronic space. While Librarian 2.0 might act as a facilitator and provide support, he or she is not necessarily primarily responsible for the creation of the content. Users interact with and create resources with one another and with librarians. In some ways, it is a virtual reality for libraries, a Web manifestation of the library as place. A library's presence on the Web in Library 2.0 includes the presence of that library's constituency and utilizes the same applications and technologies as its community, a concept recognizes in a very useful model for Library 2.0 in regards to academic libraries.

While these conceptual tenets of Library 2.0 might be rather dependable, envisioning the technological specifics of the next generation of electronic library services is at once both fraught with inevitable error and absolutely necessary. The details of how the applications so common to Web 2.0 will continue to evolve, and how libraries might utilize and leverage them for their patrons, are inherently hidden—they are wholly about innovation. But the conceptual underpinning of a library's web-presence and how it must evolve into a multi-media presence that allows users to be present as well, both with the library or librarian and with one another, are clearly in need of development. Prognostications are meant to conceptually explore and provide context to the relationship between the evolving Web and the evolving library, as a means to facilitate innovation and experimentation in library electronic services.

GENERAL PRINCIPLES OF LIBRARY 2.0

Much has been written about the meaning of Library 2.0. The parameters of Library 2.0 can be related these principles:

- *Libraries engage in rapid change mobilized by assessment.*
- *Libraries give users a participatory role in developing services modeled on their information culture.*
- *Libraries look to Web 2.0 as a model for developing services and building applications.*
- *Libraries make collections available via open, personalized, interactive services that encourage content creation, editing, commenting, bookmarking, rating, tagging, etc. by users.*

- *Libraries construct online spaces managed by interoperable, scalable components, e.g., content management systems, APIs, Web services, widgets, mashups, blogs, wikis.*
- *Libraries embrace radical trust.*
- *Libraries give up some measure of control.*
- *Library applications are in perpetual beta.*
- *Librarians draw users to the library, and also take the library to users, especially in networked spaces.*
- *Librarians are knowledgeable about and utilize information tools favored by users.*
- *Librarians are flexible, skilled, highly tolerant of experimentation, and champions of change to meet users' evolving needs.*

STEPS TOWARDS IMPLEMENTATION OF LIBRARY 2.0

1. *Librarian should ask the Management Committees to become familiar with the concepts and emerging practices of Library 2.0, and to address the following questions:*
    a. *What is the view of Library 2.0 and its applicability to the particular types of libraries?*
    b. *What trends do librarians see regarding respective users and their use of the Libraries that 2.0 concepts can address?*
    c. *What are library is lacking in its vision and practices that 2.0 concepts might help achieving?*
    d. *What attracts library to 2.0 concepts and practices that might become goals?*
    e. *What reordering of priorities is library willing to make?*
    f. *How can library reconfigure current positions to meet 2.0 goals?*

g. *What 2.0-related knowledge and skills should library expect from academic and professional staff, and how will it bring this about?*

SELECTED ACTION STEPS

1. *Library should implement an assessment program that seeks regular faculty and student input, focusing especially on the research process and the Libraries' ability to support this process with the appropriate services and tools. One component of this might be a faculty/student advisory group.*
2. *Library should investigate users' engagement in social networking, blogging, wiki editing, file sharing, social bookmarking, tagging, instant messaging and other online tools, and determine the interest in applying these types of tools to the Libraries' information environment.*
3. *Library should reserve a few work-study positions for students to become members of library committees – possibly as rovers - so that the Libraries can gain ongoing student input.*
4. *Initiate a wiki program for the Libraries. This should be a priority, as wiki requests have already come in.*
5. *Actively position the Libraries at the center of scholarly communication on campus. Begin with establishing a campus-wide blog and wiki program by working with ITS and other stakeholders to implement this. ITS has begun platform tests but its plans are unclear.*
6. *Migrate the Staff Intranet site to a wiki.*
7. *Use blogs and wikis to open up the process of developing in-library documents to include comments and trackable revisions, e.g., University Libraries Goals, Policies and Procedures.*
8. *Migrate the public Web site to a Content Management*

System; migrate selected content to wiki pages and blogs as described below.

9. *Consider the use of editable wiki pages on our Web site, e.g., subject and reference resource pages, pathfinders, help pages, FAQs. Invite participation by affiliated members of the University community.*
10. *Encourage the use of blogs for public communication with constituencies about library resources and services, e.g., blogs about public service points, electronic resources, library technology, etc.*
11. *Sponsor blogs to encourage civic engagement by the University community. For example, create a current events blog that features entries by library and teaching faculty and invites comments by the university community.*
12. *Encourage blogging by library administration.*
13. *Consider a redesign of Minerva, ERes and ILLiad to match the redesign of the public Web site.*
14. *Incorporate widgets, Web services and other technologies into our online spaces to enhance their functionality.*
15. *Explore enhancements that offer collaboration and content manipulation on the Libraries' Web presence.*
16. *Implement RSS distribution of library content, e.g., new resources on Minerva, TOC e-journal alerts, new additions to subject pages, etc.*
17. *Ask bibliographers and reference librarians to incorporate, when appropriate, external RSS feeds on our Web site from scholarly sites, blogs, news, etc. Various scripts and third party RSS aggregators can be used to accomplish this.*
18. *Ask bibliographers and reference librarians to incorporate, when appropriate, custom search tools on*

our Web site on specific topics or across a specific scope of Web sites using such services as Eurekster Swicki, Rollyo and Google Co-op.

19. *Identify the Libraries with podcasting. Create a podcast series with news, tips, research advice, interviews, features, tours, etc., and make the podcasts available on our Web site and via RSS feed. (Note that the RSS feed is the defining characteristic of a podcast.) Consider the creation of a campus podcasting studio, for example in the Interactive Media Center or Information Commons.*
20. *Establish improved procedures for and assessment of technical support. This might include creation of more online FAQs and how-to's, establishment of question tracking, etc.*
21. *Hire work-study students to serve as greeters and roving helpers to provide peer-to-peer assistance at the point of need within the University Library building.*
22. *Create a UA Libraries presence on MySpace, Facebook, and/or other social networking spaces.*
23. *Experiment with creating topical resource lists on one or more social bookmarking sites; publicize these efforts and invite student participation.*
24. *Regularly upload publicity, event and other photos to Flickr. Create a collection of these photos identified with the UA Libraries. Ask other staff (e.g., Special Collections) to identify their Flickr photos with the Libraries' collection.*
25. *Enhance the Libraries' presence in the University's course management system.*
26. *Utilize instant messenger software to communicate with users.*
27. *Seek student and faculty input when revamping,*

developing and enhancing the Libraries' physical spaces.

28. *Create a space on the staff wiki that serves as a resource collection about Library 2.0, including links to useful articles, blogs/RSS feeds, wikis and library initiatives.*
29. *Organize a day-long retreat in-house to promote 2.0 concepts, offer practice with 2.0 tools, create small 2.0 implementations, and develop plans for follow-up projects. Students should also be included among the presenters.*
30. *Offer a monthly self-paced learning day for all academic librarians and some professional staff based on their positions.*
31. *Include requirements for skills with Web 2.0 tools in the position descriptions of all relevant new positions for academic and professional staff.*

All together, the use of these Web 2.0 technologies and applications, along with others not here mentioned and others not yet invented, will constitute a meaningful and substantive change in the history of libraries. The library's collection will change, becoming more interactive and fully accessible. The library's services will change, focusing more on the facilitation of information transfer and information literacy rather than providing controlled access to it. This paper posits four conceptual underpinnings to Library 2.0: it is user-centered; a multi-media experience; socially rich; and communally innovative.

The best conception of Library 2.0 at this point in time would be a social network interface that the user designs. It is a personalized OPAC that includes access to IM, RSS feeds, blogs, wikis, tags, and public and private profiles within the library's network. It is virtual reality of the library, a place where one can not only search for books and journals, but interact with a community, a librarian, and share knowledge and understanding with them. Library 1.0 moved collections and sparse services into the online environment, and Library 2.0 will move the full suite of library services into this electronic medium. The library has had a web-presence for many years, and with Library 2.0, its patrons will be joining it.

While Library 2.0 is a change, it enables the access to information across society, the sharing of that information, and the utilization of it for the progress of the society. Library 2.0, really, is merely a description of the latest instance of a long-standing and time-tested institution in a democratic society. Despite this change fitting so well with the history of libraries and their mission, it is still a major paradigmatic shift for librarianship to open access to their catalogs and collections, as well as access to their control. Library 2.0 demands libraries focus on collaborative discovery systems. There is synchronicity between librarianship and Web 2.0; Library 2.0 has the capacity to revolutionize the profession. Rather than creating systems and services for patrons, librarians will enable users to create them for themselves. The profession will need to continue moving toward embracing facilitation and ambiguity. This shift corresponds to similar changes in library history, including the opening of book stacks and the inclusion of fiction and paperbacks in the early 20th century.

MOVING FROM LIBRARY 1.0 TO LIBRARY 2.0

Library 2.0 is about finding; and sharing. Library 2.0 recognizes that human beings do not seek and utilize information as individuals, but as communities. Some examples of the move from Library 1.0 to Library 2.0 include:

- *Email reference/Q&A pages —> Chat reference*
- *Text-based tutorials —> Streaming media tutorials with interactive databases*
- *Email mailing lists, webmasters —> Blogs, wikis, RSS feeds*

- *Controlled classification schemes —> Tagging coupled with controlled schemes*
- *OPAC —> Personalized social network interface*
- *Catalog of largely reliable print and electronic holdings —> Catalog of reliable and suspect holdings, web-pages, blogs, wikis, etc.*

It is, finally, also necessary to consider that the Web will continue to change rapidly for some time. Web 2.0 is an early one of many. Libraries must adapt to it, much as they did the Web originally, and must continually adapt for the foreseeable future.

CREATING LIBRARY 2.0 SUBJECT GUIDES

The World Wide Web has brought some amazing tools for creating online subject guides. These tools offer the addition of multimedia and multi-format elements such as photos, videos, social bookmarks, RSS feeds, and widgets to traditional resource guides, as well as an interactive dimension which makes them particularly 2.0. Few tools are given here for creating 2.0 guides.

1. Squidoo

Experts in any field can create subject guides which are referred to here as "lenses". These are able to add narrative sections, link to websites, online articles, blogs, RSS feeds and much more including pulling in multimedia and external content such as images from Flickr, bookmarks from del.icio.us, videos from You Tube, books from Amazon, and even inserting Google maps. Lenses can be made interactive by inserting user polls, enabling user voting on recommended resources, inviting users to add to resource lists, and allowing reader feedback.

Examples:

- *Using Web 2.0 Principles to Become Librarian 2.0 Available at http://www.squidoo.com/*

library2point0/

- *Library 2.0 Reading List Available at http://www.squidoo.com/library20/ Resources for LIS753 Available at http://www.squidoo.com/lis753dom*

2. Libguides

LibGuides is a white-label subscription service which enables libraries to create a branded community of librarian-created subject guides or portals for their users. These subject guides, or libguides can incorporate all kinds of content including pulling in RSS feeds, embedding videos and podcasts, pulling in del.icio.us tag clouds, uploading documents, and running user polls, etc. These guides are very widget-friendly. Libguides can be shared through a Facebook application. Libguides creators – librarians – get their own individual profiles which aggregate all of their guides and contact information, and they can even embed a live IM chat widget.

Examples:

- *Dalhousie University Libraries http://dal.ca.libguides.com/http:/dal.ca.libguides.com/*
- *Boston College University Libraries http://libguides.bc.edu/*
- *Utah State University Libraries http://libguides.usu.edu/*

3. Koonji

In 'Hindi' language, it means "key". This koonji is a how-to or resource guide for a particular subject which is broken down into steps. Each step describes a process and can include narrative, recommended links lists, tips, videos, and images. User is free to add and recommend links, vote for and add tips, discuss guides in forums, and rate koonji guides.

Examples:

- *How to get your book published http://www.koonji.com/showKoonji.htm?koonjiId=813*
- *Fortune telling with Turkish coffee http://www.koonji.com/showKoonji.htm?koonjiId=866*
- *How to sell your house http://www.koonji.com/showKoonji.htm?koonjiId=940*

4. Library Subject Guides using del.icio.us

Here is a resource guide and a technique for using the linkrolls feature of del.icio.us combined with an RSS feed service such as Feed2JS in order to output a dynamic list of resources onto any website. This guide is helpful in knowing how to get started with creating own subject guides utilizing user's own del.icio.us bookmarks. This technique is perfect for those who want to keep their existing subject guides, with their formatting, on their own websites, etc. but want to be able to offer fresh content regularly without the hassle of updating pages.

LIBRARY 2.0: EVOLUTION OR REVOLUTION?

Libraries need a revolutionary change in their services to help patrons. In the current scenario libraries have to stay on top of current technologies to make sure that they do not become obsolete and that they provide the best services for their patrons. Libraries have to provide the same or better information and service than what a patron may get from their peers or web sites that do not have verified information. And if the patron prefers to text than face-to-face interaction, then Library must text too. It is believed that Library 2.0 is a more improved, patron oriented library. The details of how the applications so common to Web 2.0 will continue to evolve, and how libraries might utilize and leverage them for their patrons, are inherently hidden—they are wholly about innovation. But the conceptual underpinning of a library's web-presence and how it must evolve into a multi-media presence that allows users to be present as well, both with the library or librarian and with one another, are clearly in need of development. The related aspects are meant to conceptually explore and provide context to the relationship between the evolving Web and the evolving library as a means to facilitate innovation and experimentation in library electronic services, and this list is by no means comprehensive.

Library 2.0 may seem and sound controversial concept that stirs debate on many fronts. As the concept continues to arrest the attention of most library users and practitioners, a number of issues relating to its real nature emerge. One of these is the character of change it represents. While many library scholars and practitioners agree that Library 2.0 represents a change, they disagree on the nature of this change. Using a critical review of documentation and arguments on this subject, the three points of view on this change are identified.

(i) The change is revolutionary and may drastically transform the profession - including renaming.

(ii) It as an evolution of the current best practices to mould a better, user-centered service using modern technology.

(iii) Library 2.0 as neither revolutionary nor evolutionary. There is need to clarify the points of view on the character of Library 2.0 change in libraries, as institutions, and in librarianship as a profession.

(iv) Library 2.0 should be seen as the latest instance in the development of the library and the services it offers, its role in facilitating participatory user-centric services should not be ignored.

Library should have no barriers. The concept that the library is everywhere is where the future of librarianship going. It is in context with taking the library beyond the walls and into a person's life. Everyone can say that libraries have an important role to play in the future of how information is accessed and retrieved. One of the biggest challenges that people are beginning to understand is that it is difficult at times to assert the legitimacy of information sources. The future will show the capacity of libraries to play a role in that. As trained professionals librarians can help people find information they need and want and find legitimate sources. What 2.0 does, is let that resource be more accessible to a person. Libraries need to use the tools of 2.0 to connect with their patrons and provide them with a creditable link to information. There is both an evolution and revolution going on with information.

TRANSFORMATION OF LIBRARY IN THE CONTEXT OF LIBRARY 2.0

The library does not transform itself in a single act but takes a lot to shape its destiny. This can be explained as below:

1. Traditional Library : This is a basic platform for initiating the library services.

2. Augmenting the traditional library : Augmentation of traditional library paves way for search engines, online databases, and email reference. This development and exposure can augment their traditional services. These tools can be stand-alone services instead of simply augmenting traditional services.

3. Change and Scanning the Horizon : Library started watching trends and meeting current and especially future demand, required to change/grow.

4. Pilot Projects : With the support of emerging tools libraries took a leap into the web 2.0 phenomena. It allowed digital conversations, experiment with video, or start podcasting.

5. Customer Participation : The concept of customer participation compelled the library to evolve their website into a digital branch that offers participation to customers rather than just information. Conversations took place in different forms in digital manner. The library saw potential as radical change=growth.

6. Community Engagement : The ultimate goal of the library was to engage the community. With some basic trusts the library allowed the community enough to allow real-time customer participation.

The evolution as a series of circles, libraries will always be books and knowledge. The tools librarians use to share it and how they interact and network with the community expands in different ways out from the center of the library. The Library 2.0 Ripple is doing something else. This library 2.0 stuff would not happen without there being a library 1.0. Traditional Library was at the center of the development. Everything starts moving outward towards the edge of the technology.

REFERENCES

1. *http://www.oclc.org/reports/sharing/default.htm*
2. *http://liblogs.albany.edu/library20/2007/04/social_scholarship_on_the_rise.html*
3. *http://www.oclc.org/reports/sharing/default.htm*
4. *http://liblogs.albany.edu/library20/2007/04/social_scholarship_on_the_rise.html*
5. *Squidoo http://www.squidoo.com/ChemistryOfDailyLife/*
6. *Using Web 2.0 Principles to Become Librarian 2.0 Available at http://www.squidoo.com/library2point0/Library 2.0 Reading List Available at http://www.squidoo.com/library20/Resources for LIS753 Available at http://www.squidoo.com/lis753dom*
7. *Libguides http://libguides.bc.edu/content.php?pid=1286&sid=5490*
8. *Dalhousie University Libraries http://dal.ca.libguides.com/*
9. *Boston College University Libraries http://libguides.bc.edu/*
10. *Utah State University Libraries http://libguides.usu.edu/*

11. Koonji http://www.koonji.com/showKoonji.htm?koonjiId=837

12. How to get your book published http://www.koonji.com/showKoonji.htm?koonjiId=813

13. Fortune telling with Turkish coffee http://www.koonji.com/showKoonji.htm?koonjiId=866

14. How to sell your house http://www.koonji.com/showKoonji.htm?koonjiId=940

15. Library Subject Guides using del.icio.us

16. http://www.herzogbr.net/blog/?p=164

17. Library 2.0 Ripples – Another Go at the Graph

18. David Lee King on August 24, 2007 http://www.davidleeking.com/2007/08/01/am-i-a-20-librarian-and-the-library-20-spectrum/

19. http://www.flickr.com/photos/davidking/978106280/

20. Abram, S., Casey, M., Blyberg, J., & Stephens, M. (2006). A SirsiDynix Institute Conversation: The 2.0 Meme - Web 2.0, Library 2.0, Librarian 2.0, February 2006.

21. Blyberg, John. (2005). ILS Customer Bill of Rights, Blyberg.net

22. Blyberg, John. (2006). 11 reasons why Library 2.0 exists and matters, Blyberg.net

23. Boog, J. (2005). Library 2.0 Movement Sees Benefits in Collaboration with Patrons, Publish, November 2005.

24. Casey, Michael. (2005). Working Towards a Definition of Library 2.0, LibraryCrunch, 21 October 2005.

25. Casey, M. & Stephens, M. (2005). Where Do We Begin? A Library 2.0 Conversation with Michael Casey, ALA TechSource Blog, December 2005.

26. Casey, M. & Stephens, M. (2006). Better Library Services for More People, ALA TechSource Blog, January 2006.

27. Casey, Michael & Savastinuk, Laura. (2007) Library 2.0: A Guide to Participatory Library Service, Information Today Press, 2007. ISBN 978-1-57387-297-3 ISBN 1-57387-297-0

28. Casey, Michael & Savastinuk, Laura. (2006) Library 2.0: Service for the Next-generation Library, Library Journal, September 1, 2006.

29. Courtney, Nancy. (2007) Library 2.0 and Beyond: Innovative Technologies and Tomorrow's User, Libraries Unlimited, 2007. ISBN 978-1-59158-537-4

30. Crawford, Walt. (2006). Library 2.0 and 'Library 2.0'" Cites and Insights 6, 2. January 2006.

31. *Farkas, Meredith G. (2007). Social Software in Libraries : Building Collaboration, Communication, and Community Online. Information Today, 2007. ISBN 978-1-57387-275-1 ISBN 1-57387-275-X*

32. *Harris, Christopher. (2006). Library 2.0 Week (Updated), Infomancy, January 2006.*

33. *Harris, Christopher. (2006) School Library 2.0, School Library Journal, May 1, 2006.*

34. *Holmberg, K., Huvila, I., Kronqvist-Berg, M. & Widén-Wulff, G. (2009). What is Library 2.0?. Journal of Documentation, 65(4): 668-681.*

35. *Levine, Jenny. (2005). Hello, Library (1.0) World!, ALA TechSource Blog, 10 October 2005.*

36. *Maness, J. (2006). Library 2.0 Theory: Web 2.0 and Its Implications for Libraries. Webology, 3 (2), Article 25.*

37. *Miller, P., (2005). Web 2.0: Building the New Library. Ariadne, No.45 October 2005.*

38. *Miller, P., Chad, K. (2005). Do libraries matter? - The rise of Library 2.0, Talis November 2005.*

39. *Miller, P. (2006). Library 2.0: The Challenge of Disruptive Innovation, Talis February 2006.*

40. *Stephens, Michael. (2006). Web 2.0 & Libraries: Best Practices for Social Software, Library Technology Reports, 42:4.*

41. *Talis Talk (31 January 2006). Podcast with Thomas Brevik, Michael Casey, Ken Chad, Paul Miller, T. Scott Plutchak, Michael Stephens and Richard Wallis.*

42. *Library 2.0 - 9/1/2006 - Library Journal*

43. *Library Juice » The Central Problem of Library 2.0: Privacy*

44. *http://www.libraryjournal.com/article/CA6365200.html*

45. *Steve Lawson, A Library 2.0 skeptic's reading list, http://stevelawson.name/seealso/archives/2006/05/a_library_20_sk.html*

46. *Wikipedia contributors, "Web 2.0," Wikipedia, The Free Encyclopedia, http://en.wikipedia.org/w/index.php?title=Web_2.0&oldid=206758560*

47. *Jessamyn West and friends, What We Want: An OPAC Manifesto, http://www.librarian.net/opac/*

48. *http://liblogs.albany.edu/library20/2008/02/im_retiring_this_blog_is_ending.html*

49. *http://www.blyberg.net/2008/01/17/library-20-debased/*

50. *http://www.oclc.org/reports/sharing/default.htm*

51. *http://liblogs.albany.edu/library20/2007/04/social_scholarship_on_the_rise.html*

52. *http://liblogs.albany.edu/library20/*

53. *http://www.addthis.com/bookmark.php?pub=VOWOSWLCZRXHFC5I&url=http://oedb.org/blogs/ilibrarian/2007/a-librarians-guide-to-creating-20-subject-guides/&title=A%20Librarian%E2%80%99s%20Guide%20to%20Creating%202.0%20Subject%20Guides*

6

RSS Applications

INTRODUCTION

The recent availability of social software encourages the exploration of some new support systems for library instruction and outreach. Social software has various definitions, but can be broadly described as an online application that moves beyond traditional static web page viewing, or individual user website customization, to encourage further interaction between users of the content, or between users and the online content creator. Some well known examples are blogs, wikis, online bookmarks, instant messaging, listservs, course management systems, RSS, and podcasts. Since social software enhances the accessibility of both content and content creators, it has significant potential for the educational support mission of academic (and other) libraries. As library users and technology change, instruction and liaison librarians are continually evaluating and implementing improved methods to communicate the availability of relevant services, resources, and assistance to their users. The development of social software continues this cycle of both change and new opportunity.

Also, since these applications share a social focus, there is the additional potential for value-added synergy by seamlessly integrating them with each other. Since social software enhances the accessibility of both content and content creators, it has significant potential for the educational support mission of academic (and other) libraries. As library users and technology change, instruction and liaison librarians are continually evaluating and implementing improved methods to communicate the availability of relevant services, resources, and assistance to their users. The development of social software continues the additional potential for value-added synergy by seamlessly integrating them with each other. RSS ("Really Simple Syndication") is simply a format that allows receiving updated content from sources of choice of user. For example, the library's RSS feeds deliver all the news and information that is posted to the Library News & Events Blog without having to visit the news page. The Blog has an accompanying RSS file that is updated everytime a new post is added, and in order to read that file, user needs an RSS reader.

"RSS is a format for syndicating news and the content of news-like sites, including major news sites like Wired, news-oriented community sites like Slashdot, and personal weblogs. But it's not just for news. Pretty much anything that can be broken down into discrete items can be syndicated via RSS: the "recent changes" page of a wiki, a changelog of CVS checkins, even the revision history of a book. Once information about each item is in RSS format, an RSS-aware program can check the feed for changes and react to the changes in an appropriate way."

— Mark Pilgrim (http://rss-net.sf.net/)

RSS is a new way to publish information online, through "RSS Feeds". RSS is an XML application that allows users to gather content as it is created and as sites are updated. When such a web feed is created, interested users can subscribe to it. Syndicated web pages are viewed with feed readers. RSS distributes a list of headlines, update notices, and sometimes full-text content. At the heart of the technology is special Web coding, called XML, which displays headlines and information on another page or "RSS Reader". This is a simple way to syndicate content. Anyone can use the RSS codes and with the appropriate web software, display the information automatically.

RSS is really a family of different XML languages. Each pf them have their own definition of the acronym (or initialism), and within those families there are several versions:

- RDF Site Summary (RSS 0.9 and 1.0)
- Really Simple Syndication (RSS 2.x)
- Rich Site Summary (RSS 0.9x)

WHAT IS RSS READER?

An RSS reader (also called an aggregator) is a software application that allows you to read blogs and Web sites that publish RSS feeds. There are a number of RSS readers available freely on the Web. For example, Google Reader and Bloglines are very popular among users. RSS is format for syndicating content on the Web. Few features are given below:

- based on XML
- RSS breaks websites into discrete chunks of information
- RSS enables user to view content from different sites on a single page.
- Many Web sites have RSS feeds these days if they have information that is updated regularly (examples: CNN, NY Times).
- User should look for the icons RSS XML to find sites with RSS feeds
- RSS lacks information about how the file should be presented.

- *To be able to read RSS feeds, user needs to use an aggregator.*

RSS FEEDS

RSS feeds are a way to distribute content between computers and displaying it to people. RSS allows users to see when specific internet pages have added new content. It helps them to keep up to date. They can get the latest headlines, articles and audiovisual files without having to visit each site.

RSS USES AND FUNCTIONS

Without RSS, users were supposed to check needed sites daily for updates. An RSS feed (often called a news feed) can check sites using an RSS aggregator (a program that gathers and sorts out feeds). RSS data is small and fast-loading. It can easily be used with services like cell phones or PDAs (w3schools, 2008). RSS uses XML to distribute web content from one web site to many other sites. RSS feeds are RDF-compliant, and RSS files contain metadata that describes the content. A website that wants to allow other sites to publish some of its contents, create an RSS document and register the document with RSS publisher. Syndicated data can contain data like news, event listings, news stories, headlines, project updates etc. The special XML-format file that makes up an RSS feed is usually created in variety of ways. News sites and blogs are maintained using content management systems that often create RSS feeds as they are updated. It is significant to know that websites produced with tools like Dreamweaver generally do not create feeds automatically.

BASICS TO RECEIVE RSS FEEDS

At the outset, user needs a "feed reader". Most of the software are free or at little cost. Websites that publish an RSS feed displays a tiny orange box or button labeled "RSS" or "XML" as described further. By clicking the button the web browser typically goes to a page of cryptic code. Now user needs to copy the Web "address" or URL of that page and plug it into his feed reader. The software then automatically retrieve and display that site's latest information.

USING THE RSS

Users need a piece of software called a news reader. It checks RSS feeds and lets them read any new articles. There are many different versions. Some of them are accessed using a browser, others are downloadable applications. Browser-based news readers let users catch up with their RSS feed subscriptions from any computer. Once a user has chosen a news reader, then he decides what content he wants to receive in news reader, by finding and subscribing to the relevant RSS feeds. This graphic indicates that there is an RSS feed available. It may be read in an RSS aggregator. To subscribe to a feed user need to simply right click on the link, select copy shortcut, and then paste the URL into their RSS reader. The graphic indicates that the RSS feed can be added to the iGoogle or Google Reader page by clicking on the Google graphic and following the instructions.

FEATURES OF RSS

1. It is an XML technology for the syndication of a website's content.
2. It has been used for this purpose for several years by mass media vendors (newspapers, etc), and is now experiencing increased usage in some academic libraries.
3. In current practice, syndication of a website means that the content creator/provider maintains an RSS "feed" or stream of information, and users can choose to subscribe to that feed.

4. *Feeds can deliver a variety of information, such as organizational news and events, journal table of contents, course content and multimedia and database search results.*

ADVANTAGES

This communication model has advantages for both content creators and users:

- *Feeds can be tailored to deliver focused content that is of interest to a specific audience, so that users aren't required to explore an entire website to find a particular content*
- *There is no cost to subscribe to a feed, and subscription only involves finding the feed URL (i.e., there is no need for private user information such as e-mail addresses, names, etc.)*
- *Feeds are enormously convenient to use. The user only has to navigate once to the website (to subscribe), since RSS feeds automatically update with any new content. All RSS feeds, from numerous sources, can be collected and viewed in one location, using a desktop or web-based aggregator such as Bloglines, or in a web browser). This means that much more material can be scanned for value to the user, in much less time.*
- *The free Mozilla Firefox and Apple Safari browsers currently provide the capability to collect RSS feeds*
- *The user chooses to opt in to the feed, and can cancel it at any time*
- *RSS is well established, reliable, and relatively easy to implement RSS is not without its limitations. The issue of content discovery remains a significant one for providers, since users must still initially identify and locate feeds they find interesting.*

  The subscription process for a feed is not yet completely

transparent to users. There are several versions of RSS (RSS 0.91, RSS 1.0, RSS 2.0, Atom) with different structure and capabilities that may create slight confusion for end users. Microsoft's Windows Internet Explorer browser does not yet support RSS, although the upcoming version 7 (currently in beta as of this writing) is expected to have this capability. Nevertheless, RSS feeds are now being successfully used by some libraries, and the technology has significant future potential.

HOW RSS READERS WORK?

RSS readers, also known as news aggregators or feed readers are an invaluable tool in today's information-rich legal industry. RSS readers automatically pull in content from variety of online sources including blogs, articles, forums, web site content and news sources, and "feed" them directly to users' desktop or smart phone for easy perusal. Users can subscribe to the feeds that interest them most and control the quantity and quality of information they receive. Popular Web-based aggregators are given below:

- *Bloglines*
- *Rojo*
- *Netvibes*

ADVANTAGES OF RSS FEED READERS

RSS feed readers are a free and easy way to stay abreast of the information most important to any user. RSS readers allow to:

- *Stay informed of the latest legal news, trends, technology, case law, technology innovations and other information by retrieving the latest content from the sites that most interest the user.*
- *Save time by not visiting each site individually or scouring the Internet for information on topics that interest the user.*

- *Control the flow and quality of information user receives.*
- *View and scan multiple content streams simultaneously.*
- *Stay up to date in users' work area.*
- *Ensures privacy by preventing the need to join each site's e-mail newsletter.*
- *Obtain fresh content automatically.*

SETTING UP RSS READER

Many legal web sites and blogs offer a feed of their content in RSS format. As RSS grows in popularity, a growing number of sites will offer their own RSS feeds. Users do not need advanced technical knowledge to set up the RSS feed reader. They need to follow the instructions on the home page of the RSS reader of their choice. Once user has set up the RSS reader, (s)he can locate sites that syndicate content and add their RSS feed to the list of feeds the feed reader checks. Many sites display a small icon with the acronyms RSS, XML, or RDF to let user know a feed is available. If the site does not display an RSS feed icon, user can copy the URL that corresponds to the topic that interests him or her and paste the URL into the reader.

POPULAR RSS FEED READERS

A number of RSS feed readers are available. Several of the most popular include:

- *Google reader*
- *Newsgator*
- *Feedreader*
- *Netvibes*
- *My Yahoo*
- *Bloglines*

NEED AND BENEFITS IN LIBRARIES:

RSS feeds and other related technologies provide users a way to syndicate and republish content on the Web. Users republish content from other sites or blogs on their sites or blogs, aggregate content on other sites in a single place, and ostensibly distill the Web for their personal use. Such syndication of content is another Web 2.0 application that is already having an impact on libraries, and could continue to do so in remarkable ways. Already libraries are creating RSS feeds for users to subscribe to, including updates on new items in a collection, new services, and new content in subscription databases. They are also republishing content on their sites.

But libraries have yet to explore ways of using RSS more pervasively. A new product from a company called BlogBridge, BlogBridge: Library (BBL), "is a piece of software that libraries can install on their own server, inside the firewall. It's not the content of the library (the books), it's the software to organize the library (the building)." It is conceivable that this kind of syndication will replace browsing and searching through library websites for content. BBL and similar RSS aggregator applications will enable users to have a single, customized, personal library page. Such page syndicates all the library content of interest to them and their research, eliminating irrelevant information. And users will, of course, control that page and that content. RSS is useful for websites that are updated frequently such as those of news sites, corporations, calendars, database producers, and libraries and information centers.

LIBRARY WEB FEEDS

Libraries should consider whether the information contained in a feed meets the needs of the user, and whether obtaining the information via a feed from the publisher will help to compact and provide focused information to users.

It may be necessary to subscribe to the resource in order for the feed to be useful. Feeds should be updated frequently and expiration dates should be considered. Libraries are increasingly creating feeds to promote and services. Libraries that offer web feeds for announcements include:

- *Georgia State University Library*
- *Lunar and Planetary Institute, Center for Information and Research Services*
- *Minneapolis Public Library*
- *Northwestern University Library*
- *Ohio University Libraries*
- *Rowland Institute at Harvard Library*
- *Suburban Library System*
- *University of North Carolina at Chapel Hill Libraries*
- *University of Windsor, Leddy Library*

a. *There are various RSS feed applications for libraries such as :*

(i) *announcements,*

(ii) *extended services,*

(iii) *e-journals and table of contents services,*

(iv) *reference service,*

(v) *library blogs,*

(vi) *web resource announcements,*

(vii) *search resource, books, newsgroups, search results, and*

(viii) *RSS-based search engines.*

(ix) *RSS feeds provide a way to disseminate or publish information.*

(x) *As publishing trends change, librarians will have to communicate with patrons using up-to date methods.*

(xi) *RSS can be used for current awareness information and to provide targeted information to patrons. RSS can be an affordable and relatively easy way to communicate with users and colleagues.*

b. *For information producers advantages include:*

(i) *increasing web traffic,*

(ii) *easy updating*

(iii) *dissemination of information, and*

(iv) *efficiency for webmasters.*

c. *For web content managers, there is:*

(i) *delivery of targeted information and*

(ii) *value-added services.*

d. *For information users, there is:*

(i) *control over the flow of information,*

(ii) *easy sharing, and*

(iii) *a more efficient delivery method.*

RSS will probably be even more prevalent in the future, making information easier to find. Browsers are beginning to include RSS features and plug-ins. RSS is such a technology that allows organizations to deliver news to a desktop computer or other Internet device. By subscribing to RSS feeds, users can easily stay up-to-date with areas of the Library's site that are of interest. The Library of Congress offers several RSS feeds for use in an RSS reader or RSS-enabled Web browser. Library feeds consist of headline, brief summary, and a link that leads back to the Library's Web site for more information.

RSS is used to deliver content syndication, or feeds, in XML metadata format. A so-called "channel" is a list of items, typically Web-published articles, and each feed item is a summary of the resource with a URI (hyperlink) to the full article. A user can locate an item of interest, and then select it to take him or her to the full article. News sites and Web logs (blogs) are the most popular source of these feeds.

Typical metadata encoded in one of these formats includes:

- *a title for the article*
- *a URI (link) to the resource*
- *the author (or creator)*
- *a description of the contents*
- *the publication date and time*
- *a classification of the content*

As the name implies, Really Simple Syndication is the easiest format for the content developer to started get with.

NEED OF RSS IN LIBRARY ENVIRONMENT:

1. *To enhance in-person library electronic classroom instruction, liaison and outreach*
2. *To create a visible, web-based presence for both sciences/engineering support services and library social software initiatives*

WHAT RSS FEEDS DOES THE LIBRARY OFFER?

User can subscribe to an RSS feed for his search results from the Library Catalogue. Usually, the Library blog publishes the few or more of the following RSS feeds:

All Library News : all posts published to the blog (includes everything below)

Alerts: interruptions in service (like an unexpected library closure or downtime of an e-Resource)

Archives and Research Collections: Archives and Research Collections news

e-Resources: pertaining to e-Resources (for example: announcements about new e-Resources)

Events: upcoming events in the libraries

Hot Docs!: government resources in the news

Instruction: upcoming library instruction & orientation sessions

Maps/Data/Gov Pubs: news and resources from Maps, Data, and Government Publications

New Books: new books in the libraries

Trial e-Resources: e-Resources being evaluated for possible purchase

Web Resources: free Web sites of interest to the academic community

To subscribe to a feed from the Library Blog or the Catalogue, user needs to right-click on the button, select "Copy Shortcut" (or "Copy Link Location"), and paste the URL of the feed into his RSS reader. There are a number of major organizations and publishers that offer RSS feeds that can be useful current awareness tools. Here are a select few:

- *Globe and Mail : a feed for each section of the newspaper*
- *New York Times : feeds for different content areas of the paper*
- *Nature Journals : provides table of contents feeds (with article abstracts) for all Nature journals.*
- *Ingenta Connect : table of contents feeds for the latest issues of Ingenta journals*
- *BioMed Central : feeds for the latest articles published in BioMed Central journals.*
- *PubMed : feeds for PubMed searches.*
- *Oxford University Press Journals : OUP provides current issue feeds for all their journals.*
- *IEEE Computer Society : offers current issue feeds for all magazines and transactions.*
- *Government of Canada News : feeds by province/*

territory, audience, or department/agency.

RSS FEEDS FOR VIDEO TUTORIALS AND BLACKBOARD CLASS CONTENT

Because of the syndication capabilities of RSS, this technology has tremendous potential for educators using online classes. Students can be automatically updated with new class content. This is especially significant for librarian instructors. It is potentially a significant advantage to be able to send relevant information to students in an RSS feed. Library RSS feeds are not limited to instruction services, and these initiatives support the increasingly familiar idea of libraries providing several feeds for their resources, services, and events. For example, one of the limitations of the currently available version of Blackboard at VCU (version 6.2) is the absence of built-in RSS. Some strategies can be used to deal with this issue.

1. *The first plan is to write, and maintain XML code for several subject-specific RSS feeds, upload them to the Blackboard Content System, and provide links to these feeds in all Blackboard classes.*
2. *The use of these feeds (to link to video tutorials) can be demonstrated to students at the beginning of every library instruction class taught, usually using the Firefox browser.*
3. *For the specialized RSS/current awareness classes, the online Bloglines aggregator, and occasionally, the library Portal (which supports RSS feeds) should also be demonstrated.*
4. *It can invariably be noticed that students (and faculty) can be quite interested in the RSS demonstration at the beginning of each class, perhaps because it is so untraditional to have access to class content this way.*
5. *Another strategy may be to open another pathway to the video tutorials and Blackboard classes by creating*

a new, subject-focused libraries blog.

THE WAY LIBRARIES ARE USING RSS

- *Syndicating blog content (on Web sites, into online courseware, etc.)*
- *Journal feeds*
- *Subject guides*
- *RSS feeds from the ILS*
- *New books feeds*
- *Search feeds*
- *Feeds of checked-out books and holds*
- *RSS feeds from databases*
- *Search feeds*
- *Subject bibliographies*

RSS FOR LIBRARY USERS

Library users are then able to keep up to date with what is new at the library without having to visit the website. RSS allows publishing information about a library as a syndicated feed. Library users subscribe to the feed using aggregator (also commonly referred to as a news reader) software which groups together, collates and shows the results of RSS feeds in an easy to read format. Most news readers are software that user downloads and installs. Others are web based services for that work inside the browser. RSS inform users about author visits to the library, provide information about upcoming book sales, or promote classes and programs. RSS is being incorporated into library catalogues and journal databases to inform users of new purchases and publications.

Examples:

- *The Curtin University of Technology has RSS feeds which allow user to see details of titles that are added to the library collection. Curtin Library RSS feeds library.curtin.edu.au/ research/rss/catalogue_rss_feeds.html*

- *The Australian National University has RSS feeds to lists of new titles in the catalogue. Library catalogue library.anu.edu.au/ftlist/*
- *Hennepin County Library in the US allows you to make any catalogue search into a custom RSS feed www.hennepin.lib.mn.us/pub/search/ RSS.cfm*
- *All EBSCOhost databases and interfaces support RSS feeds for search alerts and journal alerts. 'RSS enabled alerts allow librarians and users to feed results from EBSCOhost search alerts and journal alerts into their RSS readers and aggregators, as well as their websites.' support.epnet.com/knowledge_base/detail.php?id=2485&t=h*

Here is an elaborative example of RSS feeds from LOC (Library of Congress):

Categories:

- *General News*
- *Events*
- *For Teachers*
- *Collections Preservation*
- *Digital Preservation*
- *Legal*
- *Journalism*
- *Science*
- *Visual Resources*
- *Site Updates*
- *For Librarians*
- *Young Readers*
- *Copyright*
- *Folklife*
- *Music Division*
- *Poetry*
- *Veterans History*

General News from the Library

Latest News

A bulletin service of the latest news from the world's preeminent reservoir of knowledge, providing resources to Congress and the American people

Library of Congress Information Bulletin

A monthly magazine of in-depth features on the Library's treasures and programs

Library of Congress Blog

Musings on the unsurpassed collections and activities at the Library of Congress, the nation's oldest federal cultural institution, and a peek behind-the-scenes from a Library insider

News from the John W. Kluge Center

Updates on lectures, presentations and other news from this center for scholars established to bring together the world's best thinkers, to stimulate scholarly discussion and to interact with policymakers in Washington

Hours of Operation

Changes in standard hours of operation and emergency closing notices

Library of Congress Experience

Updates on the Library's interactive experience and exhibitions at its remarkable Thomas Jefferson Building in Washington

Places in the News

Maps of nations and localities in current news from the Geography and Map Division

Library Shop

The latest new books, prints, calendars, posters and other products based on the Library's incomparable collections and current exhibitions

Center for the Book and read.gov

The Center for the Book in the Library of Congress promotes books, reading, libraries and literacy through its many programs, as well as through its website at Read.gov, which offers resources specifically tailored for Kids, Teens, Adults and Parents & Teachers. Also, learn about Center for the Book activities

Library Web Site Updates

New on the Web

Updates on new collections, features, reference materials and other services available on the Library's award-winning Web site

New Webcasts

The latest webcasts and podcasts of lectures and events sponsored by the Library

The Wise Guide to loc.gov

Through little-known facts, the Wise Guide is an introduction to the fascinating and useful Web resources available from the Library.

Events at the Library

Upcoming Events

Listing of the dozens of free concerts, lectures, exhibitions, symposia, films and other special programs offered at the Library on Capitol Hill in Washington, D.C.

Poetry Events

Notifications of upcoming poetry readings, presentations, symposia, guidelines and other poetry activities at the Library of Congress

Folklife Events

Notifications of upcoming folklife concerts, lectures, symposia, and other events and programs at the American Folklife Center

Law Library Events

The latest news and upcoming events from the Law Library of Congress

Music Division Concerts and Events

Notifications of upcoming concerts, lectures, symposia and other events and programs hosted by the Library's Music Division

Topics

Collections Preservation

Preservation News

News from the Preservation Directorate on new breakthroughs and technology, upcoming lectures, training, internships and emergency alerts and topics on caring for collections.

Copyright: All Notices from the U.S. Copyright Office

Legislative Developments

Notices of current copyright-related legislation

Federal Register Notices

Announcements, rules, proposed rules and other notices published in the Federal Register

NewsNet

Alerts on hearings, deadlines for comments, new and proposed regulations, new publications and more

What's New at the Copyright Office

Alerts on new Copyright Office website postings and other announcements

Digital Preservation

Provides updates and announcements about the Library's program to preserve the nation's digital heritage

Folklife and Culture: American Folklife Center

Folklife News & Events

The latest information on programs, scholarships, awards, publications, and notifications of upcoming folklife concerts, lectures, symposia, and other events and programs at the American Folklife Center.

Legal Issues: Law Library of Congress

Global Legal Monitor

News of legal developments from around the world, drawn from the Global Legal Information Network, official national legal publications, and reliable press sources.

News & Events

The latest news and upcoming events from the Law Library of Congress

Legal Research Reports

Guides published by the Law Library of Congress providing legal commentary and recommended resources on issues and events with legal significance

THOMAS: Bills Presented to the President

Lists bills that have passed both the House and Senate and have been sent to the White House for the President's signature.

THOMAS: Daily Digest

Provides notification of the Daily Digest, which details the chamber action, committee meetings, and joint meetings of Congress.

THOMAS: House Floor Today

Identifies the latest bills and resolutions considered on the floor of the U.S. House of Representatives

THOMAS: Senate Floor Today

Identifies the latest bills, resolutions, nominations, and treaties considered on the floor of the U.S. Senate.

Webcasts

Notices of new webcasts from the Law Library of Congress

Music Division

Concerts and Events

Notifications of upcoming concerts, lectures, symposia and other events and programs hosted by the Library's Music Division

News

The latest news from the Library's Music Division

Newspapers and Journalism

Chronicling America: Historic American Newspapers

Updates on new content, points of interest, research and re-use of the Chronicling America digitized newspapers

Poetry

Poetry News

The latest poetry news from the Poetry & Literature Center and updates on new poetry resources available on the Library's Web site

Poetry 180

Read a poem each weekday of the school year from the Library's Poetry 180 project.

Poetry Events

Notifications of upcoming poetry readings, presentations, symposia, guidelines and other poetry activities at the Library of Congress

Science, Technology & Business

What's New in Science Reference

New products and services on the subject of science and technology from the Library's Science, Technology & Business Division

Inside Adams Blog

The blog from the Science, Technology, and Business Division will share the Library's collections, events, guides, and other happenings relative to science and business.

Veteran's History Project

Updates from the Veterans History Project (VHP)

Rare interviews, notices of events, and special features from this collection of more than 60,000 first-hand stories as told by America's war veterans from WWI through current conflicts.

Visual Resources

News from the Prints & Photographs Division

Noteworthy online collections, acquisitions, research aids, and public programs.

For Librarians

Library of Congress Classification Weekly Lists

Listing of new and revised Library of Congress Classification numbers and captions approved by the weekly editorial meeting of the Policy and Standards Division of the Acquisitions and Bibliographic Access Directorate

Library of Congress Subject Headings Weekly Lists

Listing of new and revised Library of Congress subject headings approved by the weekly editorial meeting of the Policy and Standards Division of the Acquisitions and Bibliographic Access Directorate

For Teachers

News for Teachers

Updates on new Web content, professional development opportunities and Library programs, events and services of special interest to educators

Young Readers

Exquisite Corpse Adventure

This adventure story written by America's best writers for young people will unfold exclusively on the read.gov website.

HOW TO PUBLISH OWN RSS FEEDS

There's little doubt that RSS is a great technology for staying on top of news and announcements that are important to an organization and its mission. User can leverage other sites' RSS feeds, the nonprofit can also create its own feeds in order to deliver new and important information to the constituents and supporters? Syndicating the organization's content in an RSS feed that user make available on his Web site is different from using someone else's RSS feed and reprinting their syndicated content on own site. Think of the former as publishing an outgoing RSS feed and the latter as making use of an incoming feed.

There are a handful of options for creating outgoing RSS feeds that don't require a major technical effort. For instance, someone's own organization's blog software may already have a feature that automatically transforms his posts into RSS feeds his audience can subscribe to. The same is true of many content management systems. Alternatively, there is a number of inexpensive Web-based feed-creation services that can generate an RSS feed of almost any page on Web site.

No matter which method user chooses, giving his supporters a convenient way to access his content without having to regularly check his organization's Web site can help make it easier for them to stay active and involved in his cause.

Blog-Driven News Feeds

In addition to content-publishing tools, the majority of popular blogging services include features that will serve up the posts as news feed. If user needs to add multiple feeds to his site, check to see if his blogging platform supports this functionality, since some free, popular blogging platforms — such as Blogger — only provide one feed per blog.

While many blogging services allow you to create an RSS feed, others instead support Atom, a type of syndicated XML feed that is very similar to RSS. Most of the newer feed-reading applications and services support both syndication formats, but keep in mind that older versions of news-reading software might only be compatible with RSS. In any case, no matter which of the two formats user choose, the feeds will look about the same once they reach his subscribers' aggregators. If a nonprofit organization is seeking a Web-based blogging service that supports both Atom and RSS feeds, consider LiveJournal or TypePad. By contrast, Blogger only creates feeds in the Atom format, while WordPress.com only offers support for RSS.

RSS from the CMS

Many organizations that regularly publish their own articles and news stories — or repurpose them through a Creative Commons license — have chosen to implement a content management system (CMS), an application specifically designed to organize, store, and publish content. In addition to their main features, some CMSs also include tools for adding RSS feeds to the site. For instance, Drupal and Plone — two free, open-source CMSs — both allow adding feeds natively to individual items or entire sections of the Web site. By contrast, some other CMSs require extensions to enable this functionality or don't support it at all. And while it's highly unlikely that user'd ever spend the time to implement a CMS just because he wanted to add news feeds to his site, he may want consider RSS support (or lack thereof) if he is already considering installing content-management software.

Online Services for Building Feeds

If creating an RSS feed using a CMS or a blogging platform isn't a feasible or ideal solution, user should try experimenting with a few of the many Web-based tools that allow anyone with an Internet connection to build a feed. Many of these services are free, though some will feature ads on free feeds and will charge him a monthly fee if he wishes to create more than one RSS feed or need technical support. It's also important to consider how much time his organization's staff members can spend maintaining the feed, as some online services will require him to manually add the new headlines, links, and descriptive text he wants delivered to his subscribers

Smaller organizations can look for FeedYes or Ponyfish which are low-maintenance RSS-creation option might investigate. Though these services are primarily intended to allow Web surfers to receive updates from sites that lack their own RSS feeds, his nonprofit can also use them to serve up his own headlines and content. Both of these services work by "scraping" the links and text off a given page on his Web site and saving the links and text into an XML document. (An RSS feed is basically an XML document that is formatted so that an aggregator can read it.) Both FeedYes and PonyFish are similar to configure and simple to use. First, enter the URL of the page he wants to create a feed for. Then, when his shown all the links on that page, choose the ones he wants to include in the feed (since some are navigation links that user doesn't want in the feed). Finally, select the button to generate the XML document. User can then add a link to that document from his Web page. And there he goes — that's his RSS feed, available for anyone to access. Though FeedYes will allow creating as many RSS feeds as anyone would like, user will have to pay a small yearly subscription fee to remove the ads. Ponyfish also lets users create an unlimited number of feeds, though if user wants the service to refresh the feeds every hour (instead of every four hours) for a minimal fee.

If a nonprofit organization or user wants to create a feed that consists of articles and links from a number of different pages, it can do so by creating a free account at sites like LinkRSS, Publi.sh, HitRSS, and FeedPublish.com. Services such as these do not update feeds automatically and will require someone at the organization to manually enter URLs and headlines each time he wants to add a new item to the feed. On the plus side, users who subscribe to the feed won't have to take any additional steps to receive the latest articles and news. For a more thorough list of feed-creation services, any user can check out RSS Compendium's directory of RSS editors.

Feed-Creation Software

RSS files, based on XML, provide an open method of syndicating and aggregating Web content. Using RSS files, anyone can create a data feed that supplies headlines, links, and article summaries from his Web site. These files describe a channel of information that can include a logo, a site link, an input box, and multiple "news items." Other sites can incorporate this information into their pages automatically. A website can also use RSS feeds from other sites to provide the current news headlines. These techniques let website draw more visitors and also provide them with up-to-date information.

The RSS format originated with the sites My Netscape and Radio UserLand, both of which aggregate content derived from XML news feeds. Because it's one of the simplest XML applications, RSS found favor with many developers who need to perform similar tasks. Users include Moreover, UserLand, and XML Tree. While building a feed using a free online site is cost-effective and simple, this approach does have a couple of potential downsides. First of all, a free Web-based service may not offer any kind of tech support should the user has problems building the feed or your subscribers stop receiving updates. Also, since these types of sites typically host his organization's feed on their own servers, he could run into trouble in the event that they have technical problems or simply cease to exist.

If user wants to ensure that his news feed is always up and running properly, he may want to host it on his own servers. Unless user would have access to technically skilled volunteers or staffers who can build the news feeds themselves, he might try a specialized piece of software to make the feed-creation process easier.

User can seek a program that's geared toward novices, for example, applications such as Alnera FeedWorkshop, ExtraLabs Feed Editor, FeedForAll, and Jitbit RSS Feed Creator all offer wizards, step-by-step, interactive guides that walk users through the process of building an unlimited number of feeds. In addition to their user-friendly interfaces, these programs all offer features that attach images to feeds; generate XML code; and upload completed feeds to the Web server via FTP. The aforementioned feed-creation applications all offer some sort of trial period, so user can test and compare them before he buys. RSS Compendium's directory of RSS editors also lists a large number of feed-creation software packages, which can be consulted to research additional utilities there.

Users can add a graphical icon that says "RSS" or "XML". Both acronyms are often used interchangeably, though the term "RSS" might be a bit more familiar to non-technical visitors. Few free online tools can be used to build a custom button. It's also worth noting that many sites are moving toward a standard icon to denote the presence of news feeds. Many site owners also make their news feeds available through Mozilla Firefox's Live Bookmarks feature, which acts as the browser's built-in feed-reading tool. To ensure that the visitors will be able to subscribe to the RSS or Atom feed from directly within Firefox's address bar, user should follow the instructions. Doing everything correctly makes a feed icon visible to the far right side of Firefox's address bar when user launches his organization's Web site.

Though adding an RSS or Atom feed to a Web site might call for a bit of creativity. It does not require a large budget or extensive technology skills. Best of all, equipping a site with a feed brings an organization one step closer to making sure that its supporters never miss another fundraising event, rally, or meeting and that's something that all nonprofits can benefit from.

In the context of metadata:

RSS files are metadata. RSS files are a type of metadata. Metadata are:

- *units of information about information.*
- *commonly used to provide descriptive information about the content, context, and characteristics of data.*

HTML keywords and description metatags are examples of metadata, and are used to provide information about Web pages. RSS files are easy to create. An RSS file commonly contains four main types of elements: channel, image, items, and text input. These elements are easy to identify and code. In headline collections published as results of RSS file aggregations, HTML normally renders the specified title as a headline. The title usually also serves as a link, using the URL listed in the link element. Finally, the description is normally displayed as a summary of the article underneath the headline.

HOW TO CREATE RSS FILES

RSS files can be built to either the proposed RSS 1.0 specification, or to the popular RSS 0.91 spec. For production applications, use RSS 0.91, because the 1.0 proposal is still under consideration. The 1.0 proposal differs from the 0.91 format in one main way: It incorporates Resource Description Framework (RDF) elements that allow greater flexibility at the expense of some increased complexity. This proposed specification is more extensible, creating a W3C standard for RSS files that will meet current needs, will be as backwards-compatible as possible, and will be adaptable to future requirements. Both versions of the specification share the characteristic of being a lightweight format that developers can use for many purposes. RSS is an XML application. Because of this, all RSS documents begin with the XML 1.0 declaration followed by the RSS document type declaration, as shown in Listing 2.

Example:

The XML declaration

```
<?xml version="1.0"?>
<!DOCTYPE rss PUBLIC "-//the message//DTD RSS 0.91//EN"
"http://myxlibrary.com/publish/formats/rss-0.91.dtd">
<rss version="0.91">
```

The first line declares the document to be an XML document. The second line, the DTD declaration, specifies that this XML file is based on the RSS 0.91 document type definition, DTD, at the meassage. Finally, the root element marks the beginning of the RSS file content, all of which goes between the <rss version "0.91"> tag and the </rss> tag.

The four main sections of an RSS file

After the root element come the four main sections of the RSS file. These are the channel, image, item, and text input sections. In practical use, the channel and item elements are requirements for any useful RSS file, while the image and text input are optional.

1. The channel section: The channel element contains metadata that describe the channel itself, telling what the channel is and who created it. The channel is a required element that includes the name of the channel, its description, its language, and a URL. The URL is normally used to point to the channel's source of information. Following example shows the beginning of the channel element. This part of the channel element defines the channel and begins the channel information.

THE CHANNEL ELEMENT

<channel>

<title>libraryZine</title>

<link>http://www.myxlibrary.org</link>

<description>Your source for library news, advocacy, interviews, builds, and more! </description>

<language>en-us</language>

</channel> The channel element contains the remaining channel tags, which describe the channel and allows it to be displayed in HTML. The title can be treated as a headline link. The Channel Language definition allows aggregators to filter news feeds and gives the rendering software the information necessary to display the language properly.

The </channnel> tag is used after all the channel elements to close the channel. As RSS conforms to XML specs, the element must be well formed; it requires the closing tag. User can include nine optional tags in a 0.91 channel definition. Some examples are PICS Rating, Copyright Identifier, Publication Date, and Webmaster. These additional elements can be used for a variety of purposes. For example, sites that aggregate content can use this additional meta information to allow users to filter news feeds on the basis of Platform for Internet Content Selection (PICS) ratings.

2. The image section

The image element is an optional element that is usually used to include the logo of the channel provider. The default size for the image is 88 pixels wide by 31 pixels high, but user can make his logo as large as 144 pixels wide by 400 pixels wide. Here is a sample image element:

Example: The image element

```
<image>
 <title>Librarymagzine</title>
<url>http://www.myxlibrary.org/image/mypic988.gif</url>
 <link>http://www.myxlibrary.org</link>
 <width>88</width>
 <height>31</height>
</image>
```

The image's title, URL, link, width, and height tags allow renderers to translate the file into HTML. The title tag is normally used for the image's ALT text. It is advisable to keep the image to 88 x 31 or smaller if possible, because many renderers translate channels into fixed width tables as narrow as 100 pixels. Larger graphics could cause the tables to break inappropriately, or cause the image to be left out when displayed.

The items

Items, the most important elements in a channel, usually form the dynamic part of an RSS file. While channel, image, and text input elements create the channel's identity and typically stay the same over long periods of time, channel items are rendered as news headlines, and the channel's value depends on their changing fairly frequently. Here is an example of a channel item:

LISTING 5. THE ITEM ELEMENT

<item>

<title>Java2 in Navigator 5?</title>

<link>http://www.myxlibrary.org/talkback.html?article=607</link>

<description>Will Java2 be an integrated part of Navigator 5?

Find more about it in this discussion...</description>

</item>

Fifteen items are allowed in a channel. This is a reasonable limitation, because most people use channels to distribute recent Web content. Titles should be less than 100 characters, while descriptions should be under 500 characters. The item title is normally rendered as a headline that links to the full article whose URL is provided by the item link. The item description is commonly used for either a summary of the article's content or for commentary on the article. News feed channels use the description to highlight the content of news articles, usually on the channel owner's site, and Web log channels use the description to provide commentary on a variety of content, often on third-party sites. Items are easy for developers to define and easy for users to read.

4. The text input

The text input area is an optional element, with only one allowed per channel. Usually rendered as an HTML form, text input lets the user respond to the channel. This feature enables the users to subscribe to particular newsletter or search particular site. Here is an example of a text input element:

Example: The text input element

<textinput>

<title>Send</title>

```
<description>Comments about Cookbook?</description>
<name>responseText</name>
<link>http://www.cookbook.org/cgi-bin/sampleonly.cgi</link>
</textinput>
```

The title is normally rendered as the label of the form's submit button, and the description as the text displayed before or above the input field. The text input name is supplied along with the contents of the text field when the submit button is clicked. These are the four main elements of an RSS file. After adding the image, item, and text input elements, remember to close the channel with the </channel> tag and the RSS file with the </rss> tag.

Working with RSS files

There are several ways to start working with RSS files. Because RSS files are so simple, they can be created easily using any text or XML editor. Also, there are sites with Web forms that let user create a custom RSS file online. Finally, user will also want to try creating RSS files automatically. Open-source tools for Java, PHP, and Perl can help getting started.

Publishing RSS file

Once a valid RSS file is available on Web site, the content can be syndicated. It can be done in publish and subscribe fashion. The information is published and it is available for subscription. The URL can be submitted to content aggregators such as Moreover or Userland. Aggregators take content from a variety of sites and publish it in feeds. While site's information could be mixed in with content from a variety of other suppliers, aggregators can help dramatically extending the reach of the distribution. RSS files can be used for private distribution on intranets or *extranets. Their simplicity makes RSS files a good way to publish information to a variety of systems.*

Parsing RSS files

The RSS file can be parsed back into discrete units of information. It can be done with the help of a variety of open-source tools written in Java, Perl, PHP, and even ASP. The parser reads a stream of XML text, identifies the opening and closing tags, finds the text enclosed in each tag, and creates handles to work with the parsed information. Once parsed, this information can be incorporated into dynamically generated pages. Perl is a great language for manipulating RSS files. For example, the XML::RSS module, which writes and parses RSS files. To take advantage of this parser, the XML::Parser module will also be required. These two Perl modules are available for free at CPAN.

The code sample passes a URL to a Perl script for parsing. Once parsed, the elements of the RSS file can be used in many ways. The XML::RSS module can be read with any text editor; it is heavily commented with suggestions for using it effectively. There are number of ways to usee RSS files. For example, scripts that generate RSS summaries every time your site is updated can be written, or scripts that periodically retrieve news from other sites and automatically update own news page.

RSS.NET

RSS.NET is an open-source .NET class library for RSS feeds. It provides a reusable object model for parsing and writing RSS feeds. It is fully compatible with RSS versions 0.90, 0.91, 0.92, and 2.0.1, implementing all constructs. Commercial, internal, open-source and all other developers can use RSS.NET. End users can not use RSS.NET directly.

RSS.NET powered applications & websites

- *si.blogs - slovenian blogs list.*

- *FeedJumbler - Aggregate/Merge/Combine and Convert RSS and Atom Feeds.*
- *devtoys - stuff for geeks.*
- *Leadit.SharePoint.Services - Generating RSS Feeds for SharePoint Sites.*
- *developerfood - A directory of ASP.NET, C#, and VB.NET controls, components, and development tools.*
- *RssPlug - Messenger Plus RSS Reader Plugin.*
- *RSS Xpress - freeware RSS reader.*
- *BlogWeaver - categorized feed directory focusing .NET and Longhorn.*
- *SpsRssGen - Sharepoint RSS Generator.*
- *Monologue - A blog aggregator for Mono blogers.*
- *SQLTeam.com - Website displaying SQL Server news.*
- *PopHeadlines - RSS to Inbox!*
- *GtkSharpRSS - A RSS and RDF client written in C#.*

THE CHALLENGE OF THE SOCIAL WEB

Customers once visited corporate websites to research products and form opinions about brands. Now, they are just as likely to discover a company on a friend's Facebook profile. They form opinions by searching tweets and connect with companies by subscribing to syndicated content. That means companies/organizations need to reach customers through social networks and RSS feeds to succeed in today's real-time social web.

Marketing through RSS Software

To make the social web as valuable as organizational website, it needs to publish, manage and measure "off website" content in social and syndicated environments in an automated, scalable way. With the help of software, company/organization can capitalize on this opportunity by:

- *Connecting with customers and prospects. Automatically publish any web content based on business rules including real-time search results to RSS readers, social networks and syndicated environments.*
- *Providing a consistent off website experience. Organization can present brand in the feeds and social content.*
- *Analyzing your feeds and social content. Organization can measure responses so it can increase content relevancy and develop best practices that drive real results.*

Benefits to RSS

RSS streamlines communication between publishers and readers. Since RSS has had a popularity surge, webmasters have been experimenting and using RSS feeds to deliver content in new and innovative ways. Typically, RSS feeds contain news headlines and content summaries. The content summaries contain just enough information without overwhelming the reader with superfluous details. If the reader is interested and wants additional information they can click on the item in the feed, accessing the website which contains additional details. RSS readers aggregate multiple feeds, making it easy for individuals to quickly scan information contained within each feed. Feeds are generally themed, allowing users to opt-in to feeds that are of interest. The big benefit to RSS is that individuals opt-in to content of interest, totally controlling the flow of information that they receive. If the quality of the content in the feed declines, users simply remove the feed from their RSS reader and they will not receive any additional updates from that source. The RSS reader acts as an aggregator, allowing users to view and scan multiple content streams in a timely fashion.

RSS is a great supplemental communication method that does not burden the publisher with maintaining lists or following strict privacy guidelines. RSS feeds are compiled according to the user's choices, removing any burden that is placed on publishers of email newsletters. Publishers no longer need to be concerned with spam, privacy policies, and age guidelines. Publishers using RSS as a communication vehicle are able to create keyword-rich, themed content, establishing trust, reputation, and ongoing communication with current and prospective customers.

KIND OF INFORMATION DELIVERED BY RSS FEEDS

Blogs Feed: Many blogs are catalogued in an RSS feed, with each blog entry summarized as a feed item. This makes it easy for visitors to scan blog posts for items of interest.

Article Feed: Articles are often placed into feeds to alert readers when new articles and content are available. The feed entry is typically an article summary or introduction. Readers can then ascertain if the article is of interest and read further.

Forum Feed : Many forums now have add-ons that allow participants to receive forum posts via RSS. The RSS feeds often will show the latest discussion topics; if users are interested they simply click to enter the forum to participate in the discussion. As the topic is updated they will see new entries in the RSS feed.

Schedule Feed : Schools, clubs and organizations will often use feeds to communicate meeting times, places and events that might be occurring. The RSS feeds are often used to publicize events, notify the community of schedule changes or meeting agendas.

Discounts / Specials Feed: Retail and online stores have begun using RSS feeds to deliver their latest specials and discounted offers. Some online retailers have taken this step further, allowing users to create their own feeds based on keywords or phrases. For example, this service will generate a URL than can be entered into a news reader. The feed is updated each time an item is added to Amazon that meets the specified criteria or keywords - Amazon Search Feed.

Ego / News Monitoring : Companies or individuals interested in receiving headline news based on a specific brand or keyword can use RSS feeds to monitor news sources. For example, users can use the following tool to create a feed that will allow them to receive filtered news from Google News. They will only receive items related to a specific keyword or phrase they setup.

Industry-Specific RSS Feed Uses Include: Technical professionals in specific industries have also developed RSS feeds as way to market, promote or communicate within their specific industries. In many cases, this has expanded their reach and increased communication with current and prospective customers and clients.

RSS feeds can be used by realtors to communicate the time and location for open houses, announce new property listings or promote decreased mortgage rates. Content feeds can also be used by universities to communicate sports scores or event schedules. Computer service professionals can create feeds to notify clients of potential security breaches, virus risks or outbreaks. Ultimately, RSS is molded to meet the communication needs of many sectors.

REFERENCES:

1. *http://www.libraryjournal.com/RSS*
2. *Abram, S. (2005). Web 2.0 — huh?! library 2.0, librarian 2.0. Information Outlook, 9 (12), 44-46.*
3. *BlogBridge (2006).Announcing BlogBridge: Library. http://www.blogbridge.com/archives/2006/06/announcing_blog_2.php*
4. *Breeding, M. (2006). Web 2.0? let's get to web 1.0 first. Computers in Libraries, 26 (5), 30-33.*
5. *Casey, M. (2006a). Born in the biblioblogosphere. LibraryCrunch, January 3, 2006. http://www.librarycrunch.com/2006/01/post_1.html*

6. Casey, M. (2006b). LibraryCrunch: bringing you a library 2.0 perspective. http://www.librarycrunch.com/

7. Crawford, Walt. (2006). "Library 2.0 and 'Library 2.0'" Cites and Insights, 6, 2. http://cites.boisestate.edu/civ6i2.pdf

8. Del.icio.us.http://del.icio.us/

9. FaceBook. http://www.facebook.com/

10. Flickr. http://www.flickr.com/

11. Frappr. http://www.frappr.com/

12. Habib, M. (2006). Conceptual model for academic library 2.0. Michael Habib's weblog on library and information science. http://mchabib.blogspot.com/2006/06/conceptual-model-for-academic-library.html

13. Hale, M. (1991). Paradigmatic shift in library and information science. In Library and Information Science Research: Perspectives and Strategies for Improvement, McClure, C. and Hernon, P., eds. Ablex: Norwood, NJ.

14. Lawson, S. (2006). Library 2.0: rapid response to rapid change. Colorado Libraries, 32 (2), 19-21.

15. LibraryThing. http://www.librarything.com/

16. Litwin, R. (2006). The central problem of library 2.0: privacy. Library juice: on the intersection of libraries, politics, and culture. http://libraryjuicepress.com/blog/?p=68

17. Mashups (web application hybrids). (2006). Wikipedia article. http://en.wikipedia.org/wiki/Mashup_(web_application_hybrid)

18. Miller, P. (2005a). Do libraries matter?: The rise of library 2.0 (A Talis White Paper), Talis. http://www.talis.com/downloads/white_papers/DoLibrariesMatter.pdf

19. Miller, P. (2005b). Web 2.0: building the new library. Ariadne, 45 (October, 2005). http://www.ariadne.ac.uk/issue45/miller/

20. Miller, P. (2006). Coming together around library 2.0: a focus for discussion and a call to arms. D-Lib Magazine, (12) 4, 2006. http://www.dlib.org/dlib/april06/miller/04miller.html

21. Miller, P. (2006). Library 2.0 - the challenge of distruptive innovation (A Talis White Paper). Tallis. http://www.talis.com/resources/documents/447_Library_2_prf1.pdf

22. MySpace. http://www.myspace.com/

23. Notess, G. R. (2006). The terrible twos: web 2.0, library 2.0, and more. Online, 30 (3), 40-42.

24. *O'Reilly, T. (2005). What is web 2.0? http://www.oreillynet.com/pub/a/oreilly/tim/news/2005/09/30/what-is-web-20.html#mememap*
25. *Peek, R. (2005). Web publishing 2.0. Information Today, 22 (10), 17-18.*
26. *Peer Reviewed Instructional Materials Online (PRIMO). http://www.ala.org/ala/acrlbucket/is/iscommittees/webpages/emergingtech/primo/index.htm*
27. *Public Library Interface Kit (Plinkit). http://www.plinkit.org/*
28. *Retrivr. (2006). http://labs.systemone.at/retrievr/*
29. *RSS (file format). Wikipedia article. http://en.wikipedia.org/wiki/RSS_(protocol)*
30. *Shanhi, R. (2006). Web 2.0: data, metadata, and interface. http://www.rashmisinha.com/archives/05_08/web2-data-metadata-interface.html*
31. *Tebbutt, D. (2006). Is all the talk of web 2.0 just a lot of codswallop? Information World Review, (221), 9-9.*
32. *Varnum, K. (2006). RSS4Lib: Innovative ways libaries use RSS. http://blogs.fletcher.tufts.edu/rss4lib/*
33. *WikiBios. http://www.wikibios.com/*
34. *Wikipedia. www.wikipedia.com/*
35. *Maness, J. (2006). "Library 2.0 Theory: Web 2.0 and Its Implications for Libraries". Webology, 3 (2), Article 25. http://www.webology.ir/2006/v3n2/a25.html*
36. *http://www.loc.gov/rss/*
37. *http://www.cnn.com/services/rss/*
38. *http://www.nytimes.com/services/xml/rss/index.html*
39. *http://library.open.ac.uk/services/lib20servs/rssfeed/*
40. *http://bloglines.com/*
41. *http://www.rojo.com/*
42. *http://www.netvibes.com/*
43. *http://www.google.com/reader/view/#welcome-page*
44. *http://www.newsgator.com/*
45. *http://www.feedreader.com/*
46. *http://my.yahoo.com/*
47. *http://www.bloglines.com/*
48. *http://webology.ir/2006/v3n2/a25.html#29*

49. http://library.mcmaster.ca/php/blog.php?id=841&display=full
50. http://www.theglobeandmail.com/generated/headlines/rdf/
51. http://www.nytimes.com/services/xml/rss/index.html
52. http://npg.nature.com/npg/servlet/Content?data=xml/02_newsfeed.xml&style=xml/02_newsfeed.xsl
53. http://www.ingentaconnect.com/about/researchers/subscribing_to_rss_feeds
54. http://www.biomedcentral.com/info/about/rss/
55. http://www.nlm.nih.gov/pubs/techbull/mj05/mj05_rss.html
56. http://www3.oup.co.uk/jnls/help/rss.html
57. http://bell.computer.org/rss/index.jsp
58. http://news.gc.ca/cfmx/view/en/index.jsp?categoryid=12&category=Choose+Your+News
59. http://library.mcmaster.ca/php/blog.php?id=94&display=fu
60. http://bloglines.com/
61. http://www.feedster.com/
62. http://meredith.wolfwater.com/webct.gif
63. http://www.hsl.wisc.edu/bjd/journals/rss/index.cfm
64. http://www.kclibrary.org/rss/
65. http://www.library.ualberta.ca/newbooks/index.cfm
66. http://catalog.spl.org/rss?index=.SW&term=Landscape gardening — West (U.S.)&limit=&sort=3100049&npp=10&uri=link=direct
67. http://support.ebsco.com/support_news/detail.php?id=109&t=r&page=&private=true
68. http://proquest.com/syndication/rss/
69. http://encyclopedia2.thefreedictionary.com/Web+based
70. Brian Satterfield, September 18, 2006. Easy Ways to Publish Your Own RSS Feeds: Use RSS to help your constituents stay on top of news and announcements. http://www.techsoup.org/learningcenter/internet/page5820.cfm#rate
71. http://www.techsoup.org/learningcenter/webbuilding/page1439.cfm
72. http://www.blogger.com/
73. http://www.intertwingly.net/wiki/pie/Rss20AndAtom10Compared
74. http://www.livejournal.com/

75. *http://www.wordpress.com/*
76. *http://www.typepad.com/*
77. *http://www.techsoup.org/learningcenter/internet/page4817.cfm*
78. *http://drupal.org/*
79. *http://plone.org/*
80. *http://www.feedyes.com/*
81. *http://www.ponyfish.com/*
82. *http://www.linkrss.com/*
83. *http://publi.sh/*
84. *http://www.hitrss.com/*
85. *http://www.feedpublish.com/*
86. *http://allrss.com/rsseditors.html*
87. *http://www.alnera.com/en/feedworkshop/*
88. *http://www.extralabs.net/feed-editor.htm*
89. *http://www.feedforall.com/feedforall.htm*
90. *http://www.jitbit.com/rssfeedcreator.aspx*
91. *http://feedicons.com/*
92. *http://www.ibm.com/developerworks/library/w-rss.html#ibm-pcon*
93. *http://www.ibm.com/developerworks/library/w-rss.html#resources*
94. *James Lewin. An introduction to RSS news feeds, Using open formats for content syndication http://www.ibm.com/developerworks/library/w-rss.html#*
95. *http://www.rssdotnet.com/documents/license.html*
96. *http://sourceforge.net/projects/rss-net/*
97. *http://www.rssdotnet.com/documents/class_library_reference/index.html*
98. *Amazon Search Feed - http://www.oxus.net/amazon/*
99. *http://www.justinpfister.com/gnewsfeed.php*
100. *FeedForAll - http://www.feedforall.com/*
101. *Sharon Housley manages marketing for NotePage, Inc. http://www.notepage.net/*

7

AJAX TECHNOLOGIES

INTRODUCTION

In the past few years, developers could choose between two approaches when building a web application. The first approach was to create a screen-based system with very rich interactions using a sophisticated, powerful technology such as Java or Flash. The alternative approach was to create a page-based system using easier-to-learn core web standards like XHTML and CSS whose more basic capabilities force less-rich interactions. A new technological approach, dubbed Ajax, might just be the right mix between the two.

Ajax is a group of interrelated web development techniques used. These techniques are on the client-side to create interactive web applications. With the help of Ajax, web applications can retrieve data from the server asynchronously in the background. It happens without interfering with the display and behavior of the existing page. The use of Ajax techniques has led to an increase in interactive or dynamic interfaces on web pages. Data is usually retrieved using the XMLHttpRequest object. Despite the name, the use of XML is not actually required, nor do the requests need to be asynchronous. Like DHTML and LAMP, Ajax is a group of technologies. It uses a combination of HTML and CSS to mark up and style information. We can say that AJAX is about updating parts of a web page, without reloading the whole page.

There are certain points to keep in mind:

- *Classic web pages, (which do not use AJAX) must reload the entire page if the content should change. Examples of applications using AJAX: Google Maps, Gmail, Youtube, and Facebook tabs.*
- *AJAX is a technique for creating fast and dynamic web pages.*
- *AJAX allows web pages to be updated asynchronously by exchanging small amounts of data with the server behind the scenes. This means that it is possible to update parts of a web page, without reloading the whole page.*
- *AJAX is not a new programming language, but a new way to use existing standards. AJAX is the art of exchanging data with a server, and update parts of a web page.*

GRADUAL DEVELOPMENTS

Ajax is only a name given to a set of tools that previously existed. XMLHttpRequest is a server-side object usable in JavaScript. It was implemented into Internet Explorer since the 4.0 version. In Internet Explorer, it is an ActiveX object that was first named XMLHTTP some times, before to be generalized on all browser under the name XMLHttpRequest, when the Ajax technology becomes commonly used. The use of XMLHttpRequest is found in 2005 by Google, in Gmail and GoogleMaps. It has contributed to the success of this format. But this is the when the name Ajax was itself coined that the technology started to be so popular.

WHY AJAX IS NEEDED

AJAX is required for following aspects:

- *Mainly to build a fast, dynamic website, but also to save resources.*
- *For improving sharing of resources, it is better to use the power of all the client computers rather than just a unique server and network. Ajax allows performing processing on client computer (in JavaScript) with data taken from the server.*
- *The processing of web page formerly was only server-side, using web services or PHP scripts, before the whole page was sent within the network. But Ajax can selectively modify a part of a page displayed by the browser, and update it without the need to reload the whole document with all images, menus, etc...*

Example of components of web page: fields of forms, choices of user, may be processed and the result displayed immediately into the same page.

TECHNOLOGIES BEING USED IN AJAX

The term Ajax has come to represent a broad group of web technologies that can be used to implement a web application that communicates with a server in the background, without interfering with the current state of the page. Ajax isn't a single technology. It's really several technologies, coming together in powerful new ways. Ajax incorporates:

- *standards-based presentation using XHTML and CSS;*
- *dynamic display and interaction using the Document Object Model;*
- *data interchange and manipulation using XML and XSLT;*
- *asynchronous data retrieval using XMLHttpRequest;*
- *and JavaScript binding everything together.*

Since then, however, there have been a number of developments in the technologies used in an Ajax application. In particular, it has been noted that:

- *JavaScript is the most popular language for Ajax programming due to its inclusion in and compatibility with the majority of modern web browsers. JavaScript is not the only client-side scripting language that can be used for implementing an Ajax application. Other languages such as VBScript are also capable of the required functionality.*
- *JavaScript Object Notation (JSON) is often used as an alternative format for data interchange, although other formats such as preformatted HTML or plain text can also be used.XML is not required for data interchange and therefore XSLT is not required for the manipulation of data.*

Classic Ajax involves writing ad hoc JavaScript on the client. A simpler if cruder alternative is to use standard JavaScript libraries that can partially update a page, such as ASP.Net's UpdatePanel. Tools such as Echo2 and ZK enable fine grained control of a page from the server, using only standard JavaScript libraries. Introducing XMLHttpRequest and pseudomultithreading, it is possible to swap the role of client and server (web browser may start behaving as a server and web server may start behaving as a client) in Client-Server model.

In a summarized manner, Ajax is a set of technologies, supported by a web browser. The elements of AJAX has following functions:

HTML and CSS : for presenting.

JavaScript (ECMAScript) : for local processing, and DOM (Document Object Model) to access data inside the page or to access elements of XML file read on the server (with the getElementByTagName method for example)...

The XMLHttpRequest object : used to read or send data on the server asynchronously.

This wonderful tool has facilitations of few flexibilities such as:

- *DOMParser may be used*
- *PHP or another scripting language may be used on the server.*
- *XML and XSLT to process the data if returned in XML form.*
- *SOAP may be used to dialog with the server.*

Summarizing, AJAX

- *Asynchronous JavaScript And XML*
- *Originated in 1997, but was not popular at that time because browsers didn't support JavaScript*
- *Not a technology in itself, but refers to the use of a group of technologies that provide interactivity (XHTML, CSS, DOM, XMLHttpRequest)*

The "asynchronous" word, means that the response of the server while be processed when available, without to wait and to freeze the display of the page. Examples of services that use AJAX are:

- *MyYahoo*
- *Google/IG*
- *Start.com*
- *Flickr*
- *Google Mail*
- *Google Maps*

How AJAX Works

Ajax uses a programming model with display and events. These events are user actions, they call functions associated to elements of the web page.

Interactivity is achieved with forms and buttons. DOM allows to link elements of the page with actions and also to extract data from XML files provided by the server.

To get data on the server, XMLHttpRequest provides two methods:

i. *open: create a connection*

ii. *send: send a request to the server. Data furnished by the server will be found in the attributes of the XMLHttpRequest object:*
    - *responseXml for an XML file or*
    - *responseText for a plain text.*

Ajax and DHTML

Dynamic HTML has same purpose and is a set of standards as AJAX:

- *HTML,*
- *CSS,*
- *JavaScript.*

DHTML allows changing the display of the page from user commands or from text typed by the user. Ajax allows also sending requests asynchronously and loading data from the server. It is DHTML plus the XHR object.

The XMLHttpRequest object

Allows interacting with the servers, thanks to its methods and attributes.

Attributes

1.	*readyState*	*the code successively changes value from 0 to 4 that means for "ready".*
2.	*status*	*200 is OK404 if the page is not found.*
3.	*responseText*	*holds loaded data as a string of characters.*
4.	*responseXml*	*holds an XML loaded file, DOM's method allows to extract data.*

5.	*onreadystatechange*	*property that takes a function as value that is invoked when the readystatechange event is dispatched.*

Methods:

1.	*open(mode, url, boolean)*	*mode: type of request, GET or POSTurl: the location of the file, with a path.boolean: true (asynchronous) / false/(synchronous) optionally, a login and a password may be added to arguments.*
2.	*send("string")*	*null for a GET command.*

The steps for building a request

(i) First step: create an instance

This is just a classical instance of class, but two options must be tried, for browser compatibility.

```
if (window.XMLHttpRequest)     // Object of the current windows
{
  xhr = new XMLHttpRequest();  // Firefox, Safari, ...
}
else
if (window.ActiveXObject)   // ActiveX version
{
xhr = new ActiveXObject("Microsoft.XMLHTTP"); // Internet Explorer
}
```

Or exceptions may be used instead:

```
try {
xhr = new ActiveXObject("Microsoft.XMLHTTP"); // Trying Internet Explorer
}
catch(e) // Failed
```

```
{
 xhr = new XMLHttpRequest(); // Other browsers.
}
```

(ii) Second step: wait for the response

The response and further processing are included in a function and the return of the function will be assigned to the onreadystatechange attribute of the object previously created.

```
xhr.onreadystatechange = function() { // instructions
to process the response };
if(xhr.readyState == 4)
{
 // Received, OK
} else
{
 // Wait...
}
```

(iii) Third step: make the request itself

Two methods of XMLHttpRequest are used:

- *open: command GET or POST, URL of the document, true for asynchronous.*
- *send: with POST only, the data to send to the server.*

The request below read a document on the server.

```
xhr.open('GET', 'http://www.xul.fr/somefile.xml',
true);
xhr.send(null);
```

AJAX AND INTERNET STANDARDS

AJAX applications are browser- and platform-independent! AJAX was made popular in 2005 by Google, with Google Suggest. Google Suggest is using AJAX to create a very dynamic web interface: When user starts typing in Google's search box, a JavaScript sends the letters off to a server and the server returns a list of suggestions. AJAX is based on internet standards, and uses a combination of:

- *XMLHttpRequest object (to exchange data asynchronously with a server)*
- *JavaScript/DOM (to display/interact with the information)*
- *CSS (to style the data)*
- *XML (often used as the format for transferring data)*

DRAWBACKS OF AJAX

Ajax is not all good but having few side effects as well.

- *Owing to their dynamic nature, Ajax interfaces are often harder to develop when compared to static pages.*
- *Pages dynamically created do not automatically register themselves with the browser's history engine, so clicking the browser's "back" button may not return the user to an earlier state of the Ajax-enabled page, but may instead return them to the last full page visited before it. Workarounds include the use of invisible IFrames to trigger changes in the browser's history and changing the URL fragment identifier (the portion of a URL after the '#') when Ajax is run and monitoring it for changes.*
- *Dynamic web page updates also make it difficult for a user to bookmark a particular state of the application. Many of the solutions to this problem use the URL fragment identifier (the portion of a URL after the '#') to keep track of, and allow users to return to, the application in a given state.*
- *Depending on the nature of the Ajax application, dynamic page updates may interfere disruptively with user interactions, especially if working on an unstable*

internet connection. For instance, editing a search field may trigger a query to the server for search completions, but the user may not know that a search completion popup is forthcoming, and if the internet connection is slow, the popup list may show up at an inconvenient time, when the user has already proceeded to do something else.

- *Because most web crawlers do not execute JavaScript code, publicly indexable web applications should provide an alternative means of accessing the content that would normally be retrieved with Ajax, to allow search engines to index it.*
- *Any user whose browser does not support JavaScript or XMLHttpRequest, or simply has this functionality disabled, will not be able to properly use pages which depend on Ajax. Similarly, devices such as mobile phones, PDAs, and screen readers may not have support for the required technologies. Screen readers that are able to use Ajax may still not be able to properly read the dynamically generated content. The only way to carry out functionality is to fall back to non-JavaScript methods. This can be achieved by making sure links and forms can be resolved properly and do not rely solely on Ajax. In JavaScript, form submission could then be halted with "return false".*
- *The same origin policy prevents some Ajax techniques from being used across domains. Techniques exist to sidestep this limitation by using a special Cross Domain Communications channel embedded as an iframe within a page.*
- *Like other web technologies, Ajax has its own set of vulnerabilities. Developers familiar with other web technologies may have to learn new testing and coding methods to write secure Ajax applications.*

- *Ajax-powered interfaces may increase the number of user-generated requests to web servers and their back-ends (databases, or other). This can lead to longer response times and/or additional hardware needs.*

Building an Ajax website

User needs for some wrapper. A short list of frameworks is provided below. The JavaScript program, integrated into a web page, sends request to the server to load files for rebuilding of pages. The received documents are processed with Dom's methods or XML parsers and the data are used to update the pages.

— *If JavaScript is not activated, Ajax can't work. The user must be asked to set JavaScript from within options of the browser, with the "noscript" tag.*

— *Since data to display are loaded dynamically, they are not part of the page, and the keywords inside are not viewed by search engines.*

— *The asynchronous mode may change the page with delays (when the processing on the server take some times), this may be disturbing.*

— *The back button may be deactivated*

POPULARITY OF PERSONALIZATION

Web users who keep personalized webpages are more likely to come back to the site often and will surely visit everyday to check their custom homepage content.a number of good sites listed above support drag and drop interfaces, RSS feeds, integration with search engines, and the ability to add and remove content. Statistics have shown that users prefer these features over many of the currently implemented MyLibrary sites. MyLibrary is currently used by a number of institutions, but has proven less desirable due to the burden of high maintenance and low usage. AJAX is being used for real-time data validation and auto completions in a number of different applications.

Examples included:

- *Yahoo Finance – Streaming Stock Quotes*
- *Google Suggest – Predictive text entries listed in search box*

NEW APPROACH TO WEB APPLICATIONS

Web interaction designers can't help but feel a little envious of our colleagues who create desktop software. Desktop applications have a richness and responsiveness that has seemed out of reach on the Web. The same simplicity that enabled the Web's rapid proliferation also creates a gap between the experiences we can provide and the experiences users can get from a desktop application.

Google Suggest, the way the suggested terms update as user types, almost instantly. For example, in Google Maps, after zooming in, use of the cursor to grab the map and scroll around a bit and everything happens almost instantly, with no waiting for pages to reload. Google Suggest and Google Maps are two examples of a new approach to web applications. The name is shorthand for Asynchronous JavaScript + XML, and it represents a fundamental shift in what's possible on the Web.

In the classic web application model, most user actions in the interface trigger an HTTP request back to a web server. The server does some processing — retrieving data, crunching numbers, talking to various legacy systems — and then returns an HTML page to the client. It's a model adapted from the Web's original use as a hypertext medium.

How Different is Ajax

An Ajax application eliminates the waiting nature of interaction on the Web by introducing an intermediary — an Ajax engine — between the user and the server. It seems like adding a layer to the application would make it less responsive, but the opposite is true. Instead of loading a webpage, at the start of the session, the browser loads an Ajax engine — written in JavaScript and usually tucked away in a hidden frame. This engine is responsible for both rendering the interface the user sees and communicating with the server on the user's behalf. The Ajax engine allows the user's interaction with the application to happen asynchronously. It is independent of communication with the server. Any response to a user action that doesn't require a trip back to the server (such as simple data validation, editing data in memory, and even some navigation). The engine handles on its own. If the engine needs something from the server in order to respond, if it's submitting data for processing, loading additional interface code, or retrieving new data — the engine makes those requests asynchronously, usually using XML, without stalling a user's interaction with the application.

Ajax Usage

Google is making a huge investment in developing the Ajax approach. All of the major products Google has introduced over the last year (Orkut, Gmail), the latest beta version of Google Groups, Google Suggest, and Google Maps are Ajax applications. Many of the features in Flickr depend on Ajax, and Amazon's A9.com search engine applies similar techniques. These projects demonstrate that Ajax is not only technically sound, but also practical for real-world applications. Ajax applications can be any size, from the very simple, single-function (Google Suggest) to the very complex and sophisticated (Google Maps). Ajax applications can provide the combination of the rich interaction and responsiveness,. Ajax is an important development for Web applications.

AJAX ASP/PHP Example

The following example demonstrates how a web page

can communicate with a web server while a user type characters in an input field:

Example

Start typing a name in the input field below:

First name: [ ]

Suggestions:

Example Explained - The showHint() Function

When a user types a character in the input field above, the function "showHint()" is executed. The function is triggered by the "onkeyup" event:

```
function showHint(str)
{
if (str.length==0)
 {
 document.getElementById("txtHint").innerHTML="";
 return;
 }
if (window.XMLHttpRequest)
 {// code for IE7+, Firefox, Chrome, Opera, Safari
 xmlhttp=new XMLHttpRequest();
 }
else
 {// code for IE6, IE5
 xmlhttp=new ActiveXObject("XYZ.XMLHTTP");
 }
xmlhttp.onreadystatechange=function()
 {
 if (xmlhttp.readyState==4 && xmlhttp.status==200)
  {
```

```
        document.getElementById("txtHint").innerHTML=
xmlhttp.responseText;
        }
      }
    xmlhttp.open("GET","gethint.asp?q="+str,true);
    xmlhttp.send();
    }
```

Source code explanation

If the input field is empty (str.length==0), the function clears the content of the txtHint placeholder and exits the function. If the input field is not empty, the showHint() function executes the following:

- *Create an XMLHttpRequest object*
- *Create the function to be executed when the server response is ready*
- *Send the request off to a file on the server*
- *Notice that a parameter (q) is added to the URL (with the content of the input field)*

The AJAX Server Page - ASP and PHP

The page on the server called by the JavaScript is an ASP file called "gethint.asp".

Two versions of the server file are created, one written in ASP and one in PHP.

1. The ASP File

The source code in "gethint.asp" checks an array of names, and returns the corresponding name(s) to the browser:

```
<%
response.expires=-1
dim a(30)
```

```
'Fill up array with names
a(1)="Anna"
a(2)="Brittany"
a(3)="Cinderella"
a(4)="Diana"
a(5)="Eva"
a(6)="Fiona"
a(7)="Gunda"
a(8)="Hege"
a(9)="Inga"
a(10)="Johanna"
a(11)="Kitty"
a(12)="Linda"
a(13)="Nina"
a(14)="Ophelia"
a(15)="Petunia"
a(16)="Amanda"
a(17)="Raquel"
a(18)="Cindy"
a(19)="Doris"
a(20)="Eve"
a(21)="Evita"
a(22)="Sunniva"
a(23)="Tove"
a(24)="Unni"
a(25)="Violet"
a(26)="Liza"
a(27)="Elizabeth"
a(28)="Ellen"
a(29)="Wenche"
```

```
a(30)="Vicky"
'get the q parameter from URL
q=ucase(request.querystring("q"))
'lookup all hints from array if length of q>0
if len(q)>0 then
 hint=""
 for i=1 to 30
  if q=ucase(mid(a(i),1,len(q))) then
   if hint="" then
    hint=a(i)
   else
    hint=hint & " , " & a(i)
   end if
  end if
 next
end if
'Output "no suggestion" if no hint were found
'or output the correct values
if hint="" then
 response.write("no suggestion")
else
 response.write(hint)
end if
%>
```

The PHP File

Below is the code above rewritten in PHP. To run the example in PHP, change the value of the url variable (in the HTML file) from "gethint.asp" to "gethint.php".

```
<?php
```

```
// Fill up array with names
$a[]="Anna";
$a[]="Brittany";
$a[]="Cinderella";
$a[]="Diana";
$a[]="Eva";
$a[]="Fiona";
$a[]="Gunda";
$a[]="Hege";
$a[]="Inga";
$a[]="Johanna";
$a[]="Kitty";
$a[]="Linda";
$a[]="Nina";
$a[]="Ophelia";
$a[]="Petunia";
$a[]="Amanda";
$a[]="Raquel";
$a[]="Cindy";
$a[]="Doris";
$a[]="Eve";
$a[]="Evita";
$a[]="Sunniva";
$a[]="Tove";
$a[]="Unni";
$a[]="Violet";
$a[]="Liza";
$a[]="Elizabeth";
$a[]="Ellen";
```

```
$a[]="Wenche";
$a[]="Vicky";
//get the q parameter from URL
$q=$_GET["q"];
//lookup all hints from array if length of q>0
if (strlen($q) > 0)
 {
 $hint="";
 for($i=0; $i<count($a); $i++)
  {
 if (strtolower($q)==strtolower(substr($a[$i],
0,strlen($q))))
   {
   if ($hint=="")
    {
    $hint=$a[$i];
    }
   else
    {
    $hint=$hint." , ".$a[$i];
    }
   }
  }
 }

// Set output to "no suggestion" if no hint were found
// or to the correct values
if ($hint == "")
 {
 $response="no suggestion";
```

```
  }
else
  {
  $response=$hint;
  }

//output the response
echo $response;
?>
```

AJAX DATABASE INTERACTION

AJAX can be used for interactive communication with a database.

AJAX Database Example

The following example will demonstrate how a web page can fetch information from a database with AJAX:

Example

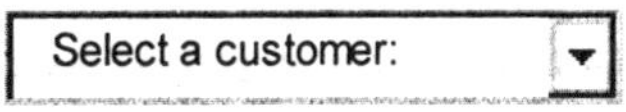

Customer info will be listed here.

Example Explained - The showCustomer() Function

When a user selects a customer in the dropdown list above, a function called "showCustomer()" is executed. The function is triggered by the "onchange" event:

```
function showCustomer(str)
{
if(str=="")
  {
  document.getElementById("txtHint").innerHTML="";
  return;
```

```
 }
if(window.XMLHttpRequest)
 {// code for IE7+, Firefox, Chrome, Opera, Safari
 xmlhttp=new XMLHttpRequest();
 }
else
 {// code for IE6, IE5
xmlhttp=new ActiveXObject("Microsoft.XMLHTTP");
 }
xmlhttp.onreadystatechange=function()
 {
 if(xmlhttp.readyState==4 && xmlhttp.status==200)
  {
 document.getElementById("txtHint").innerHTML=
xmlhttp.responseText;
  }
 }
xmlhttp.open("GET","getcustomer.asp?q="+str,true);
xmlhttp.send();
}
```

The showCustomer() function does the following:

- *Check if a customer is selected*
- *Create an XMLHttpRequest object*
- *Create the function to be executed when the server response is ready*
- *Send the request off to a file on the server*
- *Notice that a parameter (q) is added to the URL (with the content of the dropdown list)*

The AJAX Server Page

The page on the server called by the JavaScript in above

example is an ASP file called "getcustomer.asp".

The server file could easily be rewritten in PHP, or some other server languages. The source code in "getcustomer.asp" runs a query against a database, and returns the result in an HTML table:

```
<%
response.expires=-1
sql="SELECT * FROM CUSTOMERS WHERE CUSTOMERID="
sql=sql & "'" & request.querystring("q") & "'"

set conn=Server.CreateObject("ADODB.Connection")
conn.Provider="XYZ.Jet.OLEDB.4.0"
conn.Open(Server.Mappath("/db/northwind.mdb"))
set rs=Server.CreateObject("ADODB.recordset")
rs.Open sql,conn

response.write("<table>")
do until rs.EOF
 for each x in rs.Fields
   response.write("<tr><td><b>" & x.name & "</b></td>")
   response.write("<td>" & x.value & "</td></tr>")
 next
 rs.MoveNext
loop
response.write("</table>")
%>
```

AJAX uses for the Library OPAC

a. *OCLC LCSH Live Search – Instant results list of subject terms (http://lcsh.orhost.org/)*

b. *Univ. of Huddersfield Library Tag Cloud – Tag Cloud of catalog subject terms*

As blogs have been one of the most highly praised features of the Web 2.0 era, Content Management Systems (CMS) that incorporate blog and other social/collaborative features are proving to offer more useful features for library websites. A great example of this technology in action is The Ann Arbor District Library site. AADL uses Drupal. Plone is another CMS with similar features that other libraries are using.

Following are the examples of library blogs:

- *Peter Scott's list of library weblogs. Available at http://www.libdex.com/weblogs.html*
- *Yale University Harvey Cushing/John Hay Whitney Medical Library blog. Available at http://elibrary.med.yale.edu/blog/*

The goal of library websites should be to engage users with interactivity and personalization, and integrate library services into the customizable services that web users maintain regularly such as MyYahoo and Google/IG.

USING AJAX FOR CREATING WEB APPLICATIONS

a. *Screen-based Approaches : the Sophisticated Choice: Screen-based applications offer users the ability to enter and manipulate information on a small number of screens that instantly update with any submitted changes. Developers typically build these applications, which mimic the sophistication of desktop applications, with Java, Flash or a similar technology. the Gameday feature of MLB.com, and the Nike.com shoe configuration tool are some of the good examples of the screen-based approach.*

b. *Page-based Approaches : The Unsophisticated Choice:*

> *Developers who build page-based applications using standard web technologies are forced to deal with the load-reload effect of normal web pages. As a result, users who enter and manipulate information in page-based applications must sit through a page refresh in order for their changes to take place. The Amazon.com checkout sequence, Google search, and the eBay selling sequence are common examples of the page-based approach.*

While both approaches have proven successful, each has drawbacks. Screen-based approaches, for example, require significant development time and effort because they are built with difficult to learn and often proprietary programming tools. While easier to build than their screen-based counterparts, page-based approaches provide a less seamless experience.

Ajax: A Middle-of-the-Road Approach

Ajax is a new web approach that marries the benefits of both screen and paged-based approaches. By allowing more sophisticated functionality using easier-to-implement web standards, Ajax is proving a real alternative for creating powerful web applications.

Developers building Ajax interfaces leverage the same technologies as page-based approaches: XHTML, CSS, and JavaScript. Ajax became suddenly popular. Several large companies including Google have created amazing applications using the technology: Google Maps, Google Gmail, and Google Suggest are all built using Ajax. Another reason is the continuing adoption of standards compliant-browsers that support Ajax technology, most notably Firefox, Safari, Opera, and Internet Explorer 6.

Typically, when users enter information into an input field on a page-based web application, nothing is done with that information until they press "submit". After they press "submit" the information is sent to the server, a response is returned, notifying the user of success or failure. During this time, the user sits and waits while the page refreshes. The users desire (and expect) immediate response to their queries.

Ajax applications don't need to refresh the entire page to update information on it. Ajax apps can simply update parts of the page at any time. This technique gives users an instantaneous response to their inputs and queries. This allows users to continually see what they're working on and react to any changes, errors, or updates the interface notifies them of.

Instant field Checking & Saving

Fortunately, Ajax allows instant field checking and saving. It is easy to check fields on the client side using JavaScript. This produces an immediate effect, and mimics the behavior of a desktop application. However, for security reasons it is necessary to check all fields on the server end as well.

Single Screen Interface

One of the biggest reasons to use the screen-based approach is the simplicity of a single-screen interface. Single screen interfaces proved very useful for people, providing several advantages over page-based applications.

Advantages of a single-screen are:

- *(i)* *users can see the big picture of the application, seeing all of the steps necessary to complete the application.*
- *(ii)* *this gives users a clear idea of what is expected of them during a transaction.*
- *(iii)* *On a page-based application, they might have to click through several pages without knowing what is ahead of them.*
- *(iv)* *Single-screen interfaces also allow users to modify and*

change information in the order that they choose.

(v) *In a single-screen interface this is easy. On the other hand, most page-based approaches force users into a specific sequence.*

Most of Ajax's benefits mirror those of sophisticated screen-based applications. However, there is a big hurdle to creating these sophisticated applications: they are full-fledged programming environments that require advanced programming skills and a long-term commitment to proprietary technology. This makes creating interfaces in this way expensive and time-consuming. Because Ajax applications are built using nothing more than current web standards, they are relatively easy to create. Enterprising Ajax developers have created easy-to-use building blocks that allow developers unfamiliar with the approach to migrate their applications over without having to write code from scratch.

Pros and Cons

- *Speedy browsing*
- *Updates information without the need to refresh the browser*
- *Complex, browser specific, requires JavaScript to be enabled, debugging is required, and poses a security risk (source code viewable)*
- *Browser back button will not work*
- *Difficult to track use statistics*

AJAX is a smorgasbord of web technologies put together to allow dynamic client-server interactions to occur in web applications without requiring pages to reload or refresh. It is a combination of technologies used in a certain way. AJAX uses the following:

- *XHTML (or HTML) and CSS to create an interface and visually style information. The XHTML and CSS elements can be dynamically modified to display new information or styling. These changes are typically done using the Document Object Model.*

- *JavaScript is used to manipulate the interface elements and is also used to establish a communication with a web server through XMLHttpRequest. This allows data (typically in XML format) to be transmitted between the client and the web server without requiring page reloads or refreshes.*

Ajax must not be used when the menu content is dynamically fetched using Ajax. This is wrong because:

- *Search engines like google cannot see it.*
- *Users cannot bookmark the pages.*
- *It doesn't indicate anything is happening, which can be bothering over slow connections. This can be remedied by an "in progress" message like GMail.*

Ajax is good for dynamic content update within a page. It should not be used to replace the page paradigm of web documents.

Using AJAX, web applications can allow high levels of interactivity and processing, but do not require the standard type of client-server interaction, specifically:

1. *A web page interface is presented.*
2. *User information is collected (via forms, links, etc.).*
3. *The user submits information (submits form, activates link, etc.).*
4. *The server processes submitted information.*
5. *A new web page interface is sent to the user.*

(i). One Interface : With AJAX, all of these steps can be handled in one interface. Examples of AJAX implementation are mapping applications, real-time searches, chats, real-time form validation and processing, live shopping cart applications, e-mail applications, and the list

goes on. The types of web applications and interactions allowed by using AJAX has given rise to the term "Web 2.0" — something that surely indicates a major revolution in the way the web can be used. While none of the technologies that comprise AJAX are new or groundbreaking, the increased popularity and awareness of AJAX development brings with it a need for developers to be aware of the accessibility implications these technologies bring.

(ii). Dynamic Applications : AJAX allows feature-rich, dynamic web applications which use server-side processing without requiring the traditional "submit data — retrieve web page" methodology. Using XMLHttpRequest, data is transmitted behind the scenes of the web application and JavaScript is used to manipulate the application interface and display dynamic information. This allows more streamlined applications that require less processing and data transmission because entire web pages do not need to be generated for each change that occurs. Instead, one web application reflects all of the changes that occur. JavaScript can also be used to allow higher levels of interactivity than allowed through HTML itself (e.g., keyboard shortcuts, click and drag, etc. on Google Maps).

(iii). Use of Javascript : AJAX will not work in all web browsers. As its name suggests, AJAX requires JavaScript. This alone means that AJAX applications will not work in web browsers and devices that do not support JavaScript. For this reason it is not accessible to many typical Web users. The Web Content Accessibility Guidelines also require that web applications function when JavaScript is disabled or not supported. AJAX also requires that XMLHttpRequest be supported, which many browsers do not.

The current solution to these problems is to either provide a non-AJAX alternative to the application or to allow the AJAX application to continue to function if JavaScript and XMLHttpRequest are not supported. Such a requirement may be very difficult to achieve. While developers may choose to require the users to use a browser that supports AJAX, they must understand that such requirements may not be possible for all users - especially those using portable devices or older web browsers.

(iv). Quick Updating : By its nature, AJAX tends to update and manipulate interface elements 'on the fly'. AJAX also can submit information to the server without user interaction or may do so in methods that are not obvious to the user. For example, most users expect forms to be submitted, validated, and processed when a submit button is selected, but with AJAX this submission and processing can occur at any time (e.g., every 5 seconds, when a form element loses focus, etc.). It may not be apparent to users that information is being processed and saved - and this confusion can be intensified by the fact that AJAX can perform these operations very quickly. Most users expect there to be some delay before feedback or additional information is presented and typically expect the entire page to refresh indicating a new display - with AJAX, none of these visual cues may be apparent.

Another issue with AJAX is how the application interface is updated. When updates to the interface occur, it may not be visually apparent that a change has occurred. The problem is even more troublesome for screen reader users. Screen readers typically read in a linear fashion. When changes happen in the interface, the screen reader user may not be aware of the change and the new content will likely not be read. In short, to allow dynamic interface changes to be accessible, the application must alert the user that a change has occurred, allow direct access to the new content, and then allow continued functionality of the web application. This process, while difficult to achieve, especially for screen reader users, is possible to achieve in many AJAX applications.

AJAX FOR JAVA DEVELOPERS: BUILD DYNAMIC JAVA APPLICATIONS

Ajax, or Asynchronous JavaScript and XML, is an approach to Web application development that uses client-side scripting to exchange data with the Web server. As a result, Web pages are dynamically updated without a full page refresh interrupting the interaction flow. With Ajax, usercan create richer, more dynamic Web application user interfaces that approach the immediacy and usability of native desktop applications.

Ajax isn't a technology. It's a way to identify and describe a useful design technique. Ajax is new in the sense that many developers are just beginning to be aware of it, but all of the components that implement an Ajax application have existed for several years. The current buzz is because of the emergence long ago in 2004 and 2005 of some great dynamic Web UIs (User interfaces) based on Ajax technology, most notably Google's GMail and Maps applications and the photo-sharing site Flickr.

CHALLENGES OF USING AJAX

a. Availability of XMLHttpRequest : One of the biggest issues facing Ajax developers is how to respond when XMLHttpRequest isn't available. While the majority of modern browsers support XMLHttpRequest, there will always be a minority of users whose browsers do not, or whose browser security settings prevent XMLHttpRequest from being used. If you're developing a Web app to be deployed on a corporate intranet, user probably has the luxury of specifying which browsers are supported and assuming XMLHttpRequest is always available. If developer is deploying on the public Web, however, user must be aware that by presuming XMLHttpRequest is available, user is potentially preventing users of older browsers, browsers for people with disabilities, or lightweight browsers on handheld devices from using his application.

Therefore, user should endeavor to make the application "degrade gracefully" and remain functional in browsers without XMLHttpRequest support. In the shopping-cart example, the best way to degrade the application would be to have the Add to Cart buttons perform a regular form submission, refreshing the page to reflect the cart's updated status. The Ajax behavior could be added to the page through JavaScript once the page was loaded, attaching a JavaScript handler function to each Add to Cart button only if XMLHttpRequest was available. Another approach would be to detect XMLHttpRequest when a user logged in, and then serve up either an Ajax version of the application or a regular forms-based version as appropriate.

b. Usability concerns : Some of the usability issues surrounding Ajax applications are more general. For instance, it can be important to let users know that their input has been registered, because the usual feedback mechanisms of the hourglass cursor and spinning browser "throbber" do not apply to XMLHttpRequests. One technique is to replace Submit buttons with a "Now updating..." type message so that users do not repeatedly click on buttons while waiting for a response. Another issue is that users may fail to notice that parts of the page they're viewing have been updated. User can alleviate this problem by using a variety of visual techniques to subtly draw the user's eye to updated areas of the page. Other issues caused by updating the page with Ajax include "breaking" the browser's back button, and the URL in the address bar not reflecting the entire state of the page, preventing bookmarking.

c. Server load : Implementing an Ajax UI in place of a regular forms-based one may dramatically increase the number of requests made to the server. For instance, a regular Google Web search causes one hit on the server, occurring when the user submits the search form. However, Google Suggest, which attempts to autocomplete the search terms, sends several requests to the server as the user types. When developing an Ajax application, be aware of how many requests user will be sending to the server and the resulting server load this will cause. User can mitigate server load by buffering requests on the client and caching server responses in the client, where applicable. User should also attempt to design the Ajax Web applications so that as much logic as possible can be performed on the client, without needing to contact the server.

d. Dealing with asynchrony : It's very important to understand that there is no guarantee that XMLHttpRequests will complete in the order they were dispatched. Indeed, usershould assume that they will not and design the application with this in mind. In the shopping-cart example, a last-updated timestamp was used to make sure that newer cart data would not be overwritten by older data.

User should now have a good understanding of the fundamental principles of Ajax and a nuts-and-bolts knowledge of the client- and server-side components that participate in an Ajax interaction. These are the building blocks of a Java-based Ajax Web application. In addition, user should understand some of the high-level design issues that come with the Ajax approach. Creating a successful Ajax application requires a holistic approach — from UI design through JavaScript design to server-side architecture — but user should now be armed with the core Ajax knowledge needed to consider these other aspects.

REFERENCES

1. *Jesse James Garrett (2005-02-18). "Ajax: A New Approach to Web Applications". AdaptivePath.com. http://www.adaptivepath.com /ideas/essays/archives/000385.php.*
2. *Ullman, Chris (March 2007). Beginning Ajax. wrox. ISBN 978-0-470-10675-4. http://www.wrox.com/WileyCDA/Section/id-*

303217.html.

3. "Code Samples and Apps: Applets". Sun Microsystems, Inc.. http://java.sun.com/applets/.
4. http://litablog.org/2006/10/improving-library-services-with-ajax-and-rss-2/
5. Http://www.uie.com/articles/email.php?article=ajax
6. Hinchcliffe, Dion (June 2006). Real-World Ajax: Secrets of the Masters. SYS-CON Media. ISBN 9780977762200. http://ajaxdevelopersjournal.com/read/338113.htm.
7. "Dynamic HTML and XML: The XMLHttpRequest Object". Apple Inc. http://developer.apple.com/internet/webcontent/xmlhttpreq.html.
8. Hopmann, Alex. "Story of XMLHTTP". Alex Hopmann's Blog. http://www.alexhopmann.com/story-of-xmlhttp/.
9. "A Brief History of Ajax". Aaron Swartz. 2005-12-22. http://www.aaronsw.com/weblog/ajaxhistory.
10. Nikki Wright. Improving Library Services with AJAX and RSS http://litablog.org/2006/10/improving-library-services-with-ajax-and-rss-2/
11. http://www.daveyp.com/blog/stuff/tags/subjects.html
12. http://www.aadl.org/
13. Gregory E. Aldridge (2003-03-09). "System and method for providing a browser-based user interface". United States Patent and Trademark Office. http://www.uspto.gov/web/patents/patog/week16/OG/html/1341-3/US07523401-20090421.html.
14. Ajax and PHP. Study of the interaction between Ajax and a PHP script by the GET and POST commands. http://www.xul.fr/ajax/ajax-php.php
15. "JSON - JavaScript Object Notation". Apache.org. http://tapestry.apache.org/tapestry4.1/ajax/json.html.
16. "Speed Up Your Ajax-based Apps with JSON". DevX.com. http://www.devx.com/webdev/Article/32651.
17. "Why use Ajax?". InterAKT. 2005-11-10. http://www.interaktonline.com/support/articles/Details/Ajax:+Asynchronously+Moving+Forward-Why+use+Ajax?.html?id_art=36&id_asc=309.
18. Designing Powerful Web Applications: An Interview with David (Heller) Malouf 07/27/2006 http://www.uie.com/articles/malouf_interview/
19. "Deep Linking for AJAX". http://blog.onthewings.net/2009/04/

08/deep-linking-for-ajax/.

20. *Ajax offline. Ajax and Gears, tutorial and demo. http://www.xul.fr/en/technologies/gears-ajax.php*
21. *Prokoph, Andreas (2007-05-08). "Help Web crawlers efficiently crawl your portal sites and Web sites". IBM. http://www.ibm.com/developerworks/library/x-sitemaps/index.html.*
22. *Edwards, James (2006-05-05). "Ajax and Screenreaders: When Can it Work?". sitepoint.com.*
23. *Quinsey, Peter. "User-Proofing Ajax". http://www.alistapart.com/articles/userproofingajax.*
24. *Designing Web Applications for Use 12/11/2006 http://www.uie.com/articles/designing_web_applications_for_use/*
25. *http://blog.taragana.com/index.php/archive/how-not-to-use-ajax/*
26. *http://www.tinkingteam.com/NL/default.asp*
27. *"Access Control for Cross-Site Requests". World Wide Web Consortium. http://dev.w3.org/2006/waf/access-control/.*
28. *"Secure Cross-Domain Communication in the Browser". The Architecture Journal (MSDN). http://msdn.microsoft.com/en-us/library/bb735305.aspx.*
29. *Tips for Designing Powerful RIAs: An Interview with David Malouf and Bill Scott 12/06/2006*
30. *Sullivan, Bryan. "Testing for security in the age of Ajax Programming". developerFusion. http://www.developerfusion.com/article/6197/testing-for-security-in-the-age-of-ajax-programming/.*
31. *Stamos, Alex; Lackey, Zane. "Attacking Ajax Web Applications". iSEC Partners. http://www.isecpartners.com/files/iSEC-Attacking_AJAX_Applications.BH2006.pdf.*
32. *JSON. The second data format for Ajax. http://www.xul.fr/ajax-javascript-json.html*
33. *Firebug. Firefox extension to debug Ajax. https://addons.mozilla.org/fr/firefox/addon/1843*
34. *Anaa. A simple framework based on this tutorial. http://www.scriptol.com/ajax/anaa/*
35. *http://nikeid.nike.com/nikeid/index.jhtml*
36. *NetBeans. IDE to build Ajax applications.*
37. *Web Apps: Where Business Needs and User Needs Collide 01/*

27/2010. http://www.uie.com/articles/web_apps_needs/

38. *Watch and Learn: How Recommendation Systems are Redefining the Web 12/13/2006 http://www.uie.com/articles/recommendation_systems/*

8

Blog and Blogging

WHAT IS A BLOG?

Blog is short from for web log. It refers to a category of website where the content is presented in a continuing sequence of dated entries. When we put it simply, it is an online diary. An online diary is a personal diary or journal that is published on the World Wide Web on a personal website or a hosting website. It is found that online diaries began in 1994. A blog can be produced by one author or carried out collaboratively by a community of authors. We can say that blogs are websites that contain brief entries displayed in reverse chronological order. The newest entry is seen at the top of the webpage. The entries can be updated at anytime—hourly, daily, weekly or monthly. This concept increased with the introduction of automated publishing systems, particularly Blogger 'www.blogger.com'. Such services are used to simplify and speed up the publishing process. It allows people with little or no technical background to update and maintain a blog. Creating a blog requires no html skills.

DEFINING THE BLOG

A blog is "a frequently updated website consisting of

dated entries arranged in reverse chronological order so the most recent post appears first."

—*Jill Walker,*
Routledge Encyclopedia of Narrative Theory

Thus a Blog can be:

- *personal or professional*
- *individual or collaborative*
- *about ANYTHING*

These are social software for the creation of instant (almost) web pages with built-in user comment and trackback capabilities. It's very obvious that many (not all) blogs are designed around a specific theme or subject. A strong feature is RSS capability. Most blogs provide a continuously updated feed of their content. It is also possible to create multiple feeds for a single blog, where each feed provides content for a specific subject category or subtopic. Another advantage of many blogs is their user-selectable arrangement of content either chronologically or by subject category. The interface also provides an easy-to-use search tool for its content. Blogs and wikis are fundamentally 2.0, and their global proliferation has enormous implications for libraries. Blogs may indeed be an even greater milestone in the history of publishing than web-pages. They enable the rapid production and consumption of Web-based publications. In some ways, the copying of printed material is to web-pages as the printing press is to blogs. Blogs are HTML for the masses.

BLOG FOR LIBRARIES

Blogs have many implications for libraries. Library managers therefore need to be aware of what blogs can do to promote the library and its services. Sometimes library blogs can be building blocks for communicating news and information to users. Libraries should aim to create a feeling of transparency by blogging about proposed projects and plans, and listening to users via comments and then responding to them. Creating a blog for a library is a free, easy, and fast way to communicate information to users. It can function as a medium for users to participate in service development. There are four major ways blogs can be used in the library:

(1) *as an information service,*

(2) *as a library service,*

(3) *as a feedback tool, and*

(4) *as a professional awareness service.*

1. *Blogs as an information service*

Libraries can use blogs as a library promotional tool to inform clients of changes and additions to library services and collections, and of news and current events. According to a study of the use of blogs, wikis and other collaborative technologies in the information industry in Australia more public libraries are using blogs than wikis and that 22 per cent of public libraries used blogs to communicate with clients. Few other examples are as following:

- *Madison Public Library in Wisconsin publishes a blog What's new www.madison publiclibrary.org/ whatsnew.html which provides basic news, new services and serves as a communications vehicle for the library.*
- *Eastern Regional Libraries in Victoria publishes a blog What's new @ Eastern Regional Libraries easternregional.blogspot. com/. Its blog is used for library announcements eg public holiday closures, refurbishments, advertising library events, providing lists of new books, cds and dvds as well as the odd book review.*
- *Yarra Plenty Regional Library in Victoria publishes a blog Yarra Plenty blog yarraplentylibrary.*

blogspot.com/. Its blog aims to be a platform for interaction between the library and its users, including staff. Input and suggestions for content are welcome from the community.

2. Blogs as a library service

Libraries can list new books, videos, CDs, or DVDs as they are added to the collection. Library staff can review new titles and link them to relevant internet sites. An online book discussion can be started. Library can provide links to author interviews and list book award announcements. It can be used to promote library services and resources in order to draw people into the library. For example:

- *Madison Public Library in Wisconsin publishes a blog MADreads www.madison publiclibrary.org/ madreads/featuring a brief book review every day. Ten staff members contribute to the blog and readers are encouraged to interact with the reviews by posting comments and opinions.*

3. Blogs as a feedback tool

Blogs encourage feedback from users via the comments link. They can provide information about their library experiences and guide improvements. Polls and surveys can also be added to blogs using free software tools such as Pollhost www.pollhost.com/. Libraries can gather valuable feedback from their users.

4. Blogs as a professional awareness tool

Library can used as current awareness and professional aids, Blogs help in staying ahead of changes in technology and in the library profession. In this scenario librarians need to stay ahead to justify their existence and so that consumers will look to the library as a place of currency. By use of blog, library can become part of a very progressive segment of the education.

The most obvious implication of blogs for libraries is that they are another form of publication and need to be treated as such. They lack editorial governance and the security this provides, but many are nonetheless integral productions in a body of knowledge, and the absence of them in a library collection could soon become unthinkable. This will, of course, greatly complicate collection development processes, and the librarian will need to exercise a great deal of expertise and fastidiousness when adding a blog to a collection (or, perhaps, an automated blog-collection development system). Or, perhaps the very notions of "reliable" and "authoritative", so important to collection development, will need to be rethought in the wake of this innovation.

COMPARISON BETWEEN BLOG AND WIKI

This beginning of Library 2.0 makes collections and services more interactive and user-centered, enable information consumers to contact information producers and become co-producers themselves. It could be that Library 2.0 blurs the line between librarian and patron, creator and consumer, authority and novice. The potential for this dramatic change is very real and immediate, a fact that places an incredible amount of importance on information literacy. In a world where no information is inherently authoritative and valid, the critical thinking skills of information literacy are paramount to all other forms of learning. Blogs and wikis are relatively quick solutions for moving library collections and services into Web 2.0. This beginning of Library 2.0 makes collections and services more interactive and user-centered, enable information consumers to contact information producers and become co-producers themselves. It could be that Library 2.0 blurs the line between librarian and patron, creator and consumer, authority and novice. The potential for this dramatic change is very real and immediate, a fact that places an incredible amount of importance on information literacy. In a world where no information is inherently authoritative and valid, the critical thinking skills of information literacy are paramount to all other forms of learning.

While comparing with blogs, Wikis are essentially open web-pages, where anyone registered with the wiki can publish to it, amend it, and change it. Much as blogs, they are not of the same reliability as traditional resources, as the frequent discussions of Wikipedia (an online encyclopedia where any registered user can write, amend or otherwise edit articles) in the library world well note. This of course does not eliminate their value, it merely changes librarianship, complicates collection development and information literacy instruction. The lack of peer review and editorship is a challenge to librarians, not in that users should avoid wikis, but only in that they should understand and be critical in depending on them. Wikis as items in a collection, and the associated instruction of users in the evaluation of them, are almost certainly part of the future of libraries.

In addition, a library wiki as a service enables social interaction among librarians and patrons, essentially moving the study group room online. As users share information and ask questions, answer questions, and librarians do the same within a wiki, a record of these transactions is archived perhaps for perpetuity. And these transcripts are in turn resources for the library to provide as reference. Furthermore, wikis and blogs will almost certainly evolve into a more multi-media environment as well, where both synchronous and asynchronous audio and video collaborations will take place. Blogs are new forms of publication, and wikis are new forms of group study rooms.

Ultimately, blogs and wikis are relatively quick solutions for moving library collections and services into Web 2.0. Wikis are essentially open web-pages, where anyone registered with the wiki can publish to it, amend it, and change it. Much as blogs, they are not of the same reliability as traditional resources, as the frequent discussions of Wikipedia (an online encyclopedia where any registered user can write, amend or otherwise edit articles) in the library world well note; but this of course does not eliminate their value, it merely changes librarianship, complicates collection development and information literacy instruction. The lack of peer review and editorship is a challenge to librarians, not in that users should avoid wikis, but only in that they should understand and be critical in depending on them. Wikis as items in a collection, and the associated instruction of users in the evaluation of them, are almost certainly part of the future of libraries.

In addition, a library wiki as a service can enable social interaction among librarians and patrons, essentially moving the study group room online. As users share information and ask questions, answer questions, and librarians do the same within a wiki, a record of these transactions is archived perhaps for perpetuity. And these transcripts are in turn resources for the library to provide as reference. Furthermore, wikis and blogs will almost certainly evolve into a more multi-media environment as well, where both synchronous and asynchronous audio and video collaborations will take place. Blogs are new forms of publication, and wikis are new forms of group study rooms.

VARIOUS WAYS TO IMPLEMENT AND USE BLOG IN A LIBRARY SCENE

Disseminate news : Blogs can be very helpful in spreading the news.

Provide subject-specific information — subject guides developed on-the-fly and at the point-of-need.: Blogs can be utilized for disseminating subject specific information in a very efficient manner. Various distinguished links can be provided to cater subject related information.

To build community and start a conversation: Blogging can act as a tool to build specific and interest concerned communities. These platforms can provide forum to have conversation on the topics of interest.

Market library resources and services: Though the libraries have been instrumental in adapting variety of marketing techniques, the innovative capabilities of blog can also be explored. The way it supports information reach to each interested users is beyond any doubt.

To provide readers' advisory services: The discussion facility and capacity on the blog is impressive enough to become advisor of the library patrons.

To share information among library staff members: The blog can act as an immediate medium to share information among the library staff members. Regardless of physical and time boundaries, the blog can prove itself a omnipresent method of communication.

As a content management system : The information shared, communicated or disseminated through the blog can be retained as and technology facilitates. The features can be used as a strong content management system.

BLOGGING BASICS

A blogger (user) should keep certain things in mind such as:

- *Only create a blog if he/her sees a real need for it and have a staff committed to maintaining it.*
- *Know whom blogger blogging FOR*
- *Know what blogger blogging ABOUT*
- *Develop a mission statement for he/her blog*
- *Blogs don't update themselves*
- *Consider setting an update timeline*

One should learn to tailor the material to the medium

by finding out what usability studies reveal about how people actually read on-line and what the implications are for developing micro-content, menus, and layout. Filled with examples, tips, and tricks, various interactive on-line course are a must for library web site content contributors and webmasters who want to improve their sites and on-line writing style.

BLOGGING TOOLS

There are a number of good blogging tools, but choosing among them can be confusing. There are few blogging tools and key considerations for selecting a blogging platform including:

(i) *the skills required to set it up;*

(ii) *the ease with which blogger can post to it;*

(iii) *whether he can upload images, video, or audio to it;*

(iv) *its ability to moderate comments and prevent spam;*

(v) *how closely blogger can tailor its design to match the look and feel of web site and other collateral; and*

(vi) *tools blogger can use to track who's reading it.*

Features and Functions

Blogging tools are designed to be easy to use. They generally don't provide all the advanced features of a complex content management system. These are as following:

- *Create posts : Since the purpose of a blog is to be able to post new text or information to the site frequently, creating posts should be quick and easy.*
- *Upload pictures and multimedia : Many blogs go beyond text to include photos, video, or audio.*
- *Display posts to visitors : A blogging platform can make it easy for readers to view your posts and to comment on them.*

- *Moderate : While it's typical to allow visitors to post comments to a blog, different platforms provide varying levels of help to weed out inappropriate contributions.*
- *Publish RSS feeds : RSS feeds allow more Internet-savvy users to subscribe to the blog.*
- *Configure the appearance and layout : Tools vary widely in the degree to which they allow to configure the blog, and the methods they offer to do this.*
- *Find support : Not every blogging tool offers the same degree of support: while some offer personalized assistance, others have forums where blogger can find answers to his questions.*
- *Host the blog : While some blogging software lives on the own server, others are hosted by the vendor.*
- *Get stats on blog : Reporting features will help blogger sees how many people are visiting the blog, and which posts are most popular.*

Some features are fairly common to all blogging tools, while others are more specialized. Blogs have the typical features. There is some criteria which can be used to evaluate whether a particular blogging tool is right.

(i) Creating Posts

The procedure for creating a blog post is fairly standard across blogging platforms. Blogger has to type in a title and the text blogger wants to appear below it. Formatting options can vary from tool to tool, however; while many blogging platforms provide easy-to-use tools that allow blogger to create bold text, italics, larger font sizes, and more, not every tool offers these. Formatting tools themselves also vary. Some platforms allow changing text color and fonts as blogger likes, others limit to a particular set of styles defined for the site. It should be made sure that the blogging platform can strip out extra formatting that might otherwise interfere with online formatting and RSS feeds (more about RSS feeds in a moment). Some platforms also allow to preview the post before a blogger makes it live, or to save a draft of it.

(ii) Uploading Pictures and Multimedia

While blogger can publish pictures to blog using a variety of tools, some platforms make it easier than others. A few allow blogger to upload images easily in a single step, while others require to upload images separately and then add them to a post afterwards. Some tools also automatically size and optimize images, while others require that blogger does this using another tool (like Adobe Photoshop). Resizing photos will avoid huge image file sizes, creating long download times for the users. Any blogging tool will allow the blogger to link to video or audio files already posted on the Web. To use this type of multimedia frequently, however, blogger should look for a tool that will let upload multimedia files or even embed multimedia in a post to let the users view or listen without leaving site.

Displaying Posts to Visitors

Blog layouts tend to be standard, without much variation between platforms. There are a few factors to consider, making a final selection:

- *Navigation : Organizing the posts into categories can help visitors find and sort through previous posts.*
- *Excerpts : Some tools offer the option to show excerpts (rather than entire posts) on a blog's landing page.*
- *Front-end usability : If a blog is likely to be visited by people unfamiliar with blog conventions, the links on the blogs should be intuitive.*
    - *What does the visitor need to click on to view comments?*

— *How can they find a permanent URL for a post?*
— *Is the permanent URL easy to understand, or just a mess of numbers?*

(iii) Moderating

Moderating is necessary for the inappropriate comments. If a blogger allows comments, he will want to be able to keep an eye on them and intervene when necessary: therefore, the blogging tool should allow approving comments before they appear on the blog and delete unwanted contributions when necessary. It's also helpful to require posters to register or to submit their email address with a post. For large volume of comments, blogger may want to look for a tool that allows searching and filtering all comments, ban posts that include a particular keyword, or ban a poster by IP address. While the previously mentioned features help combat spam, additional tools also require users to verify that they are humans and not spambots by transcribing a wiggly set of letters (also known as a CAPTCHA).

(iv) Publishing RSS Feeds

One popular blog feature, particularly among more Web-savvy users, is the ability to "subscribe" to blog content via RSS. RSS allows people with the appropriate software to gather the content from many blogs so they can read it all together in one place. Providing RSS access to any blog will make it more useful and appear professional to blogger's audience.

CONFIGURING THE APPEARANCE AND LAYOUT

The configuration of the blog's appearance varies widely between blogging platforms. While some blogging sites limit to a few templates, others allow blogger to tailor everything to the exact needs.

While some tools allow a blogger to set up a blog without HTML, a blogging platform that allows blogger to use it will give him more control. There's a lot to consider such as:

- *Templates : If blogger can set up a blog quickly using a template that defines the layout and colors, how many choices does he have, and how professional are they?*
- *Fonts and colors : Can blogger tailor text and colors on the blog to match an existing Web site or organizational branding?*
- *Domain : Can the blog use blogger's organization's domain*
- *Widgets : Can blogger add in widgets, pieces of code written by third parties that allow extra functionality, like polls or images from photo-sharing site flickr?*
- *Layout updates : To what degree will the platform allow blogger to modify templates to create a custom layout or to match his Web site?*
- *Customization : Can blogger customize every single page, message, and element to create a completely tailored blog?*

ADVANTAGES AND DISADVANTAGES OF BLOGGING

1. Advantages : A long, long time ago, when people didn't know what blogging was, nor they cared, some would keep a notebook in which they wrote their daily thoughts and events called a diary, either typed or handwritten. Nowadays such activities are replaced by technologies. Of course, the idea of keeping an online diary came along with the new means of communicating facilitated by the growing virtually based communities. Nevertheless, blogging has only become a phenomenon a few years ago and the blogosphere was born. Today everybody has to have a blog but the blog how-tos underline the need for content quality. That is, in order for a blog to become popular, the articles must be original, well documented (if applied) and active. A blog writer (professional or not) must ensure a certain post fluidity (at least the same style, or, if the blog has a theme, -s-he has to make sure -s-he does not digress to much from the primary subject), pertinent feedback (comments, sharing, suggestions). Therefore, writing a blog takes time and effort and not everybody can afford that.

On the other side, the copyright issue can cause some headaches. Blogs are as different as people and they reflect their author. No matter what to what category a blog pertains to, no blogger should forget that what they post is public. There are countless boundaries that, if ignored, can get the poster into a great deal of trouble. If the text is not protected (and in most cases it is not), it does not belong to the poster any more, it can be copied and pasted everywhere in the web universe and beyond. At the same time, total subject freedom adds the risk of confusing the readers, abandoning the search because they had too many choices to handle. In conclusion, blogs open the door to the world (be it only virtual, but it still counts) to people who otherwise had no chance of making their voice heard.

There are definitely some advantages to running a business blog, however. The easy way blogger's blog can be updated does mean that blogger will be able to post new information quickly – and get it to blogger's customers and clients just as fast. Organization will also be able to keep everyone informed of new policies, products and other important info without having to send out massive emails or snail mail. Blogger can also drive traffic to blogger's business site from blogger's blog by having links on blogger's site as well as others'. The advantages of blogs from an organizational perspective include the following:

- *The consumer and citizen are potentially better*

informed and this can only be good for the long-term health of our societies and economies.

- *Blogs have potential to help the organization develop stronger relationships and brand loyalty with its customers, as they interact with the 'human face' of the organization through blogs.*
- *Blogs, in an intranet environment, can be an excellent way of sharing knowledge within the organization.*
- *Blogs can be a positive way of getting feedback, and keeping blogger's finger on the pulse, as readers react to certain pieces, suggest story ideas, etc.*
- *Blogs can build the profile of the writer, showcasing the organization as having talent and expertise.*

2. Disadvantages : Just as there are advantages to having a business site, there are disadvantages to having personal sites. One of the biggest is posting too much personal information. This can come in the form of putting in particular information (blogger's full name and address, for example) or "saying" something in one of blogger's posts that blogger may regret later. The advantages and disadvantages of Internet blogging are numerous, but ultimately it is up to blogger to decide whether or not blogging is something blogger would enjoy or profit from. Blogs are a great way to communicate and experience the Web – if used correctly.

The disadvantages of blogs are:

1. *Either lack of something interesting, and/or inability to write down their ideas in a compelling and clear manner.*
2. *The people who have most time to write have least to say, and the people who have most to say don't have enough time to write it.*
3. *Like practically everything else on the Web, blogs are easy to start and hard to maintain. Writing coherently*

is one of the most difficult and time-consuming tasks for a human being to undertake. As a result, many blogs are not updated, thus damaging rather than enhancing the reputation of the organization.

Blog software

Weblog software (also called blogging software or blogware) is software designed to simplify the creation and maintenance of weblogs. As specialized content management systems, weblog applications support the authoring, editing, and publishing of blog posts and comments, with special functions for image management, web syndication, and moderation of posts and comments. There is no doubt that blogs are massively popular now, and are set to become even more prevalent in the future. A substantial number of bloggers now write for advertisers who want to boost the reputation of their services and products.

Most sponsored post ventures ask that bloggers provide their own blog software. Those who wish to write subsidized blogs have several different blog software packages to choose from, most of which are free. Type Pad and Windows Live Writer are both popular blog software packages. On asymptomatic.net, a chart shows the features of various user-installed blog software packages side-by-side for the purpose of assessment. Of course, the blog software package someone chooses depends on his own individual needs. As with any software download, some blog software is not safe. Users should be careful for the risk of downloading malware.

- *Server models : There are weblog applications that can be downloaded and installed on user systems.*
  - *Free-software or open-source licenses, allowing them to be used, modified, and redistributed freely*
  - *Proprietary software which must be licensed*
  - *Other weblog applications are offered only*

through their developers' hosts, either free of charge or for a fee. Services are typically limited to hosting of the blog itself, but some services offer the option of using the hosted software to update a blog published elsewhere.

- *Clients : Maintenance is usually done through a browser-based interface, enabling authors to create and update content on the site. Most software also supports the use of external client software to update content using common APIs such as:*
  - *The MetaWeblog API and*
  - *The Atom Publishing Protocol. For example the WordPress website has an extensive list of clients that support most APIs (not just WordPress).*
  - *Other examples include ecto and MarsEdit.*

How to Manage the Posts and comments

All weblog software supports authoring, editing, and publishing of entries in the following format:

- *Title : the main title, or headline, of the post.*
- *Body : main content of the post.*
- *Permalink : the URL of the full, individual article.*
- *Post Date : date and time the post was published.*

Blog entries can optionally include the following too:

Comments: It allow readers to discuss blog entries, correcting errors or otherwise expressing their opinions on the post or the post's subject.

Categories (or tags): There are indexes to subjects discussed by the entry

Trackback (pingback) : It links to other sites that refer to the entry

Most weblog applications also have various linking and web syndication features. Web syndication is usually offered in the form of RSS or Atom. This allows other software (such as feed aggregators) to maintain a current summary of the blog's content. The user selects a language during installation. Post moderation requires users to register before commenting, or requires individual posts or comments to be approved by a moderator or administrator before they appear in the blog. Weblog applications use various user account systems that allow readers to post comments to a particular blog. For instance, users with Blogger accounts may comment on any Blogger blog. Other weblog applications allow users to post content or comments only to blogs where they have an account. The posting API varies among different weblog applications. The typical interface is a form to be filled out online, with a varying number of fields. Applications such as Movable Type offer a greater number of form fields and choices than applications such as Blogger. Some applications also have plugins for Firefox that integrate into the browser's menus so that right clicking on selected text on any given web page brings up a small window that allows the user to post directly to their blog. Most types of blogware support adding thumbnail images within blog posts. Photo blogging is a separate genre of blogging that deals primarily with images. A list of notable weblog software follows:

1. *User hosted platforms : Software packages installed by weblog authors to run on their own servers.*
2. *Free and open source software : These software packages are offered as free and open source software:*
    - *Apache Roller (Java-based)*
    - *b2evolution (PHP/MySQL)*
    - *blosxom (Perl)*
    - *Dotclear (PHP)*
    - *DotNetNuke (VB.NET/ASP.NET)*
    - *Drupal (PHP)*

- *Elgg (PHP)*
- *Frog CMS (PHP)*
- *Geeklog (PHP)*
- *Habari (PHP)*
- *Jaws (PHP)*
- *Joomla! (PHP)*
- *LifeType (PHP)*
- *Livejournal (Perl)*
- *Movable Type (Perl)*
- *Nucleus CMS (PHP)*
- *Pebble (Java-based)*
- *PivotX (PHP)*
- *Sandbox (PHP)*
- *Serendipity (PHP)*
- *Textpattern (PHP/MySQL)*
- *Thingamablog (Static web page, no need for CGI, PHP or MySQL)*
- *Typo (Ruby on Rails)*
- *WordPress (PHP)*

PROPRIETARY SOFTWARE

These packages are under a proprietary software license. They may require the purchase of a license key to use them. The specific licensing terms vary but some are free of charge for personal or non-commercial use.

- *Telligent Community*
- *ExpressionEngine*
- *Traction TeamPage*
- *Windows Live Writer*
- *IBM Lotus Connections*
- *IBM Lotus Quickr*

- *XCAP Community Engine*

DEVELOPER-HOSTED PLATFORMS

Software services operated by the developer, requiring no software installation by the weblog author:

- *Blogger*
- *uCoz*
- *doomby*
- *Gandi*
- *Posterous*
- *LiveJournal*
- *Maneno*
- *Moxietype*
- *MySpace*
- *Open Diary*
- *Skyrock*
- *Tumblr*
- *TypePad*
- *Vox*
- *weBlog.com*
- *Windows Live Spaces*
- *Wordpress.com*
- *XCAP Community Engine*
- *Xanga*
- *servertoday.com*

Various software on yahoo listing are given as below:

audblog : Service that provides bloggers with the ability to post audio to their blogs from any phone. www.audblog.com

AudioBlog.com : Add sound to the blog or online journal. www.audioblog.com

audioBLOGGER : Provides bloggers with the ability to post audio to their blogs from any phone. www.audioblogger.com

b2 : News and blog tool. cafelog.com

BackType : Find, follow, and share comments. Keep track of all the comments you make on blogs or other websites. www.backtype.com

Big Blog Tool : Offers a subscription based tool for web loggers. www.bigblogtool.com

blam! : Blacklist manager aiming to help bloggers in their fight against comment spam. blam.sourceforge.net

Blog Drive : Offers free blog hosting, blog templates, layouts, and a quiz maker. www.blogdrive.com

Blog Studio : Free blog service built on software services with blogs that can reside with Blog Studio or the on own site. www.blogstudio.com

Blogarithm.com : Online tool that will email you when the new postings appear on the favourite blogs. www.blogarithm.com

Blogbox.com : Free, open-source rich Internet applications for personal web sites, wikis, and blogs. www.blogbox.com

blogBuddy : Program that manages Blogger.com and other blogs which implement the Blogger API. blogbuddy.sourceforge.net

BlogFace : Cataloged collection of objects for the Zope application server. www.zope.org/Members/karl/BlogFace/BlogFace

BloggerBot : Allows AOL Instant Messenger to post to sites using Blogger from within Instant Messenger. www.fibiger.org/bloggerbot

BlogJet : Way to blog right from Windows. blogjet.com

BlogKomm : Free comment script that displays

comments below posts rather than in pop-ups with blogs running on PHP servers. www.blogkomm.com

Bloglet : Offers an email subscription service for bloggers. www.bloglet.com

BlogMax : Emacs package that turns stylized HTML stored in text files into complete HTML for blog updating. www.billstclair.com/blogmax

BlogniX : Blogger client for Linux blognix.sourceforge.net

Blogopedia : Free ASP blogging application. www.blogopedia.co.uk

Blogplates : Webring of blog and journal designs with information on how to implement them for the own personal journal. www.blogplates.net

BlogRolling : Provides a free service to manage buddy lists on the blog that works with every major blog tool and web site. www.blogrolling.com

BlogSkins.com : Offers free skins and style templates for Blogger and Movable Type powered sites. www.blogskins.com

Blogstickers : Offers free custom graphics and design utilities for using within a blog. www.blogstickers.com

Blogtracker : Offers a service that works with blogs.com and shows only recently updated or the favorite blogs. www.dansanderson.com/blogtracker

BlogWorks : XML based blogging tools. www.blogworks.com

Blosxom : Open source blog application designed from the ground up with simplicity, usability, and interoperability in mind. www.blosxom.com

Bot A Blog : Free service where "bots" send you simple text emails when the favorite blogs are updated and new entries are added. www.botablog.com

Build The Own Log : Discussses how to build the own web log using Trellix client-side software. www.danbricklin.com/log/byol.htm

CHweblog : Displays real-time statistics on web sites. www.serverlog.net

Class Blogmeister : Blogging tool designed with teachers and students in mind. Teachers can evaluate, comment on, and publish students' blog articles in a controlled environment. www.classblogmeister.com

Command Line Warriors : Open blog about computing with the help of command line, Linux, BSD, or Unix shells and applications such as Bash, Emacs, Vi, and Mplayer. commandline.org.uk

Coranto : Unofficial site dedicated to the new posting program that includes theme downloads. coranto.gweilo.org

Diary-X : Online journal software requiring no HTML experience. www.diary-x.com

Drupal : A content management and discussion engine suitable to setup or build a content driven or community driven web site. www.drupal.org

Eastgate Tinderbox : Personal content management assistant for Macintosh computers that stores notes, ideas, and plans to be shared through a web log. www.eastgate.com/Tinderbox

Edit The Home Movies : Blog provides updates and reviews on the latest video editing software and home video editing. www.edityourhomemovies.blogspot.com

Enetation : Free commenting system with template support that works with several web log generators. www.enetation.co.uk

Eye For Beauty: Journal Templates : Offers free linkware and journal templates for web logs. www.eyeforbeauty.com/Linkware/journaltemp.html

fav.or.it : Blogging platform that lets you write the own blog posts and publish them on the Internet. fav.or.it

FeedBurner : Advanced feed management technology that helps bloggers, podcasters, and commercial publishers get more value from the content they create. www.feedburner.com

frassle : Helps users read and publish blogs, track bookmarks, and find relevant content. www.frassle.rura.org

Free-Conversant : Internet server software whose standard features include tools for managing news pages and journals (weblogs), event calendars, online discussion forums, tools for publishing sites, email and mailing-list integration, and many other services. www.free-conversant.com

Geeklog : Offers a free open-source blog tool. www.geeklog.sourceforge.net

HaloScan : Free commenting system for blogs and web sites, allowing visitors to leave instant feedback. www.haloscan.com

Inknoise : Subscription-based personal publishing for blogs with multimedia and design features. www.inknoise.com

Instablogs : Asian blog network which also alllows users to read and comment via their mobile phone. www.instablogs.com

Lijit : Create a customized search engine for the content. Lijit searches the blog, bookmarks, photos, and more. www.lijit.com

MajikWidget : Blog widgets and resources from MajikWidget to help anyone make money blogging. www.majikwidget.com

MarsEdit : Weblog editor for Mac OS X that makes blog writing like composing email. Works with various blog systems. www.red-sweater.com/marsedit

MemberWing : Provides Wordpress membership site plugin featuring optimized SEO, four levels of membership, automated recurring payments, and digital download guard. www.memberwing.com

Metstatic.org: Blog Script : A Bourne-Again shell script that allows one to maintain a blog on the command-line. www.metastatic.org/blog

Miz Graphics : Offers free blog templates that are compatible with any log. www.mizjenna.com/~mizgraphics

Moby Nuke : Blogging software, photo galleries, forums, and more based on the postnuke content management system. www.mobynuke.net

Monaural Jerk : An open source blog, journal, news, diary system that allows one or more authors to regularly publish content without touching HTML. www.monauraljerk.org

Movable Type : Offering personal publishing software for the blog generation. www.movabletype.org

MozBlog : Tool to enable people to blog with Mozilla while surfing. www.mozblog.mozdev.org

MyBlogLog : Social network for bloggers and blog readers. MyBlogLog community service allows fellow blog readers to connect, share insights, and see what other members are also reading. www.mybloglog.com

Nettiez.com : Provider of web page publishing tools and community tools for online diaries and journals. www.nettiez.com

Nucleus : Blog script that uses PHP4 and mySQL to reach its goals. www.nucleuscms.org

Onclave.org : Offers tools that enable collaborative blogging and information sharing, publishing tools, and newsfeeds. www.onclave.org

Open Journal : Offers a web based interface to a perl script will manage and maintain the Web-based musings and writings. www.grohol.com/downloads/oj

Personal Weblog : Free PHP/MySQL tool for adding a blog to a home page. www.kyne.com.au/~mark/software/weblog.php

pMachine : Offers software for creating sites with a simple blog or interactive news. www.pmachine.com

Port41 : Free service which allows users to create, edit, and share content on the web and intranets. www.port41.com

Project Hurricane : Online community portal software built using the .NET Framework. www.projecthurricane.net

Radio UserLand : Blog tool that builds a site, organizes and archives posts, and publishes content. radio.userland.com

reger.com : Publishing tools and hosting for activity-specific weblogging. www.reger.com

Roller Weblogger : Server-based weblogging software that is designed to support multiple simultaneous blog users and visitors. www.rollerweblogger.org

Squishdot : News publishing and discussion product for Zope that creates a place in the web site where people can post comments, hold discussions, and more. www.squishdot.org

tBLOG : Free web log publishing tool and templates that allow users to add calendar, search, link management, voting, and commenting modules to their sites. www.tblog.com

Traction : Developers of enterprise blog software. www.tractionsoftware.com

Travel Journal : TravelJournal is an advanced online authoring and publishing platform for travel writing. Share the adventures with the family, friends, and the rest of the world. www.traveljournal.com

TypeKey : Free, open system providing a central identity that anyone can use to log in and post comments on blogs and other web sites, helping to prevent abusive or offensive content. www.typekey.com

Upsaid : Offers a complete web journaling service. www.upsaid.com

W.Bloggar : Free client for posting to several different hosts and software that support the Blogger API. www.wbloggar.com

WAPblogger : WAP interface to Blogger, LiveJournal, and other smart weblog-style tools. www.ubique.ch/wapblogger

Weblogs Inc. : Dedicated to creating niche blogs across niche industries in the same manner as a trade publication, with the focus on participatory journalism. www.weblogsinc.com

WeColumn.com : Tool helps users publish their columns to any website. Type up the column with text, pictures, links, or flash movies and then WeColumn provides the code so that a website can feature the column. www.wecolumn.com

WordPress : Semantic personal publishing platform with a focus on aesthetics, web standards, and usability. Software and documentation to get started on the blog. wordpress.org

YACCS : Free service that allows placing a comments section on the blog. rateyourmusic.com/yaccs

Zempt : Multi-platform posting software for use with Movable Type. www.zempt.com

SECURITY MEASURES FOR HIDING THE IDENTITY ONLINE

There are a number of ways a user can hide identity

when using the Internet. As a general rule, the more secure user wants to be, the more effort s-he needs to expend hiding identity. To blog anonymously user needs to consider just how paranoid s-he wants to be before deciding how hard s-he wants to work to protect identity. Some of the strategies for protecting identity online require a great deal of technical knowledge and effort.

1. Pseudonyms

One easy way user can hide identity is to use a free Webmail account and a free blog host outside the native country. (Using a paid account for either email or Web hosting is a bad idea, as the payment will link the account to a credit card, a checking account, or a Paypal account that could easily be linked back to user.) User can create a new identity — a pseudonym — when user signs up for these accounts, and when the finds authority the blog, the pseudomonas id will be found.

Examples of free Webmail account providers:

- *Yahoo Mail*
- *MSN Hotmail*

Examples of free blog-hosting providers:

- *Blogger*
- *Seo Blog*
- *Blogsome*

2. Public Computers

3. Anonymous Proxies

Some reliable lists of public proxies:

- *Publicproxyservers.com : Lists anonymous and identifiable proxies.*
- *Rosinstrument Proxy Database : A searchable database of proxy servers.*

- *Samair : Only lists anonymous proxies and includes information on proxies that support SSL.*

4. Onion Routing

Onion-routing system Tor, provides a high degree of anonymity for Web surfing. Onion routing takes the idea of proxy servers, a computer that acts on blogger's behalf, to a new level of complexity. Each request made through an onion routing network goes through two to 20 additional computers, making it hard to trace which computer originated a request. Each step of the Onion Routing chain is encrypted, making it harder to trace the posts.

MICROBLOGGING

Microblogging is a passive broadcast medium in the form of blogging. A microblog differs from a traditional blog in that its content is typically much smaller, in both actual size and aggregate file size. A microblog entry could consist of nothing but a short sentence fragment, an image or embedded video. As with traditional blogging, microbloggers post about topics ranging from the simple, such as "what I'm thinking right now," to the thematic, such as "sports cars." Commercial microblogs also exist, to promote websites, services and/or products, and to promote collaboration within an organisation. Some microblogging services offer features such as privacy settings, which allow users to control who can read their microblogs, or alternative ways of publishing entries besides the web-based interface. These may include text messaging, instant messaging, E-mail, or digital audio.

Services

Initially the microblogs were known as tumblelogs. The term was coined in a blog post on April 12, 2005, However, by 2006 and 2007, the term microblog came into greater usage for such services provided by Tumblr and Twitter. In May

2007, 111 microblogging sites were counted internationally. Among the most notable Microblog services are Twitter, Tumblr, Plurk, Emote.in, Beeing, Jaiku and identi.ca. More recently, varieties of services and software with the feature of microblogging have been developed. For example, Plurk integrates video and picture sharing and Emote.in has a concept of sharing emotions, built over microblogging, with a timeline. Pownce integrated microblogging with file sharing and event invitations. Later on Pownce was merged into SixApart in 2008. Other leading social networking websites Facebook, MySpace, LinkedIn, and XING also have their own microblogging feature, better known as status updates.

With the growth of microblogging, many users want to maintain presence in more than one or more social networks. For example, Lifestream and Profilactic aggregate microblogs from multiple social networks into a single list. Services such as Ping.fm send out blogger's microblog to multiple social networks..

Microblogging in organizational usage

Users and organizations can set up their own microblogging service with the help of open source and free software. Hosted microblogging platforms are also available for commercial and organizational use. Microblogging has become a new informal communication medium, especially for collaborative work within organizations. Over the last few years communication patterns have shifted primarily from face-to-face communication to more online communication in email, IM, and other tools. However, some argue that email is now a slow and inefficient way to communicate.

- *The 'one to many' broadcasting offered by microblogs is thought to increase productivity by circumventing this.*

- *Another implication of remote collaboration is that there are fewer opportunities for face to face informal conversations.*
- *However, microblogging has potential to support informal communication among co-workers.*
- *Microblogging is therefore is expected to improve the social and emotional welfare of the workforce, as well as streamlining the information flow within the organization.*
- *It can increase opportunities to share information, help realize and utilize expertise within the workforce, and help build and maintain common ground between co-workers.*
- *As microblogging use continues to grow every year, it is quickly becoming a core component of Enterprise Social Software.*

Email vs. Microblogging

email	*Microblogging*
Actionable Paradigm	*Passive Communication*
Sender to Recipient	*Broadcast*
Expectation of being read	*Viewer's discretion*
Only visible to parties in the thread	*Visible to all followers*
good for task assignment	*not so good for task assignment*
pre-exisiting connection required	*no explicit invite or connection required*
brainstorming cumbersome	*excellent for brainstorming*

Issues with microblogging

Some issues with microblogging are privacy and security.

(i) *Privacy is arguably a major issue, because users may broadcast sensitive personal information to anyone who views their public feed. Microblog platform providers can also cause privacy issues, through altering or presetting users' privacy options, in a way users feel compromises their personal information. An example would be Google's Buzz platform, which incited controversy in 2010 by automatically publicising users' email contacts as 'followers'.*[16] *Google later amended these settings.*

(ii) *Security concerns have been voiced within the business world, since there is potential for sensitive work information to be publicised on microblogging sites such as Twitter.*

(iii) *Integration could be the hardest issue to overcome, since it can be argued that corporate culture must change to accommodate microblogging.*

What are Video Tutorials/Screencasts?

Video is an extremely powerful communication medium. It can communicate large quantities of complex information in a very short period of time. Although high-end video production can still be a very complex and expensive undertaking, current technology has made quality video production accessible to the average content developer. Screen capture software, such as TechSmith's Camtasia Studio or Macromedia's (Adobe) Captivate, has made it much easier to produce educational videos that demonstrate the use of library search engines, databases, and other information resources (Newest version 2005). A screen capture video is also referred to as a screencast and it can be played back on either a desktop workstation or a portable media player. Because Camtasia Studio is capable of recording any screen activity, it can also capture media generated by other software, such as PowerPoint presentations, for example. The software is designed primarily for recording and editing screen capture video, but it is also capable of recording audio and incorporating images and video from other sources. the development of online library instruction classes for the sciences, intended for use during course-integrated live instruction in a computer classroom. The Blackboard Content System (a web-based file management system) provided a flexible online location to position content suited to library instruction. Class content included assignment information, concepts and procedural details, links to useful resources, relevant screenshot images, discussion of concepts, pdf handouts, and multimedia. Initially started with course-integrated instruction in the sciences, this strategy rapidly expanded to other academic disciplines. A Blackboard class was also used to support graduate student orientation sessions in the sciences. In addition, Blackboard-based stand-alone workshops have now been taught, covering topics such as RSS for current awareness, and molecular structure searching.

PODCASTS

Podcasting is one example of integrating two established technologies, media files and RSS feeds, very effectively. This integration makes it dramatically easier for the end user to stay updated with the latest media from a selected content creator, since the content is syndicated. Podcasts are audio RSS feeds and video feeds are referred to as video podcasts. Podcasts are not limited to playback on an Apple iPod and iTunes, but can be used on other portable media players and PDAs. Also, podcasts do not have to be played back on a portable player; they are also playable on desktop workstations. Some academic institutions (e.g., Purdue University, Stanford University, and others) already podcast course content to their students.

When creating a library blog, library may want to use a library themed layout. Yet it can be challenging to find them. Searching for example, under themes on wordpress dashboard won't give many results and blogger doesn't have as many custom templates in general. Here are seven great library or book related templates for any library related blog.

1. *Law library wordpress theme : While this theme does not have anything that specifies that it must be used for a law library, it makes a great theme for any library blog.*
2. *This simple and colorful wordpress books theme has three columns and would make a great library or reading blog theme.*
3. *The library can be compared to an open book and with this wordpress theme it will be even more so. Basic colors and an open book in the banner make this a great library theme.*
4. *The easy reader wordpress theme features white background with blue highlights and a girl reading a book, another great library wordpress theme.*
5. *The library of the future will not look like libraries now. Reach out and embrace the library of the future with these futuristic looking library wordpress theme.*

VARIOUS WEBLOG TOOLS, SOFTWARE AND PLATFORMS LISTED ON GOOGLE

- *Radio UserLand : http://radio.userland.com/ Weblog software for individuals, educational institutions, and corporations. Free trial available.*
- *b2evolution : http://b2evolution.net/ Open source PHP/ mySQL weblog tool derived from the same code that later became WordPress. Supports multiple categories, sub-categories, multiple weblogs, skins, statistics, comments, anti-spam filters.*
- *Status.net : http://status.net/ Open source microblogging application, aiming to be an alternative to Twitter. Provides hosting services, a list of existing servers using this software, documentation and*

information for developers.

- *Nucleus CMS : http://www.nucleuscms.org/ A PHP/SQL blogging tool which resides on your webserver. Includes multiple weblog capabilities, and RSS syndication.*
- *Serendipity : http://www.s9y.org/ An open-source project for creating a simple CMS for blog authors.*
- *Geeklog : http://www.geeklog.net/ Free open-source blog tool. Runs on many different operating systems and uses PHP4 and MySQL.*
- *Scoop : http://scoop.kuro5hin.org/ Free collaborative media software for running community web logs . Requires Perl, mod_perl, and MySQL.*
- *Dotclear : http://dotclear.org/ Open source weblog and content management system written in PHP, featuring built-in antispam protection, automated installation and a multilingual interface.*
- *Slashcode : http://slashcode.com/ Open Source software for creating Slashdot-style discussion weblogs. Provides links to the software, and help for setting up and running the software.*
- *MarsEdit : http://www.red-sweater.com/marsedit/ A multifeatured weblog editor for Mac OS X (10.3 or higher) by Red Sweater Software. Site includes screenshots, features list, and trial download.*
- *PivotX : http://www.pivotx.net/ The next generation Pivot, a customizable weblog tool written in PHP and using flat files or a SQL database as data storage.*
- *Antville : http://www.antville.org Based on an open source project aimed to the development of an "easy to maintain and use" weblog-hosting system. It can host unlimited blogs.*
- *Thingamablog : http://thingamablog.sourceforge.*

net/ A cross-platform, standalone application for authoring and publishing weblogs. It will work on any platform on which Java can run. Thingamablog does not require a third-party blogging host, a CGI/PHP enabled web server, or a MySQL database. The only requirement to setup and manage a blog is FTP access to a web server.

- *Pebble : http://pebble.sourceforge.net/ A light weight, open source, blogger that is written as a web application to run inside J2EE web containers.*
- *Blosxom : http://www.blosxom.com/ Lightweight blogging application written in Perl.*
- *Roller Weblogger : http://www.rollerweblogger.org/ Open source weblogger written in Java and based on Struts, Velocity and Castor. Not recommended for beginners.*
- *tBLOG : http://www.tblog.com/ Integrate fully customizable weblog templates, with any website. Add calendar, search, link management, voting, and comment modules.*
- *BlogCFC : http://blogcfc.riaforge.org/ Open source (Apache License v.2) weblog software written in ColdFusion MX.*
- *BLOG:CMS : http://blogcms.com/ Blogware requires PHP and MySQL. Features include weblog, forum, wiki, news aggregator, and photo gallery.*
- *MyTripJournal.com : http://www.mytripjournal.com/ Easy-to-use blogging tool with mapping system designed specifically for travelers. Post text and photos. Includes a notification system to let your friends know when an update is posted.*
- *Python Desktop Server : http://pyds.muensterland.org/ An open source weblog, news aggregator and light weight desktop CMS system.*

- *SnipSnap.org : http://www.snipsnap.org Weblog and wiki system written in Java.*
- *boastMachine : http://boastology.com PHP/MySQL powered blogging platform.*
- *CocoBlog : http://cocoblog.sourceforge.net/ Open source blogging package based on Apache's Cocoon and Xindice products.*
- *Open Journal Project : http://www.grohol.com/downloads/oj/ Free, perl-based open source journal script.*
- *Zomplog : http://www.zomp.nl/zomplog/ An easy to use weblog application which uses php and MySQL.*
- *Traction Software : http://tractionsoftware.com/ Enterprise weblog software. System for capturing and managing knowledge in the course of a communication or business process.*
- *Presstopia : http://presstopia.com Open source ASP.NET weblog application. Supports MySQL, MS Access, MS SQL Serve, Atom 0.3, RSS 2.0 feeds, multiple authors, comment, trackbacks, update pings.*
- *NewsBruiser : http://newsbruiser.tigris.org/ Free, open source weblog program that focuses on ease of use.*
- *serwatka.net : http://serwatka.net Articles and information for weblog development with the eZ Publish CMS.*
- *BlogBinders.com : http://www.blogbinders.com/ Create a bound book out of a live journal, blog or weblog.*
- *MKDoc : http://mkdoc.com/ Web site building, serving and content management tool that has been designed to encourage the use of good information architecture and the production of accessible web sites.*

- *BlogMax : http://www.billstclair.com/blogmax/ Emacs elisp package for maintaining a web log.*
- *PHPosxom : http://sourceforge.net/projects/phposxom/ PHP rewrite of Rael Dornfest's Blosxom.*
- *Wheatblog : http://wheatblog.sourceforge.net A lightweight, open source, customizable blogging and content management solution powered by PHP and MySQL or SQLite.*
- *Blog.Mac by Largemouth Software : http://www.largemouthsoftware.com/blogmac.html Create, manage, and publish a weblog on Mac OS X using the .Mac service.*
- *Vine Type : http://vinetype.com A website management system that requires no database nor scripting language installation. Free for non-commercial use.*
- *BlogFace : http://www.zope.org/Members/karl/BlogFace/BlogFace A weblog product for the Zope application server.*
- *Nanoblogger : http://sourceforge.net/projects/nanoblogger/ Small weblog engine written in Bash.*
- *PersonalBlog : http://sourceforge.net/projects/personalblog Light-weight personal blogging application that is suitable for installing on a host provider. It's written in JAVA and uses a variety of J2EE technologies.*
- *Personal Weblog : http://www.kyne.com.au/~mark/software/weblog.php A PHP/MySQL include file for adding a weblog to a home page.*
- *SimplyBlog Software : http://www.kamat.com/community/software Tool designed to create weblogs on corporate Windows based Intranets.*
- *SnapLog Photo Blogger : http://snaplog.com/ A one*

click photo weblog publishing application that sends updates to a site via FTP.

- *Kit : http://markpasc.org/code/radio/kit/ Software package for use with Radio Userland, including search, news aggregation, file uploader, and other tools.*
- *EasyMoblog : http://sourceforge.net/projects/easymoblog/ An open-source platform for personal weblogs and moblogs. It allows the creation of customizable and easy-to-use weblogs. Update just by sending e-mail messages.*
- *Pocket Blog : http://www.pocketblog.com/ Pocket PC application for managing weblogs that support the Blogger API. Works offline, posting entries when internet connectivity is available.*
- *Easy Blogs : http://www.easyblogs.com/ Desktop-based journal publisher stores all information on the local computer and uploads content via FTP. Multiple templates and RSS feed available.*
- *Trellix : http://danbricklin.com/log/byol.htm Client-side windows based blogging software. No HTML experience required.*
- *blojsom : http://blojsom.com/ A lightweight blog package written in Java that is inspired by blosxom. Includes highly configurable flavors, templating, plugins, and the ability to run a multi-user blog.*
- *Monaural Jerk : http://monauraljerk.org Free, open-source PHP/MySQL weblog system. Includes calendar navigation, "edit this page", searching, channels, RSS, XML, tell-a-friend, and spider-friendly URLs.*
- *Somery : http://somery.danwa.net/ PHP-based 'blog software.*
- *Blog Script : http://metastatic.org/source/blog/ A simple, command-line based utility for maintaining personal weblogs. It runs easiest on Unix-like*

platforms, such as Linux.

- *Serendipity : Creating a website using S9Y : http://www.squidoo.com/serendipity-blog Collection of tutorials, articles and links about the weblog software.*
- *MeYou : http://www.meyou.com Publish own blogs with PC or mobile Java phone. Community directory available.*
- *Broadcast Builder : http://www.lionhardt.ca/bb/ Create RSS channels and weblogs. Windows.*
- *CF Blogger : http://www.daydreaminc.com/personal_blog.cfm A blog application built with ColdFusion. This is an open source project.*
- *Particle Blogger : http://www.particlesoft.net/particleblogger/ Server-side blogging tool written in PHP with integrated RSS feed and static URLs option.*
- *GoBlogGo : http://www.gobloggo.com Post pictures from a camera phone. Moblogging photoblog home.*
- *Farook.org: Blog : http://www.farook.org/bytes.htm Maintain a weblog on any site which supports FTP while keeping all your entries on your own hard disk for safety. WYSIWYG HTML editor.*
- *Pivot : http://www.pivotlog.net/ A customizable weblog tool written in PHP and using flat files as the data storage.*
- *BlogCFM : http://www.blogcfm.org An open-source blog application written in CFML, supporting both Coldfusion MX 6.1+ and Bluedragon Server 6.1+.*
- *ZuZuSoft : http://erasable-ink.tripod.com/journalscript/index.html CGI/Perl-based script for publishing a journal through text files rather than a browser interface.*
- *cLoG : https://sourceforge.net/project/showfiles.php?group_id=72934&package_id=122641 Open*

source blog system for people who have access to a provider with php and mySQL capabilities.

- *telnet7 Bloggy : http://t7_bloggy.tripod.com For websites that use free webhosting services.*
- *Greymatter : http://www.noahgrey.com/greysoft/ Weblogging software requires Perl 5 and knowledge of HTML.*
- *Blogoommer : http://blogoommer.sourceforge.net/ A standalone java application for editing, organizing and publishing weblogs by FTP. Generate a weblog site with calendar-based navigation, links, and RSS 1.0 and 2.0 news feeds.*
- *ApeJet Blog : http://www.apejet.org/sites/ apejetblog/ Simple open source tool for servers running PHP. No database needed. Produces RSS, archives, and categories.*
- *BlogLite : http://phplabs.com/scripts.php?script= BlogLite A basic, easy to use weblogging suite built with PHP and MySQL. 2 scripts, 2 HTML templates. Web journaling script.*
- *Addendat : http://deekoo.net/technocracy/ addendat/ Blogging tool for those who don't like Javascript or whose servers are running SCP, which makes using other blogging tools difficult or impossible.*
- *Bs.post : http://code.gushue.net/bspost/ A minimal news/ weblog system using PHP4 and SQL.*

BLOGGING FOR LIBRARIES

While often regarded as a platform for people to share their personal stories, a blog can also be used to tell the story of an organization. A blog can be a powerful and influential communication and public-relations tool for library organization. The Blog is a type of technology that can be used in a myriad of ways. Librarians do not have to worry about creating a site because the format is fixed by a template, thus allowing the person to focus on the content. Examples of how a Blog can be used in a library are as followed:

- *To offer information on services, new purchases, and events. For example, the Ross-Blakley Law Library Blog at the University of Arizona allows customers to search for news by categories (University of Arizona).*
- *A Blog can be use to provide specialized information. For example, the public library of Allen County in Indiana has a blog dedicated just for young people (Allen County).*
- *To reach out to patrons, especially if the blog is offered in other languages. An example is the Sacramento Public Library which offers the blog both in English and Spanish (Sacramento Public Library).*
- *The Blog allows customers to have a voice, like in the case of the Blog at Cornell University where questions about the library can be answered by anyone (Cornell University).*

An example of how the Blog is used in library that must be mentioned is that of the Ann Arbor District Library (AADL). Throughout the literature, the AADL has been mentioned as the best examples of adoption of the Blog in a library setting. While many libraries are using the blogs as a supplement, the AADL has integrated the blog into its home page (Ann Arbor District Library). Through the blog, information is regularly posted. Responses are written informally, in the first person, with minimum information and supplemented by links. Something interesting - and much appreciated by the users - is that this Blog allow to read other's comments, an unexpected function compared to other library's Blogs. Through the free use of the Blog, the AADL shows that it is possible to create a virtual

environment where all comments are respected, appreciated, and taken into consideration.

REFERENCES

1. *http://encyclopedia.thefreedictionary.com/Online+diary*
2. *http://www.thefreedictionary.com/chronological*
3. *http://www.webology.org/2006/v3n2/a25.html#34*
4. *http://library.uvm.edu/nucleus/LibNews.php*
5. *http://library.lib.binghamton.edu/mt/science/*
6. *http://www.library.ohiou.edu/subjects/businessblog/*
7. *http://collectionsnews.blogspot.com/*
8. *http://www.thefreedictionary.com/chronological*
9. *http://encyclopedia.thefreedictionary.com/Online+diary*
10. *Eldon, Eric. (2008). "2008 Growth Puts Facebook In Better Position to Make Money". VentureBeat. http://venturebeat.com/2008/12/18/2008-growth-puts-facebook-in-better-position-to-make-money/.*
11. *"Control Yourself, Inc. launches Identi.ca, the Open Microblogging Service". Control Yourself, Inc. 2008-07-02. http://controlyourself.ca/2008/07/02/control-yourself-inc-launches-identica-the-open-microblogging-service/.*
12. *Twitter - Where did the idea for Twitter come from? http://twitter.com/about#idea*
13. *Identi.ca bookmarklet*
14. *Reiss, David. "Facebook Developers News". http://developers.facebook.com/news.php?blog=1&story=110.*
15. *http://www.aadl.org/taxonomy/term/86*
16. *http://library.coloradocollege.edu/bookends/*
17. *http://referencenewman.blogspot.com/*
18. *http://mjcpl.org/*
19. *Tumblelogs (kottke.org)*
20. *Pownce website. http://www.pownce.com/*
21. *Harvard Business School. 2009-06-01. http://blogs.harvardbusiness.org/cs/2009/06/new_twitter_research_men_follo.html.*
22. *Sysomos. 2009-06-10. http://www.sysomos.com/insidetwitter/.*
23. *TechCrunch. 2009-06-10. http://www.techcrunch.com/2009/06/*

10/the-more-followers-you-have-the-more-you-tweet-or-is-it-the-other-way-around/.

24. *2009-06-21. http://www.post-gazette.com/pg/09172/978727-96.stm.*
25. *TechCrunch. 2008-11-26. http://www.techcrunch.com/2008/11/26/first-hand-accounts-of-terrorist-attacks-in-india-on-twitter/.*
26. *http://www.findingdulcinea.com/news/technology/2009/June/Twitter-on-Iran-a-Go-to-Source-or-Almost-Useless.html.*
27. *"Could this be a factor in the allure of microblogs?". http://thelaughingbuddha.wordpress.com/2009/04/19/could-this-be-a-factor-in-the-allure-of-microblogs/.*
28. *"StatusNet". http://status.net/.*
29. *Dejin Zhao & Mary Beth Rosson (May 2009). "'How and why people Twitter: the role that micro-blogging plays in informal communication at work'". ACM GROUP2009 Conference. http://portal.acm.org/citation.cfm?id=1531710.*
30. *Ross Mayfield (October 15, 2008). "'Email hell'". Forbes. http://www.forbes.com/2008/10/15/cio-email-manage-tech-cio-cx_rm_1015email.html.*
31. *Socialtext.com. http://www.socialtext.com/customers/casestudy_fona.php.*
32. *Joab Jackson (November 20, 2009). "NASA program proves the benefits of social networking". Government Computer News. http://gcn.com/Articles/2009/11/30/A-Space-side-NASA-social-networking.aspx?Page=1.*
33. *"'Google Buzz redesigned after privacy complaints'". The Telegraph. February 15th, 2010. http://www.telegraph.co.uk/technology/google/7240754/Google-Buzz-redesigned-after-privacy-complaints.html.*
34. *http://www.techsoup.org/learningcenter/webbuilding/page5516.cfm#rate*
35. *http://www.infobarrel.com/Advantages_and_Disadvantages_of_Blogging*
36. *http://www.marketingtitan.com/internet_marketing_articles*
37. *http://www.gerrymcgovern.com/new_thinking.htm*
38. *Emma Barnett (2010). "'Have business networking sites finally come of age?'". The Telegraph. http://www.telegraph.co.uk/technology/7482116/Have-business-networking-sites-finally-come-of-age.html.*

39. *"'A world of connections'". The Economist. Jan 28th, 2010. http://www.economist.com/specialreports/displaystory.cfm?story_id=15351002.*
40. *Burnham, Kristin (2009-12-01). "12 Microblogging Tools to Consider". IDG CIO.com. http://www.cio.com/article/509433/12_Microblogging_Tools_to_Consider.*
41. *http://www.thepartnership.ca/partnership/bins/calendar_page.asp?cid=2488-2321-3733*
42. *http://www.gerrymcgovern.com/new_thinking.htm*
43. *http://www.blogpublishingtool.com/2008/January/Blog-Software-Packages.htm*
44. *http://www.techsoup.org/learningcenter/internet/page6042.cfm*
45. *http://www.eff.org/Privacy/Anonymity/blog-anonymously.php*
46. *http://www.google.com/Top/Computers/Internet/On_the_Web/Weblogs/Tools/*
47. *http://www.techsoup.org/learningcenter/webbuilding/page5516.cfm#rate*
48. *http://www.wpthemehub.com/book-tree-blogger-template/*

9

Enterprise 2.0 and Applications in Library

INTRODUCTION

The idea of Enterprise 2.0 is only a couple of years old. Enterprise 2.0, which is the use of social media and social networking tools in a business setting, is having a major impact on how employees learn and share information. It is becoming increasingly important that organizations stay aware of these changes. It is needed to play a bigger role in understanding and selecting Enterprise 2.0 tools, and to partner and collaborate with the information technology Sections along the way.

Defining enterprise 2.0

Harvard Business School professor Andrew McAfee is credited with coining the "Enterprise 2.0" term when he saw the potential to apply to business the concepts of Web 2.0 tools, which until recently have been used primarily by teens and college students to build social networks.

According to the Enterprise 2.0 Conference web site, it is defined as:

"Enterprise 2.0 is the term for the technologies and business

practices that liberate the workforce from the constraints of legacy communication and productivity tools like email. It provides business managers with access to the right information at the right time through a web of inter-connected applications, services and devices. Enterprise 2.0 makes accessible the collective intelligence of many, translating to a huge competitive advantage in the form of increased innovation, productivity and agility."

Essentially, Enterprise 2.0 is the idea of creating an ecosystem of open, connected tools while growing and nurturing a culture of learning and sharing. With the help of technologies under one umbrella, Some of the more common tools related to Enterprise 2.0 are blogs (ex. WordPress), wikis (ex. MediaWiki), micro-blogging platforms (ex. Yammer or Present.ly), social bookmarking sites (ex. Scuttle), and even in-house social networks, similar to Facebook. Enterprise 2.0 is viewed as the real beginning of change to more productive tools toward open information exchange. Moreover, the bottom-up, emergent nature of these technologies provides great advantage to innovation and product development processes.

UNDERSTANDING THE ENTERPRISE 1.0 AND COMPARING WITH ENTERPRISE 2.0:

Enterprise 2.0" has a simple definition: The application of Web 2.0 technologies to the enterprise. But there are almost as many different meanings for "Web 2.0" as there are mashups, making "Enterprise 2.0" an equally nebulous concept. Enterprise 2.0 emphasize on RIAs (Rich Internet applications) that enable collaboration. Enterprise 1.0 was about the following aspects:

- *Transactional Applications : data-centric systems designed to handle core business transactions and processes.*
- *Productivity Tools : document-centric tools used by knowledge workers to manage and maintain their*

work files.

- *Communications Tools : ever-growing email messages that must get categorized organized and filed into various topic folders by each individual user.*

While still essential for any enterprise, the tools of Enterprise 2.0 lacked the ability to promote something that is becoming an increasingly important aspect of any organization i.e., social engagement. Enterprise 2.0 came into existence with a new paradigm based on enterprise social networking. It is the platform of engagement for all constituents across and beyond the enterprise, empowering them to be more engaged by staying connected with the people and activities around them. Platforms of engagement are people-centric. In doing so, they can:

(i) *participate,*

(ii) *contribute and*

(iii) *collaborate with one another more effectively, thereby achieving higher business goals for the company as a whole.*

DESIGN AND STRUCTURE

The work environment is highly structured, largely reactive, and the workflow is linear. By design, systems of record are records-centric, revolving around enterprise data, documents, messages and their surrounding business processes. Integration is Enterprise 2.0. Enterprise 2.0 should be a structure that allows great flexibility in the choice and use of applications throughout an organization, supporting the applications with APIs to allow data to be taken from and deposited into central data stores. Their mission is to facilitate collaborative tasks such as problem solving, exception handling, consensus building, and innovative brainstorming, tasks that cannot be pre-programmed into structured processes or workflows. Consequently, platform of engagement participants must thrive to be proactive, engaging in multiple activities in parallel to reach maximum geometric scalability, such as:

- *Assemble and sustain a critical mass of active members across and beyond the enterprise.*
- *Build out an ecosystem of networks and communities by these members, for these members.*
- *Establish meaningful social business connections amongst themselves.*
- *Integrate fully into all aspects of systems of record.*
- *Follow all relevant activities by anyone, from anywhere, at anytime.*

BENEFITS OF ENTERPRISE 2.0

1. *Enterprise 2.0 tools make it easier to share and organize information. Tagging and rating provide a straightforward way to find content and make judgments about what to look at. Blogs and wikis are natural collaboration and communication platforms. Social network tools help staff find the right individual or group of people. Enterprise 2.0 has the potential to provide knowledge and content management in a surprisingly cheap and easy fashion using Web-based tools.*
2. *Enterprise 2.0 refers to the concept of moving Web 2.0 tools and technologies into the enterprise to help your employees, partners, suppliers and customers work together to build networks of like-minded people and share information.*
3. *The fact is, Enterprise 2.0 concepts are gaining credibility, and it's not just startups that are paying attention to this space. More than 800 people attended the recent Enterprise 2.0 Conference in Boston, which included speakers from IBM, Microsoft and Cisco, and*

a host of other smaller players. IBM introduced the Web 2.0 Goes to Work package for the WebSphere Portal, while Microsoft promoted Sharepoint, a natural collaboration environment, as a way to implement Enterprise 2.0 ideas along with Office and other Microsoft technologies.

The following areas result in measureable gains for companies that have been using E20 the longest:

- *Greater ability to share ideas*
- *Improved access to knowledge experts*
- *Reduced costs of communication, travel and operations*
- *Decreased time to market for products*
- *Improved employee satisfaction*

TOOLS

Enterprise 2.0 takes the original concept of the Web, using websites to feed content to visitors, and turns it upside down. Instead of a one-way conversation, the organization talking to the site visitor-Enterprise 2.0 allows implementing a multiparty conversation to share information and manage knowledge inside and outside the organization using blogs and wikis, social networking and tagging, rating systems and the like. The link among these tools is the ability of the individuals involved to participate and to control the process while they work together, share information and create networks of people with similar interests. Tools to enable these functions have existed for a long time. The trouble is that few people used them, despite large amounts of resources expended to deploy these systems. What changed is the simplicity of the tools. If they're simpler, they're more likely to be used, an important component for knowledge management. Instead of trying to implement huge, all-encompassing enterprise-wide systems, the simpler Web-based tools under the Enterprise 2.0 umbrella strip away the complexity of the '90s technologies while carrying on the spirit of the ideas. This concept of reach is one of the fundamental elements of the network effects we seek from implementing blogs, wikis, and other collaborative and relationship oriented tools in the enterprise.

It takes time to create blogs, tag emails, learn how to use them, and convince other people to use such tools as well. Fortunately, a feature inherent in social networking tools enables "viral networking" to occur where people can invite others to participate in activities. This can generate "buzz" that can be even more effective than an email from the CEO about creating content that can be scanned and indexed. Three P's - People, Processes, and Projects are concerned.

- *People : refer to the people in the organization who do the work.*
- *Processes : refer to the work activities these people perform.*
- *Projects : are defined activities with beginnings and ends that people do in relation to the processes.*

USAGE OF ENTERPRISE 2.0

Enterprise 2.0 is an integrated combination of strategy, implementation, and full-lifecycle rollout that reflects the practical realities of the enterprise world including concerns around ROI, value generation, risk, control, and trust. Pragmatic Enterprise 2.0 is not a rigid, one-size-fits-all template however.

Adaptive Methods + Risk Navigation
+ Best-of-Breed Platform = Success

Implementing social media at the enterprise level can be a political, bureaucratic, and technical struggle. Though the tools themselves are usually easy to acquire, creating the right environment for demonstrable success is more challenging. Hinchcliffe & Company has created a simple, easy-to-use service that provides access to the full range of benefits of social computing while proactively reducing the downside. The Enterprise 2.0 can be used for:

- *Internal social collaboration*
- *Intranet redesigns*
- *Customer communities*
- *Government 2.0*
- *Business social networks*

OBJECTIVES

Enterprise 2.0 is all about empowering users to be more efficient in executing business goals. An important part of the enhancement is around using more flexible, collaborative tools that facilitate improved knowledge sharing - which in most cases is best served if the culture is more transparent and less hierarchical. For many organizations, comfort with transparency and lateralization will be a long-term process often involving new hires, training and new organizational incentives. Of course, increased transparency has to be moderated with regulatory and other legal requirements in many industries.

CONCERNED PRINCIPLES

In terms of the business value the difficulty is that it's very hard to show true metrics for the gains that can be made form enterprise 2.0 – there are significant anecdotal benefits that need to be extrapolated to an organization-wide benefit. Extrapolating that up through the organization, the contention is that if a simple thing like reply-all can create such costs for an organization, high level operations can drive huge benefits.

Enterprise 2.0 pre-supposes that you can upend hierarchies for the benefit of all. Yet none of that thinking has a credible use case you can generalize back to business types - except: knowledge based businesses such as legal, accounting, architects etc. Even then - where are the use cases? Five principles concerned, are as following:

- *Workforce transformation*
- *Business process/operations*
- *Intellectual property/Privacy/governance*
- *Religious wars (technology/generational biases)*
- *Bottom line business benefits*

Implementing social media at the enterprise level can be a political, bureaucratic, and technical struggle. But it doesn't have to be. Though the tools themselves are usually easy to acquire, creating the right environment for demonstrable success is more challenging. There seems to be a great deal of discussion lately of how, if at all, Enterprise 2.0 differs from Web 2.0, or indeed if there is even such a thing as Enterprise 2.0. Do you think that perhaps folks are getting too caught up in the debate and/or turned off by it that they fail to investigate the opportunities that may be there for their businesses? To a large degree, when we're describing what the term Web 2.0 means to the enterprise, we are talking about things they can do that they could not do before or things they can do more easily and cost-consciously than before. Web 2.0 represents a very fundamental shift. With Web 1.0, it is getting to know the Internet and figuring out how to use it. But now SOA, mashups and rich Internet applications are visible. This shift will be matched in importance only by the shift from the mainframe to client-server architecture.

FEW CONSIDERATIONS FOR IMPLEMENTATION OF ENTERPRISE 2.0

The organization can survey to gauge the attitudes toward Enterprise 2.0 applications and understand their policies and procedures for controlling their usage. The goal can be achieved by getting answer to few key questions such as:

- *What types of Enterprise 2.0 applications are being adopted and what security risks do they pose?*
- *What policies do organizations have in place that governs appropriate use of these applications?*
- *Which control mechanisms do IT departments have today vs. what they need?*
- *What steps can an organization take for the safe enablement of Enterprise 2.0 applications?*

Following aspects must be kept in mind while introducing an enterprise level system to maximize network effects from improved collaboration and shared intelligence:

Focus on problem areas : Enterprise social networking, shared intelligence, and collaboration tools should be introduced where they can do the most good.

Maximize staff ownership : Staff ownership and operation must be implmented as soon as possible.

Reward participation : Creating and updating certain types of information related to people, processes, and projects is now an expected and required part of their job. They should be trained and evaluated accordingly.

Promote growth : People should understand the need to invite and help others to participate. This "sales" role should be everyone's responsibility, not just management's or the Training Department's.

IN THE LIBRARY SYSTEM

Integrate Enterprise 2.0 tools with the LMS require time to experiment and identify which tools have the most value at organizations. There are few aspects to think upon:

1. *Library organizations should have the right mindset so that they will naturally figure out what works at organization. For example, if it determines to help*

connect staff to library users, and them to information, library needs to find out the areas where these tools will fit naturally in organization.

2. *Libraries should listen to their learners, run small pilot programs (many of these tools are open-source / free), and experiment. Fortunately, unlike an LMS, they can install several of these tools and experiment under the radar.*
3. *When libraries visualize potential areas of success, they can be more visible and vocal with their efforts. (Depending on their situation and their comfort-level with technology, they may want to have an ally in their IT department during their experimentation. They can help install some of the tools / systems.)*

Benefits:

Various potential benefits are as following:

1. *Productivity*
2. *knowledge retention*
3. *Information Discovery*
4. *Business Agility*
5. *Cross-Pollination*
6. *Fostering Innovation*
7. *Competitive Advantage*
8. *Modern workplace*
9. *More Transparency*
10. *Less Duplication*
11. *Better Communication*
12. *Adaptive Processes*

ENTERPRISE 2.0 ARCHITECTURE

Companies nowadays work with an Enterprise Architecture to align business, information, applications and infrastructure. There are several standards for this already, like TOGAF or the Zachman Framework. The 'Human Interaction Management System' (the so called 'Enterprise 2.0') is about processes with a lot of work from people involved. It is opposite to the more stable processes that are dealt with by BPM. The main question in this "Enterprise 2.0"-area is: "How do you get the right co-worker at the right place and time, to do the work (s)he's good at? John Hagel discusses about pull models vs. push models. A pull model exists within a situation of abundance. It knows two main processes:

1. *A process that adds meaningful artifacts/resources to a repository, with attention to the possibility to find it back.*
2. *A process that gets and uses the artifact/resource from the repository, at the moment of need.*

An example of a pull model for knowledge is Wikipedia (or any wiki)

Here is a process in which writers add knowledge and another process in which people get the information at the time they need it. Examples of pull models are scattered on the internet. Resources are normally planned and pushed in a work schedule. Enterprise 2.0 (and Enterprise 2.0 Architecture) introduces pull models for the organization. But not only with knowledge pull models, but also with people pull models. In order to get (human) resources to the right project, a modern organization does not use a push model, like planning, but takes a new approach i.e., a pull model.

Layers in Enterprise 2.0

There can be a place for a pull model within Enterprise 2.0, to get resources at the right time at the right place, then it can be said that the Enterprise 2.0 Architecture must consist of several layers, which can be following:

- *Co-workers*
- *Place within the organization (dependent on organizational structure, knowledge, social network, reputation)*
- *Process layer (turbulent 'human' processes)*
- *Business goals*
- *Context demands*

How Enterprise Architecture enables Web 2.0

The moving Web 2.0 technologies to the enterprise that is fundamentally about: integration and interaction. Web 2.0 is about building solutions in a new way. Enterprise Architecture does not inform about building the solution in the correct way, as much as it tells about building the correct solution. Enterprise Architecture is not that of IT software development to build the right systems. Enterprise Architecture is not the Central Soviet of IT. It can be explained by the example of the city planners who set zoning, inspect new construction, enforce setbacks, and protect wetlands.

BUILDING AN ENTERPRISE 2.0 APPLICATION

Building an Enterprise 2.0 application is not just building a Web 2.0 application. According to management consultants McKinsey and Company, Web 2.0 projects often are seen as grassroots experiments, and leaders sometimes believe the technologies will be adopted without management intervention-a "build it and they will come" philosophy. Enterprise 2.0 applications, in contrast, serve business objectives and have support from internal (IT, business) and external (customers, partners) stakeholders. It may adapt the follow actions:

- *An Enterprise 2.0 technology strategy should combine*

the different aspects of Web 2.0 capabilities into a secure and comprehensive platform where business conversations and tasks are executed in the context of business goals.

- *It should promote and enable rich user experiences and expose enterprise content in the most secure fashion.*
- *An Enterprise 2.0 application combines the capabilities of content management, security, search and Web 2.0. It gathers information from ERP applications, CRM systems and other backend enterprise applications and delivers this information in a form that is context-based, secure, and easy to find.*

Building Blocks of Enterprise 2.0

Enterprise 2.0 is an integrative business strategy that combines multiple disciplines, technologies, and experiences. The fundamental capabilities of any rich Enterprise 2.0 require the combination of content management, a Web 2.0 framework, security, and integration with enterprise applications.

1. Content Management : Organizations inadvertently deal with structured and unstructured data. Structured data can include documents, files, and videos, and is generated primarily from within the company. Unstructured data is generated mostly from customer interactions and could include blog postings, Wiki entries, and chat scripts. The Content Management platform provides a single and consistent infrastructure for managing, publishing, and delivering the data in a uniform fashion. Configuration of the Web 2.0 and content management layers requires the use of Single Sign-On for authentication and an LDAP provider as the identity store. To go beyond the limitations of J2EE security and to enable applications to authenticate users and enforce authorization, the most important standard is the Java Authentication and Authorization Service (JAAS), a standard security Application Programming Interface (API) that was added to the Java language through the Java Community Process. Integrating the Web 2.0 layer with Enterprise applications using SOA. SOA plays an instrumental role in orchestrating business processes using BPEL (Business Process Execution Language). BPEL automates Web services-based integration between different backend applications and humans. Integration between the Web 2.0 and SOA layers is bidirectional. Users from the Web 2.0 layer can kick-off or advance key business processes by calling BPEL processes directly. SOA, in turn, can deliver contextual enterprise data to the Web 2.0 layer.

2. Web 2.0 Framework : While the Content Management platform addresses how content is created and managed, the Web 2.0 framework provides the collaborative platform to enable rich interaction through the ability to expose enterprise data in a highly collaborative manner. Due to the social nature of Web 2.0 platforms, it's important that this collaborative presentation layer is not only user-friendly and easy to navigate, but that this single presentation layer is multi-channel accessible (by PCs, mobile devices, PDA, and other devices). Most importantly, the Web 2.0 framework enables conversational participation with users and systems through services like instant messaging, voice interaction, wikis, blogs, communities, tagging, user ratings, and personalization.

3. Security : Enterprise 2.0 systems should be built with business in mind, with security as the highest priority. Exposing and personalizing content poses very specific security challenges, especially given the highly accessible and highly interactive nature of Enterprise 2.0 solutions. Who can publish and edit content? What happens to content over time? What user role-based restrictions should be placed on content?? Enterprise 2.0 should be safe, secure, auditable, and controllable. The Security layer provides authentication, authorization, personalized delivery of content based on user roles and identities, a complete audit trail over the lifecycle of the content, and content publishing/monitoring controls. There are a number of different types of OLS users, and the security infrastructure needed to support these different types is identified below:

- *Public : Public users should only be able to view and download product manuals.*
- *Portal User : Users who registered with OLS with no Wind River license (i.e. they do not own any Wind River products) should only be able to update and add licenses to their profiles. They do not have access to OLS content.*
- *Basic : Users who registered with a valid license that has no active Wind River product support. These users own Wind River products but have either allowed their product support to lapse or did not purchase product support. These users can access OLS but are restricted to viewing only basic content such as Tech Tips, Application Notes, and Manuals.*
- *Maintenance : Users who registered with a valid license that has active product support. These users own Wind River products and also have an active support service contract with Wind River. These users should be able to view all content in OLS except content restricted to Premium users.*
- *Premium : Maintenance users attached to a Premium Support account should be able to view all OLS content as well as premium content specific to their Premium Support account.*
- *Employee : Employees should be able to view all OLS content, including premium content. Employees should also be able to view content that is inaccessible to customers, for example, unpublished defects and*

all service requests logged by customers (customers should only be able to see their own service requests).

4. Integration : Enterprise 2.0 brings information from ERP applications, CRM systems, and other backend enterprise apps together and presents it to the end user in a secure and contextual fashion. Users collaborate on information that is either coming out of or going into an enterprise application. This requires integration between enterprise applications orchestrating data and business flow, merging this data with the content management layer and presenting it to the end user in a Web 2.0 front end.

With many technology tiers comprised of several different products, it is important that these layers interact without any friction. Building Enterprise 2.0 frameworks in accordance to industry standards helps to ensure interoperability with minimal code changes required. A standards-compliant platform also ensures flexible design architecture, allowing companies to scale their Enterprise 2.0 environments and easily fold in new features on an as-needed basis.

CHALLENGES IN BUILDING ENTERPRISE 2.0 APPLICATIONS

There are certain challenges that the typical organization may have to overcome to implement emerging technologies that fall under the Web 2.0 or Enterprise 2.0 umbrella. The biggest challenge is the complexity of the existing IT landscape. Too often it has many different tiers, with many different products and vendors. Just to understand it is a big challenge. So it is recommended that organizations establish a reference architecture they can use as a guideline or blueprint. If someone is not sure where a Web 2.0 technology may fit into the enterprise, the blueprint will help to look at it from a systems standpoint.

Where is Enterprise 2.0 headed?

- *Businesses are actively seeking information about how best to implement Enterprise 2.0. This is driving significant demand for knowledge about how. The rise of the 2.0 Adoption Council is one demonstration of this need to share information about what works. Further providing evidence that there's a need for how: A survey in the near past showed that 36% of their members were currently managing multi-million dollar budgets this year for Enterprise 2.0.*
- *There is still lot of debate about how to calculate the ROI of social computing. While credible ROI numbers are essential to the business case of any IT project, the longer cause and effect chains of social software mean that the story is richer yet more complex. But some approaches are becoming increasingly apparent. For example, at the Enterprise 2.0 SUMMIT, according to Kjetil Kristensen, we spend 60-80% of our time in the workplace on interaction and collaborative activity. With payroll being one of the largest components of the yearly budget, anything that drives efficiencies in the #1 activity of the workday can create significant returns. Straightforward models that focus on improving specific collaborative activities rather than generic performance improvements will likely have the most credibility here.*
- *Certain internal groups are driving Enterprise 2.0 within organizations more than others. While there are always exceptions, in general we're seeing more social computing being run by the groups responsible for collaboration, knowledge management, line-of-business, and corporate communication and less with IT, human resources, and other support units. To me, this seems like the right groups are driving this forward, particularly when they aim at specific*

business challenges.

- *The trough of disillusionment is the next stage for Enterprise 2.0. Expectations for social software often run quite high, especially in terms of seeing immediate returns. And even though some case studies show impressive early uptake and benefits, it can often take a year or more before serious gains can be measured in many organizations. For now, especially as businesses discover the best ways to reap the benefits of social computing for them, the Enterprise 2.0 story will have to run the gauntlet of inflated expectations for a while until more maturity is reached.*
- *There is still a lot of Enterprise 2.0 discussion out of business context. Often there is this sense that it's an environment or appendage in a vacuum, without a clear connection with the business. Focus is still on the immediate understanding of what Enterprise 2.0 is instead of what it means in context of the larger organization and its processes. This is particularly true for engaging with cross-cutting concerns such as content management, document management, corporate records archiving, SoX processes, or even unified communication and messaging, the latter two which social computing environments often compete with directly (even while not usually replacing them.)*

REFERENCES

1. *https://www.yammer.com/*
2. *https://www.presentlyapp.com/*
3. *http://sourceforge.net/projects/scuttle/*
4. *http://www.elearninglearning.com/?query=social learning*
5. *http://www.wordpress.org/*
6. *http://www.mediawiki.org/wiki/MediaWiki*
7. *http://www.osscube.com/services/enterprise-2.0-development*
8. *http://www.networkcomputing.com/content-management/*

229607609?pgno=1

9. *Pehong Chen. Enterprise 2.0: Why All Business Software Must Go Social http://blogs.forbes.com/ciocentral/2011/04/22/enterprise-2-0-why-all-business-software-must-go-social/*
10. *Enterprise 2.0 is Not an Application http://ourfounder.typepad.com/leblog/2009/08/enterprise-20-is-not-an-application.html*
11. *http://blog.hbs.edu/faculty/amcafee/index.php/faculty_amcafee_v3/*
12. *http://enterprise2conf.com/*
13. *http://www-306.ibm.com/software/info/web20/*
14. *http://www.cio.com/article/123550/2#tools*
15. *Ajay Gandhi (2010). Realizing the Benefits of Enterprise 2.0 - Q&A from the KM World webcast. http://blogs.oracle.com/enterprise20/tags/Enterprise+2.0*
16. *http://hinchcliffeandcompany.com/pragmaticenterprise2/pe2_elements.html*
17. *http://www.paloaltonetworks.com/researchcenter/tag/enterprise-2-0/*
18. *http://www.paloaltonetworks.com/researchcenter/2010/06/tune-into-enterprise-2-0-webcast-featuring-forrester-research/#comments*
19. *http://www.ddmcd.com/storage/downloads/enterprise_2.0_network_effects.pdf*
20. *This fall, enterprise social computing will change forever http://hinchcliffeandcompany.com/pragmaticenterprise2/pe2_elements.html*
21. *http://www.socialtext.net/wikinomics/index.cgi?enterprise_2_0_architecture##*
22. *http://www.opengroup.org/architecture/togaf8-doc/arch*
23. *http://www.zifa.com/*
24. *How Enterprise Architecture enables Web 2.0 http://blogs.msdn.com/nickmalik/archive/tags/Enterprise+Architecture/default.aspx*
25. *Building Enterprise 2.0 Applications. Nam Doan-Huy, YiHong Xu, Narshimha Rao Kondapaka, and Melody Wood. http://www.oracle.com/technetwork/middleware/downloads/fmw-11-download-092893.html*

26. *http://www.20adoptioncouncil.com/*
27. *http://blogs.zdnet.com/Hinchcliffe/?p=334*
28. *http://twitter.com/k_kristensen*
29. *http://i.zdnet.com/blogs/enterprise_2_cause_and_effect.png*
30. *http://blogs.zdnet.com/Hinchcliffe/?p=852*

10

SEMANTIC WEB AND INFORMATION RETRIEVAL

"If HTML and the Web made all the online documents look like one huge book, RDF, schema, and inference languages will make all the data in the world look like one huge database"

Tim Berners-Lee, Weaving the Web, 1999

The Semantic Web is the extension of the World Wide Web that enables people to share content beyond the boundaries of applications and websites. It has been described in rather different ways: as a utopic vision, as a web of data, or merely as a natural paradigm shift in daily use of the Web. Most of all, the Semantic Web has inspired and engaged many people to create innovative semantic technologies and applications. It is a set of formats and languages that find and analyze data on the World Wide Web, allowing consumers and businesses to understand all kinds of useful online information. Thus we can say that the semantic web is a transformation of the existing web that is meant to enable software programs, applications, and agents to find meaning and understanding on web pages. These capabilities have been developed in the context of finding and using enormous data and information.

DEFINING IT

The Semantic Web was thought up by Tim Berners-Lee, inventor of the WWW, URIs, HTTP, and HTML that the Web as a whole can be made more intelligent and perhaps even intuitive about how to serve a user's needs. Berners-Lee observes that although search engines indexes much of the Web's content, they have little ability to select the pages that a user really wants or needs. He foresees a number of ways in which developers and authors, singly or in collaborations, can use self-descriptions and other techniques so that context-understanding programs can selectively find what users want.

SOME BASIC INFORMATION

- *The word semantic stands for the meaning of.*
- *The semantic of something is the meaning of something.*
- *The Semantic Web = a Web with a meaning*

FREQUENTLY USED ACRONYMS

There are frequently used acronyms in semantic web concept.

- *API : application programming interface*
- *HTML : Hypertext Markup Language*
- *URI : Uniform Resource Identifier*
- *W3C : World Wide Web Consortium*
- *XML : Extensible Markup Language*

The Semantic Web is a web that is able to describe things in a way that computers can understand. We can look into following statements:

- *Leo Tostoy was an author from Russia.*
- *"Anna Karenina" was authored by Leo Tolstoy.*
- *"Anna Karenina" is an intense work of fiction.*

Sentences like the ones above can be understood by people. But how can they be understood by computers? Statements are built with syntax rules. The syntax of a language defines the rules for building the language statements. But how can syntax become semantic?

This is what the Semantic Web is all about describing things in a way that computers applications can understand it.

- *The Semantic Web is not about links between web pages.*
- *The Semantic Web describes the relationships between things (like A is a part of B and Y is a member of Z) and the properties of things (like size, weight, age, and price)*

The Semantic Web is a mesh of information linked up in such a way as to be easily processable by machines, on a global scale. It can be considered as an efficient way of representing data on the World Wide Web, or as a globally linked database.

There is a dedicated team of people at the World Wide Web consortium (W3C) working to improve, extend and standardize the system, and many languages, publications, tools and so on have already been developed. However, Semantic Web technologies are still very much in their infancies, and although the future of the project in general appears to be bright, there seems to be little consensus about the likely direction and characteristics of the early Semantic Web.

NEED OF THE SEMANTIC WEB

The problem with the majority of data on the Web that is in this form at the moment is that it is difficult to use on a large scale, because there is no global system for publishing data in such a way as it can be easily processed by anyone.

All of the information is presented by numerous sites, but all in HTML. The problem with that is that, is some contexts, it is difficult to use this data in the ways that one might want to do so. The Semantic Web can be seen as a huge engineering solution but it is more than that. A large number of Semantic Web applications can be used for a variety of different tasks. It is helpful in increasing the modularity of applications on the Web.

The Semantic Web is generally built on syntaxes which use URIs (Uniform Resource Identifiers) to represent data, usually in triples based structures: i.e. many triples of URI data that can be held in databases, or interchanged on the World Wide Web using a set of particular syntaxes developed especially for the task. These syntaxes are called "Resource Description Framework" syntaxes.

BACKGROUND

Tim Berners-Lee, a software engineer at CERN knew that there had to be a better way to keep track of information about what people were working on. He wrote:

The aim would be to allow a place to be found for any information or reference which one felt was important, and a way of finding it afterwards. (Information Management: A Proposal, 1989).

What he wanted, in short, was the Web. And so he built it. He wrote the first Web browser and Web server and the protocols that they used to communicate. Years passed. More pages were linked into his Web, more users grabbed software to use it. People made and lost millions on it, papers lauded and decried it. But Tim Berners-Lee wasn't finished yet.

"Now, miraculously, we have the Web", he wrote (Business Plan for the Semantic Web, 2001).

The current Web supports documents, pages of text

and figures designed for humans. The Semantic adds support for databases, vast collections of information neatly organized to be processed by machines. The Semantic Web is not about teaching machines to understand human words or process natural language. Everything is written out in structured languages for machine. The goal is not to build thinking, but merely to collect data in a useful way, like a large database. The phrase Semantic Web is attributed to Tim Berners-Lee, inventor of the Web and Director of the World Wide Web Consortium (W3C). The Web was implemented using URIs, HTTP and HTML, the Semantic Web is built with URIs, HTTP and RDF. There are discussed as following:

1. URIs

URIs are Uniform Resource Identifiers, they are text strings that identify resources, or concepts. Commonly referred to as URLs, they come in many forms (and are extensible, so that new forms can be created) and identify many things. A URI is simply a Web identifier: like the strings starting with "http:" or "ftp:" that is often found on the World Wide Web. Anyone can create a URI, and the ownership of them is clearly delegated, so they form an ideal base technology with which to build a global Web on top of. In fact, the World Wide Web is such a thing: anything that has a URI is considered to be "on the Web". The syntax of URIs is carefully governed by the IETF, who published RFC 2396 as the general URI specification. The W3C maintains a list of URI schemes.

Here are some examples:

- *http://me.aaronsw.com/ identifies a person, Aaron Swartz.*
- *http://purl.org/dc/terms/modified identifies a concept, that of the last-modified date.*
- *uuid:04b749bf-3bb2-4dba-934c-c92c56b709df is a decentralized identifier, called a UUID. It is created by*

combining the time and the address of Ethernet card (or a random number if user doesn't have one) to create an identifier that is unique. This allows one to create identifiers without having a centralized system like domain names that must be given out by some authority. On many machines UUIDs can be created using the program uuidgen.

- *tag:sandro@world.std.org,2001-06-05:Taiko is a persistent identifier, called a TAG, it combines an email address or domain name along with a date to allow the person who "owned" that address on that date to create persistent identifiers*
- *esl:SHA1:iQAAwUBO51bkD6DK6KYhyiEEQJLqw CfSviAHvC1REXEkOGEWf9pAByCRwAni92 xgCJqNL4forLRlGIK5szDXfckCE:someName is an esl, a URI that uses cryptographic hashes and digital signatures to ensure that no one else can create URIs in a particular name. It also allows for verification of "official" information, by making sure that it is signed with the same key that signed the URI.*

This is just a small example of the many types of URIs that exist. New "URI schemes" can be registered with IANA for different purposes. However, all names are bound by Zooko's Law, which says that names are like the old joke "good, fast, cheap: choose two": names can be decentralized, secure, human-memorizable: choose two. There are URI schemes that embody each possible choice in Zooko's Law: ESLs are decentralized and secure, simple keywords are decentralized and human-memorizable and domain names are secure and human-memorizable.

2. HTTP

HTTP is a system for performing operations on resources (identified by URIs). It is widely-implemented. This is the protocol all Web browsers and servers speak. Three major "methods", or types of actions are associated:

- *GET asks for information about a resource.*
- *POST sends a request to a resource. It's what turned the Web from a way to get documents, to a platform for applications and services. When user does something like send an email over the Web, user is doing a POST, making a request of the server.*
- *PUT sends updated information about a resource. The original Web browser made editing just as easy as browsing: user had visited his page, and clicked the edit button. Then he could make changes, like fixing a typo, just like in a word processor. When he hit save, the browser could send a PUT back to the server, with the updated copy. Unfortunately this functionality was not included in most browsers. This meant that making a Web page was just too hard for most users, and that's why the Web became something of a one-way medium.*

Aside from the method and the resource to act on, HTTP includes a number of headers to provide a lot of useful functionality. It has a method of authentication that uses cryptographic hashes to avoid sending passwords "in the clear" — this prevents crackers from being able to steal them. It has something called the Accept: header, to allow browsers to tell the server what formats they support. That way the server can send HTML to HTML web browsers and RDF to Semantic Web agents. It has built-in support for compression to cut down on bandwidth, and something called ETags to let clients find out if a page has changed. By using HTTP, Semantic Web services get all of this functionality for free. It's already built-in to the many HTTP servers and clients that are available for lots of platforms in almost every programming language.

3. RDF

RDF, the Resource Description Framework, is the major

new piece of the Semantic Web. It's a format for providing information in machine-readable form, using URIs and text strings as terms.

It combines these terms into triples, sets of three which express basic concepts or statements. Web links, such as a link from X to Y create pairs, like: (X, Y). The Semantic Web adds a type to this link, making it (X, relation, Y). This expresses that X has a relation with Y. An example showing the triple:

<JJST> <website> <http://web.jjst.edu/> .

The above triple expressed facts about the world. They are also very simple, but many complex concepts can be written as triples. For those familiar with relational databases, they can be written in triples very simply:

<primaryKey> <column_name> "field value" .

RDF FORMAT

The most fundamental building block is Resource Description Framework (RDF). It is a format for defining information on the Web. Each piece of data, and any link that connects two pieces of data, is identified by a unique name called a Universal Resource Identifier, or URI. (URLs— the common Web addresses that we all use, are special forms of URIs.) In the RDF scheme, two pieces of information, and any notation indicating how they are connected, are grouped together into what is called a triple. URIs can be agreed on by standards organizations or communities or assigned by individuals. The relation "is a" is so generally useful, for example, that the consortium has published a standard URI to represent it. The URI http://en.encyclopedia.org/wiki/fish" could be used by anyone working in RDF to represent the concept of fish. In this way, different people working with different sets of information can nonetheless share their data about dolphins and television animals. And people everywhere can merge knowledge bases on large scales.

A triple can simply be described as three URIs. A language which utilises three URIs in such a way is called RDF: the W3C have developed an XML serialization of RDF, the "Syntax" in the RDF Model and Syntax recommendation. RDF XML is considered to be the standard interchange format for RDF on the Semantic Web, although it is not the only format. Once information is in RDF form, it becomes easy to process it, since RDF is a generic format, which already has many parsers. XML RDF is quite a verbose specification, and it can take some getting used to.

COMPARISONS WITH XML

XML was designed for documents, not data. Because of this, it has many features (like attributes and entities) that make sense for document-oriented systems, but only cause problems when expressing data. Also, there are many ways to say the same thing in XML. For example all these XML documents:

```
<author>
 <uri>page</uri>
 <name>Laura</name>
</author>
<person name="Laura">
 <work>page</work>
</person>
<document href="http://www.w3.org/test/page"
author="Laura" />
```

Represent the same basic RDF triple:

<page> <author> <Laura> .

Even if one were to say things slightly differently, the number of changes user can make to a triple are fairly small. User can use different URIs, but then all one needs to do is assert a new triple, saying that the two URIs are equal. Then author RDF system can do the equivalent of a find-and-replace, so that he can continue to use the information. Similarly, author can write the triple in the other direction, saying:

<Laura> <creation> <page>

But this is similarly easy to describe in RDF, and to convert. In XML, the system to convert documents is called XSLT, and it's a Turing-complete language, meaning it has the same expressive power as a programming language. It quickly becomes very complicated to convert XML documents and deal with all the different formats. But in RDF, it stays fairly easy. In addition, triples are simple things. User can simply keep a table with three columns and know that any triple user ever encounter will fit. XML's hybrid tree structure is so confusing and nonstandard that there are actually special XML databases — databases specifically designed to support all the odd features of XML.

4. RDF Schema

RDF Schema was designed to be a simple datatyping model for RDF. User can also create properties and classes, as well as doing some slightly more "advanced" stuff such as creating ranges and domains for properties. All of the terms for RDF Schema start with "http://www.w3.org/2000/01/rdf-schema#". The alias "rdfs:" is often used for RDF Schema. The first three most important concepts that RDF and RDF Schema give us are the "Resource" (rdfs:Resource), the "Class" (rdfs:Class), and the "Property" (rdf:Property). These are all "classes", in that terms may belong to these classes. For example, all terms in RDF are types of resource. To declare that something is a "type" of something else, we just use the rdf:type property:-

rdfs:Resource rdf:type rdfs:Class .

rdfs:Class rdf:type rdfs:Class .

rdf:Property rdf:type rdfs:Class .

rdf:type rdf:type rdf:Property .

This simply says that "Resource is a type of Class, Class is a type of Class, Property is a type of Class, and type is a type of Property". These are all true statements. It is quite easy to make up the own classes. For example, let's create a class called "knowledge", which contains all of the subjects in the world:-

Knowledge rdf:type rdfs:Class .

Now we can say that "Language is a type of subject":-

:Language rdf:type :Knwoledge .

We can also create properties quite easily by saying that a term is a type of rdf:Property, and then use those properties in RDF:-

:name rdf:type rdf:Property .

:Language :name "Language" .

RDF Schema also has a few more properties that user can make use of: rdfs:subClassOf and rdfs:subPropertyOf. These allow saying that one class or property is a sub class or sub property of another. For example, we might want to say that the class "Language" is a sub class of the class "Subject". To do that:

:Language rdfs:subClassOf :Subject .

Hence, when we say that Language is a Subject, we are also saying that Language is Knowledge. We can also say that there are other sub classes of Animal:-

:Human rdfs:subClassOf :Animal .

:Duck rdfs:subClassOf :Animal .

RDF Schema is very simple, and allows building up knowledge bases of data in RDF quickly. The next concepts which RDF Schema provides are ranges and domains. Ranges and domains let us say what classes the subject and object of each property must belong to. For example, we might want to say that the property ":bookTitle" must always apply to a book, and have a literal value:-

rdfs:domain always says what class the subject of a triple using that property belongs to, and rdfs:range always says what class the object of a triple using that property belongs to. RDF Schema also contains a set of properties for annotating schemata, providing comments, labels, and the like. The two properties for doing this are rdfs:label and rdfs:comment, and an example of their use is:-

:bookTitle rdfs:label "bookTitle";

rdfs:comment "the title of a book" .

ONTOLOGIES AND INFERENCES

a. Ontology Languages

Individuals or groups may want to define terms and data they frequently use, as well as the relations among those items. This set of definitions is called an ontology. Ontologies can be very complex (with thousands of terms) or very simple. Web Ontology Language (known as OWL) is one standard that can be used to define ontologies so that they are compatible with and can be understood by RDF.

b. Inference Engines

Ontologies can be imagined as operating one level above RDF. Inference engines operate one level above the ontologies. These software programs examine different ontologies to find new relations among terms and data in them. For example, an inference engine would examine the three RDF triples below and deduce that Flipper is a mammal. Finding relations among different sources is an important step toward revealing the "meaning" of information.

DAML

DAML is a language created by DARPA as an ontology

and inference language based upon RDF. DAML takes RDF Schema a step further, by giving more in depth properties and classes. DAML allows one to be even more expressive than with RDF Schema, and brings us back on track with our Semantic Web discussion by providing some simple terms for creating inferences.

DAML+OIL

DAML provides us a method of saying things such as inverses, unambiguous properties, unique properties, lists, restrictions, cardinalities, pairwise disjoint lists, datatypes, and so on. One DAML construct that is the daml:inverseOf property. Using this property, it can be said that one property is the inverse of another. The rdfs:range and rdfs:domain values of daml:inverseOf is rdf:Property. Here is an example of daml:inverseOf being used:-

:hasName daml:inverseOf :isNameOf .

:Ben :hasName "Ben" .

"Ben" :isNameOf :Ben .

The second useful DAML construct that is the daml:UnambiguousProperty class. Saying that a Property is a daml:UnambiguousProperty means that if the object of the property is the same, then the subjects are equivalent. For example:-

foaf:mbox rdf:type daml:UnambiguousProperty .

:x foaf:mbox .

:y foaf:mbox .

It implies that:-

:x daml:equivalentTo :y .

Many Semantic Web applications now involve DAML, though it is only one in a series of languages and so forth that are being used.

INFERENCE

The principle of "inference" is quite a simple one: being able to derive new data from data that is already known. In a mathematical sense, querying is a form of inference. Inference is one of the driving principles of the Semantic Web, because it will allow creating SW applications quite easily. With the help of inference, the system could easily be scale up. Merging databases simply becomes a matter of recording in RDF somewhere that "Person Name" in a particular database is equivalent to "Name" in another database, and then throwing all of the information together and getting a processor to think about it.

LOGIC

For the Semantic Web to become expressive enough to help us in a wide range of situations, it will become necessary to construct a powerful logical language for making inferences. A great range of tools are available with which to build the Semantic Web: assertions (i.e. "and"), and quoting (reification) in RDF, classes, properties, ranges and documentation in RDF Schema, disjoint classes, unambiguous and unique properties, datatypes, inverses, equivalencies, lists, and much more in DAML+OIL.

Notation3 introduces a "context" construct, enabling one to group statements together and quantify over them using a specially designed logic vocabulary. Using this vocabulary, for example, one can express "or", using NANDs:-

```
{ { :Nancy :loves :TheHouston } a log:Falsehood .
 { :Nancy :is :Fruit } a log:Falsehood .
} a log:Falsehood .
```

Which can be read as "it is not true that Nancy does not love The Houston and is not fruit". Here Nancy a universally quantified variable. The above example does not serialize "properly" into XML RDF, because XML RDF does not have the context construct as denoted by the curly brackets in the example above. However a similar effect can be achieved using reification and containers.

SEMANTIC WEB MARKUP FOR BLOGS

In the perspective of semantic web WordPress, MovableType, or TypePad theme does not correspond to a simple test for truly semantic XHTML markup. At the same time, though, it is extremely unsettling that an inferior markup structure is prevailing in the face of an absolutely correct way of doing things.

PROPER XHTML STRUCTURE FOR BLOGS AND FOR GOOGLE!

The goal is to describe each page to the search engines through the use of hierarchical XHTML tags (<title>, <h1>, <h2>, <h3> etc.) and to present them in a logical, meaningful order.

Regarding blog architectures, there are five areas:

1. Title of web pages

Page titles are the most important link between pure web page and the human readers. Although their apparent impact on a website's pages may appear minimal, their true impact in the search engines is undeniable. Google pulls the contents of the <title> tag and links it as the most prominent piece of information in the search result. Users scan content rather than reading it, so it is needed to provide them with value.

2. Coding up the logo and tagline

Usually site logos are served inside <h1> tags. Besides the <title> tag, the <h1> tag is supposed to tell both Google and users exactly what they can expect to find on the current Web page. In addition, search engines assign a hierarchical *rank to the different headline markup tags, and except for the <title>, the <h1> tag is the most powerful piece of information user can serve to the search engines about a particular page. The title can be served inside a <div> instead. The tagline should be laser-focused on the unique value proposition, the primary subject of the Web site.*

3. Heading

The heading-titles being served inside <h2> tags is far and away the biggest markup mistake. This title is the single most important piece of information developer can serve to the search engines about an individual page. It should be featured as prominently as possible within the markup. The best way to serve the title inside <h1> tags. Developer should only have one set of <h1> tags on any given Web page.

4. Sub-headlines and Sidebar headlines

Breaking up the posts into sub-sections is a great idea both stylistically and also for reader comprehension. The most common way to delineate these sub-sections is through the use of sub-headlines. For sub-headlines, <h3> and <h4> tags are the most popular choices. When title is kept within <h1> tags, then it stands to reason that the sub-headlines ought to be highly-focused, relevant, and served inside <h2> tags. Under this setup, the sub-headlines facilitate the title in the most powerful way possible while still maintaining the hierarchy of semantic markup.

The sidebar items can add some value to a page, they can't (and shouldn't) touch the main content area with regard to overall value on a page. Therefore, the sidebar headlines must not go inside high and mighty <h2> tags. They can be put inside <h3> or <h4> tags at the most. When the sidebar headlines are closely focused around the primary subject matter, then serving them inside <h3> tags is a great idea because they will carry as much weight and adding as much value as possible. Heading tags should appear in the code in *order, to signify a hierarchy of content. For example, to use h4 for the sidebar headings, then _semantically_ what developer is saying is "these sections are a sub-section of the previously declared h3, which in turn is a sub-section of the previous h23 .*

EVOLVEMENT OF SEMANTIC WEB

The Semantic Web is an evolving development of the World Wide Web in which the meaning (semantics) of information and services on the web is defined, making it possible for the web to "understand" and satisfy the requests of people and machines to use the web content. It derives from World Wide Web Consortium director Sir Tim Berners-Lee's vision of the Web as a universal medium for data, information, and knowledge exchange. Semantic Web and information systems research is a multidisciplinary field that welcomes contributions for intelligently labeling, linking, integrating, analyzing, and making sense of data in all forms on the Web and networks, using theory and practice from such disciplines as artificial intelligence, natural language processing, soft computing, databases, information retrieval, social networks, distributed computing, web engineering, information systems, human-computer interaction, and economics. Semantic Web is a maturing field of technology that continues to be the emphasis of much focused research.

THE RESOURCE DESCRIPTION FRAMEWORK

The RDF (Resource Description Framework) is a language used for describing information and resources on the web. Putting information into RDF files, makes it possible for computer programs ("web spiders") to search, discover, pick up, collect, analyze and process information from the web. The Semantic Web uses RDF to describe web resources. For example, if information about music, cars, tickets, etc. were stored in RDF files, intelligent web applications could collect information from many different sources, combine information, and present it to users in a meaningful way. RDF will be helpful for Information like this:

- *Computer prices from different resellers*
- *Information about medicines*
- *Plane schedules*
- *Spare parts for the industry*
- *Information about books (price, pages, editor, year)*
- *Dates of events*

The Semantic Web is not a very fast growing technology. One of the reasons for that is the learning curve. RDF was developed by people with academic background in logic and artificial intelligence. For traditional developers it is not very easy to understand. One fast growing language for building semantic web applications is RSS.

JENA

Jena is a Java framework for building Semantic Web applications. It provides a programmatic environment for RDF, RDFS and OWL, SPARQL and includes a rule-based inference engine. Jena is open source and grown out of work with the HP Labs Semantic Web Programme. The Jena Framework includes:

- *A RDF API*
- *Reading and writing RDF in RDF/XML, N3 and N-Triples*
- *An OWL API*
- *In-memory and persistent storage*
- *SPARQL query engine*

Currently the World Wide Web is the largest single information resource. Unfortunately, despite its dependence on computers to operate at all, most of the information is only understandable by humans and not by computers. While computers can use the syntax of HTML documents to display them to user in a browser, Web computers can't understand the content—the semantics.

The Web was originally all about documents. The simple act of clicking on a link in Web browser triggers the browser to ask a Web server to send a document, which it then displays. The document might be an e-mail from a friend. The Web browser doesn't really care; it just follows its internal rules for displaying the page. It's up to user to understand the information on the page. Structuring data adds value to that data. With consistent structure, it can be used in more ways. User can see the demand for structured data today in the proliferation of APIs that have sprung up around Web sites as a part of the Web 2.0 trend—an API is structured data, and structured data from a variety of sources is what powers mashups. The idea behind mashups is that data is pulled from various sources on the Web and, when combined and displayed in a unified manner, this combination of elements adds value over and above the source information alone. The individual APIs that everyone is busy building are to solve the exact same problem that the Semantic Web is intended to address: to expose the content of the Web as data and then combine disparate data sources in different ways to build new value. Rather than build and maintain user's own API, he can build his Web site to take full advantage of the Semantic Web infrastructure which is already in place. If his Web site is his API, he can reduce the overall development and maintenance. Similarly, rather than build custom solutions for every Web site user wants to pull data from, he can implement one solution based on Semantic Web technologies and have it work interchangeably across many Web sites—including Web sites he weren't even aware of before he began development.

SEMANTIC WEB TECHNOLOGY OVERVIEW

Semantic Web technologies can be considered in terms

of layers, each layer resting on and extending the functionality of the layers beneath it. Although the Semantic Web is often talked about as if it were a separate entity, it is an extension and enhancement of the existing Web rather than a replacement of it. The Semantic Web technology stack is explained as following:

- *SPARQL*
- *RDF/OWL*
- *XML*
- *GRDDL*
- *RDFa/OWL*
- *XHTML*
- *HTTP and URI*

The base layer of the Semantic Web is HTTP and URIs. These are commonly considered 'Web' rather than 'Semantic Web', but every proposed Semantic Web technology rests upon these Web fundamentals. URIs are the nouns of the semantic Web. HTTP is the verbs: GET, PUT and POST as well as a number of thoroughly tested solutions in the fields of authentication and encryption. The Resource Description Framework (RDF) is the workhorse of the Semantic Web. It is a grammar for encoding relationships. An RDF triple has three components: a subject, a predicate (or verb), and object. Each can be expressed as a resource on the Web that is a URI. This is far less ambiguous than encoding data in random XML documents.

In the early days of the Semantic Web, it was hoped that content will be available in RDF and soon make a plethora of data available. Unfortunately, perhaps because the main XML expression of RDF looked unnecessarily complex, uptake was slow. More succinct RDF representations, like Notation3 (N3) and Terse RDF Triple Language (Turtle) are now available but have been unable to overcome the inertia. A solution to the problem was inspired by the Microformats approach. With Microformats, semantic value is added to existing HTML content by using consistent patterns of standard HTML elements and attributes. Microformats exist for narrow but common items of data such as contact information and calendar items. The W3C equivalent is RDFa, RDF data embedded in XHTML. The implementation is slightly more complex than Microformats but it is far more generic, anything which developer can express in RDF, he can add to XHTML documents using RDFa. Through this technique the Semantic Web can be bootstrapped by existing Web content.

Of course, the RDF embedded in XHTML documents as RDFa is no good for all the Semantic Web tools, which require RDF as input. There needs to be an automatic method to recognize the presence of RDFa content and extract the RDF out of it. The W3C solution for this is Gleaning Resource Descriptions from Dialects of Languages (GRDDL). The idea is that you run an existing XHTML document through an XSL transform to generate RDF. You can then link the GRDDL transform either through direct inclusion of references or indirectly through profile and namespace documents. If developer has expressed an author relationship in an RDF file on site, could the computer assume they were the same thing? What if he instead had a writer relationship in RDF triple? What he need is a way to express a common vocabulary, to be able to say that 'author' and 'writer' are analogous. On the Semantic Web this problem is solved by ontologies, and the W3C standard for expressing ontologies is the Web Ontology Language (OWL).

Once the developer has some sources of data in RDF, and he has ontologies to let others determine the relationships between them, he needs a way to get useful information out of them. The Simple Protocol and RDF Query Language (or SPARQL, pronounced 'sparkle') is an SQL-like syntax for expressing queries against RDF data, and the queries themselves look and act like RDF data. The fundamental paradigm for SPARQL is pattern matching and it is designed to work across the Web on data combined from disparate sources and to be flexible. For example, matches can be described as optional, which makes it much better than SQL at querying ragged data. Ragged data has an unpredictable and unreliable structure, which is what he might expect to find if his data is combined from various sources on the Web rather than from a single well-contained SQL database.

PLANNING A SEMANTIC WEB SITE

Developer can save time if he plans from the start to embrace Semantic Web technologies and turn Web site into an API, rather than create a separate API for the Web site. A Semantic Web approach gives you free API-like functionality. Usually an API is a way to get structured data, in XML or JSON format, out of an otherwise unstructured Web site. This leads to a dual approach: He has Web pages for human consumption and he have an API where computers can pull out structured information for automatic processing. However, this creates extra work for him; if he expects people to make use of the API, then he have to document it and support it and keep it synchronized with new features on the Web site. With a Semantic Web approach, the Web site is the structured data. He doesn't need a separate implementation. He and the users can take advantage of other Semantic Web tools to do automatic processing.

While designing an API, an object model is considered for conceptual organization so developers can understand when they get collections of items or just items, and which collections their items belong in. On a Semantic Web site this will be partly determined by the ontology choices, but also by the URI scheme. Approaches to making the URIs usable as part of the API is must. On an existing Web site, updating the content is must to take advantage of GRDDL, RDFa and Microformats.

EVALUATING THE DATA IN THE CONTEXT OF EXISTING ONTOLOGIES

To design an ontology that matches up to the data is more complex part of the Semantic Web. Arriving at the right ontology is usually a critical element of successful implementation of Semantic Web projects. Fortunately, many ontologies already exist. Table 1 lists some of them.

Table: Some ontologies in use on the Web today

Dublin Core	This metadata element standard for cross-domain information resource description provides a simple and standardised set of conventions for describing things online in ways that make them easier to find.
SIOC	Semantically-Interlinked Online Communities Project is an ontology that expresses the information contained both explicitly and implicitly in Internet discussion methods, such as blogs or forums mailing lists.
FOAF	The Friend of a Friend ontology describes individuals, their activities and their relations to other people and objects. FOAF allows the description of social networks in a distributed fashion.
DOAP	Description Of A Project is an ontology to describe open-source projects
ResumeRDF	This ontology expresses a Resume or Curriculum Vitae (CV), including information such as work and academic experience or skills.

In addition, many ontologies are domain specific in fields such as technology, environmental science, chemistry and linguistics.

SEMANTIC URI SCHEME

When a Web site is the API, then the URIs are the methods that programmers will access to get data. A sensible, succinct and consistent structure is therefore very important, because frequent changes will cost the goodwill of the target audience. The components of an RDF triple are usually URIs. To change them will invalidate most existing RDF which *refers to the Web site. The categorization hierarchy is fixed. As the Web advanced, dynamically generated sites became the norm. Flexibility, with structure no longer tied to a particular layout of files, the amount of semantic information in the URI decreased. Consequently the URI gives very little semantic value. More recently, content management systems and Web development frameworks have started to have semantically structured URIs yet retain the flexibility of dynamic pages. This is achieved through URIs that refers to content which can be delivered from a script or page in a different location. This is achieved through routes (rules that map matching URLs to specific controllers and actions).*

The filename extensions (.html and .cgi) provide no semantic information that is relevant to the user and actually cause problems in the long run. Changing the Web site to use PHP instead of CGI scripts, there are different URIs but serve exactly the same content. This is bad for the semantic value of the URIs, as well as the Google ranking! A Web browser will generally indicate its preferred content type using the Accept HTTP header. When asked for this resource, the Web server can check that header, note that text/html is one of the options, and serve an HTML page. If there is a mashup application that wants RDF, then the Accept header in the HTTP request should contain application/rdf+xml and the Web server, from the same URI, can serve an RDF version of the page.

It depends upon the choice of developer to shake hand with the Semantic Web in the Web site infrastructure; there are probably several opportunities to add structure to existing content on the Web site. This is the domain of Microformats, RDFa and GRDDL. The strong collaboration trends in Web 2.0 will only lead to more requirements for structured and semantically encoded data being available on the Web.

VARIOUS RESOURCES TO LEARN

- *The ultimate mashup : Web services and the semantic Web (Nicholas Chase, developerWorks, August 2006): Practice using Semantic Web techniques with this six-part tutorial series.*
- *Introduction to Jena : Use RDF models in the Java applications with the Jena Semantic Web Framework(Philip McCarthy, developerWorks, June 2004): Developer can find out how to use the Jena Semantic Web Toolkit to exploit RDF data models in the Java applications.*
- *Programmable Web : A great place to stay up to date with the latest on mashups and the new Web 2.0 APIs.*
- *The Structured Web : A Primer: An efficient reading of a general introduction to the value of structured data.*
- *The W3C's RDF Primer : A good source to use it effectively.*
- *A Semantic Web Primer for Object : Oriented Software Developers: A primer to learn how to use Ontologies, such as RDF Schema and OWL, in the context of OOP.*
- *The W3C's OWL Overview : A programmer can get an understanding of what OWL can do for apps that process information content instead of just presenting it to humans.*
- *The SPARQL Query Language for RDF specification: A source to explore the syntax and semantics of this query language for RDF.*
- *Notation3 : Developer can read about N3, a compact and readable alternative to RDF's XML syntax.*
- *Terse RDF Triple Language : Turtle is a textual syntax for RDF that writes RDF graphs in a compact and natural text form, with abbreviations for common usage patterns and datatypes. Turtle is compatable*

with existing N-Triples and Notation 3 formats and the triple pattern syntax of SPARQL.

COMPONENTS OF THE SEMANTIC WEB STACK

The semantic web comprises the standards and tools of XML, XML Schema, RDF, RDF Schema and OWL that are organized in the Semantic Web Stack. The OWL Web Ontology Language Overview describes the function and relationship of each of these components of the semantic web:

- *XML : It provides an elemental syntax for content structure within documents, yet associates no semantics with the meaning of the content contained within.*
- *XML Schema : It is a language for providing and restricting the structure and content of elements contained within XML documents.*
- *RDF : It is a simple language for expressing data models, which refer to objects ("resources") and their relationships. An RDF-based model can be represented in XML syntax.*
- *RDF Schema : It is a vocabulary for describing properties and classes of RDF-based resources, with semantics for generalized-hierarchies of such properties and classes.*
- *OWL : It adds more vocabulary for describing properties and classes: among others, relations between classes (e.g. disjointness), cardinality (e.g. "exactly one"), equality, richer typing of properties, characteristics of properties (e.g. symmetry), and enumerated classes.*
- *SPARQL : It is a protocol and query language for semantic web data sources.*

SEMANTIC WEB SOLUTIONS

The Semantic Web takes the solution further. It can be explained in the following steps:

1. *It involves publishing in languages specifically designed for data: Resource Description Framework (RDF), Web Ontology Language (OWL), and Extensible Markup Language (XML).*
2. *HTML describes documents and the links between them.*
3. *RDF, OWL, and XML, by contrast, can describe arbitrary things such as people, meetings, or airplane parts.*
4. *Combination of these technologies provides descriptions that supplement or replace the content of Web documents.*

Thus, content may manifest itself as descriptive data stored in Web-accessible databases, or as markup within documents (particularly, in Extensible HTML (XHTML) interspersed with XML, or, more often, purely in XML, with layout or rendering cues stored separately). The machine-readable descriptions enable content managers to add meaning to the content. It describes the structure of the knowledge about that content. A machine can process knowledge itself, instead of text, using processes similar to human deductive reasoning and inference. This process obtains more meaningful results and helping computers to perform automated information gathering and research.

SEMANTIC WEB LANGUAGES

RDF Schema and DAML are very powerful languages for creating languages. The Semantic Web works on a principle: the less rules, the better. This means that anyone can say anything about anything. The answer is (perhaps unfortunately!) no. Although the basic parts of the Semantic

Web and RDF are very minimally constraining, applications that are built on top of the Semantic Web will be designed to perform specific tasks, and as such will be very well defined. These are of following kinds:

a. *Scripting languages are lightweight and easy to learn, but on the other hand mature enough to be used within complex applications, as the Mozilla, Zope and CWM projects show. Large parts of the current Web rely on scripting languages such as Python, PHP, Perl, JavaScript, ASP, JSP, ActionScript and ColdFusion. These languages are the tools of a generation of web programmers who use them to quickly create server-side and client-side web applications. Support for scripting languages is widely deployed within the current web infrastructure: PHP for example is installed on 16 million domains. It is therefore likely that scripting languages will also play a crucial role in the Semantic Web gaining critical mass. Many deployed Semantic Web applications are already using these languages e.g. in the FOAF and RSS communities. It is likely that the process of RDF-izing existing database-backed websites, wikis, weblogs and CMS will largely rely on scripting languages.*

b. *A proof language is simply a language that helping to prove truth ness of a statement. An instance of a proof language will generally consist of a list of inference "items" that have been used to derive the information in question, and the trust information for each of those items that can then be checked. The file speaks for itself, and when processed using CWM, does indeed work, producing the intended output. CWM doesn't have the capability to automatically check file checksums or digital signatures, but it is only a matter of time before a proper Semantic Web trust engine is written.*

LIFE CYCLE OF SEMANTIC WEB SERVICES

Semantic Web services do have a life cycle, right from deployment to its invocation. The life cycle of Semantic Web services comprises different stages like service modeling, service discovery, service definition and service delivery.

1. Beginning : The life cycle begins with modeling the web service and the service request by the provider and the consumer respectively.

2. Development of web services descriptions : Web service descriptions are developed using models like OWL-S, WSMO.

3. Service definition : Service descriptions are used in the discovery stage on which discovery algorithms, matchmaking techniques are applied.

4. Delivery stage : Once a set of service providers are identified for a service requester, service definition takes place to select the concrete service. Finally, the concrete service is delivered to the service requester in the delivery phase.

Currently, HTML pages on the web are designed to be read by humans, and information is found using internet search engines. Earlier searching for information was not a good use of people's time. Due to developments on the web, people will be able to use their PC or mobile device to access information in a seamless way, based on who they are. Information strategies are being framed. Some of the information will arise from data tagging standards that are being developed for the web. The semantic web has the ability to improve decision-making.

UNDERSTANDING THE SCHEMA LAYER

The basic model of the RDF allows doing a lot on the blackboard, but does not give many tools. It gives a model of assertions and quotations on which the data can be mapped in any new format. A schema layer is required to declare the existence of new property. Sometimes it required to constrain the types of object it can apply to. These meta-assertions make it possible to do rudimentary checks on a document. Much as in SGML the "DTD" allows one to check whether elements have been used in appropriate positions, so in RDF a schema will allow us to check that, for example, a driver's license has the name of a person, and not a model of car, as its "name".

The schema language typically makes simple assertions about permitted combinations. If the SGML DTD is used as a model, the schema can be in a language of very limited power. The constraints expressed in the schema language are easily expanded into more powerful logical layer expressions (the next layer). This uses logical expressions which are not available at this level, but that is OK so long as the schema language is, for the moment, going to be handled by specialized schema engines only, not by a general reasoning engine.

WHAT IS THE LOGICAL LAYER?

The logical layer requires ways of writing logic into documents to allow. The next layer is predicate logic (not, and, etc) and the next layer quantification (for all x, y(x)). The applications of RDF at this level are basically limited only by the imagination. The availability of a language which has the great power of predicate calculus with quotation, will allow when defining a new language for a specific application, two things are required:

- *One must settle on the (limited) power of the reasoning engine which the receiver must have, and define a subset of full RDF which will be expected to be understood;*
- *One will probably want to define some abbreviated functions to efficiently transmit expressions within the*

set of documents within the constrained language.

The RDF model does not say anything about the form of reasoning engine. There is no definitively perfect algorithm for answering questions (or, basically, finding proofs).

EVOLUTION RULES LANGUAGE

RDF at the logical level already has the power to express inference rules. Two fundamental functions required to be done by RDF engines are:

1. *for a version n implementation to be able to read enough RDF schema to be able to deduce how to read a version n+1 document;*
2. *for a type A application developed quite independently of a type B application which has the same or similar function to be able to read and process enough schema information to be able to process data from the type B application.*

QUERY LANGUAGES

A query engine has specific algorithms and indexes available with which to work, and can therefore answer specific sorts of query. A query can be thought of as an assertion about the result to be returned. RDF at the logical level is sufficient to represent this in any case. A vocabulary which helps in either of two ways:

1. *It allows common powerful query types to be expressed succinctly with fewer pages of mathematics, or*
2. *It allows certain constrained queries to be expressed, which are interesting because they have certain computability properties.*

For example, SQL is a query language. The query language can be defined in terms of RDF logic. One useful step the specification of specific query engines for example searches to a finite level of depth in a specified subset of the Web (such as a web site). Various Semantic Web languages are listed as below:

- *Ontology Inference Layer (OIL)*
- *DARPA Agent Markup Language (DAML)*
- DAML+OIL
- *Web Ontology Language (OWL)*
- *Resource Description Framework (RDF)*
- *Web Services Modeling Language (WSML)*
- *Web Services Semantics (WSDL-S)*
- *SAWSDL*

SEARCHING IN THE FUTURE

While search engines which index HTML pages return many inappropriate answers. Logical engines have typically been able to restrict their output to that which is provably correct answer, but have suffered from the inability to rummage through the mass of intertwined data to construct valid answers. If an engine combines a reasoning engine with a search engine, it may be able to construct proofs in a certain number of cases of very real impact. Indexes contain very complete lists of all occurrences of a given term. Search engines use logic to weed out all but those which can be of use in solving the given problem.

Using RDF rather than XML has two reasons:

(i) *The benefit that one gets from drafting a language in RDF is that the information maps directly and unambiguously to a model, a model which is decentralized, and for which there are many generic parsers already available. In an RDF application, user knows about the bits of data that are the semantics of the application, as well as the bits which are just syntactic fluff.*

(ii) RDF data will become a part of the Semantic Web. XML Schema is a language for restricting the syntax of XML applications. Built in BNF in RDF sets out how the language is to be used. However, using XML Schema in conjunction with RDF may be useful for creating datatypes and so on.

SEMANTIC WEB SERVICES

Semantic Web Services (like other conventional web services) are the server end of a client-server system for machine-to-machine interaction via the World Wide Web. Semantic services are a component of the semantic web because they use markup which makes data machine-readable in a detailed and sophisticated way. The mainstream XML standards for interoperation of web services specify only syntactic interoperability, not the semantic meaning of messages.

Semantic web services are built around standards, which are universal in nature, for the interchange of semantic data. This makes it easy for programmers to combine data from different sources and services without losing meaning. Web services can be activated "behind the scenes". For this a web browser makes a request to a web server, which then uses various web services to construct sophisticated reply. Semantic web services can also be used by automatic programs that run without any connection to a web browser.

Semantic Web Service frameworks are as following:

- *WSMF*
- *OWL-S*
- *QuASAR.*
- *WSMO*
- *IRS-III*
- *METEOR-S*
- *HALEY*

- *BioMOBY (Bioinformatics)*

The ESSI (European Semantic Systems Initiative) brought together six European FP6 projects working in the domains of Semantic Web Services and semantically empowered service-oriented architectures.

- o *Adaptive Services Grid (ASG)*
- o *Data Information and Process Integration with Semantic Web Services (DIP)*
- o *Knowledge Web*
- o *Semantic Knowledge Technologies (SEKT)*
- o *Semantics Utilized for Process management within and between Enterprises (SUPER)*
- o *Triple Space Communication (TripCom)*

Various other projects are listed below:

QuASAR : Quality Assurance of Semantic Annotations for Services. A project of the school of computer science, University of Manchester.

SWSI : The Semantic Web Services Initiative is an ad hoc initiative of academic and industrial researchers, many of which are involved in DARPA and research projects funded by the European Community.

METEOR-S : A project of the LSDIS Lab, University of Georgia and Kno.e.sis Center, Wright State University.

HALEY : A Web service composition project of the LSDIS Lab, University of Georgia

http://knoesis.wright.edu/. Semantics (Services, Science) : The 3S project at the kno.e.sis center, Wright State University, Dayton, OH.

SEMANTIC WEB SERVICES INITIATIVE (SWSI)

The Semantic Web Services Initiative (SWSI) is an ad hoc initiative of academic and industrial researchers, many of which are involved in DARPA and EU funded research projects. The SWSI mission is threefold:

- *to create infrastructure that combines Semantic Web and Web Services technologies to enable maximal automation and dynamism in all aspects of Web service provision and use, including (but not limited to) discovery, selection, composition, negotiation, invocation, monitoring and recovery;*
- *to coordinate ongoing research initiatives in the Semantic Web Services area;*
- *to promote the results of SWSI work to academia and industry.*

COMPOSITION OF SEMANTIC WEB

- *Metadata : Metadata is the word used to mean "data about data". This extra data that is meaningful to tools, it is sometimes described that information as being semantic (it means "meaning"). In different ways this meaningful information gets created. Content developers can embed metadata in a webpage. Filtering software uses such information. Publishers might embed metadata simply to make their pages more useful. Metadata files can be created describing something on the web and place those files on a web server that a user owns. Meta-data describes a worldview; incompatibility is an inevitable by-product of vigorous argument. It is difficult to enforce semantics on human situations; it ends up debasing the semantics, rather then making the connection more informative.*
- *On The Fly Text Parsing : Few tools attempt to discover meaningful information by scanning through the text of the document while user is viewing it. Few other tools can understand grammar structures in the sentences of the text and guess information based on that information. For example, Microsoft's MindNet and Princeton's WordNet are such two databases that*

might be used to understand the structure of sentences. The databases list of words and relationships are meant to cover the entire spectrum of commonly-used words. In future, tools that extract semantic information on the fly might be provided free with software as a value-add.

- *Service Provided by Site : Some sites (e.g. the Microsoft Developer Network (MSDN) and CNET's news.com) would offer to add their own metadata directly through an interface provided by the site. Such websites use different web-based interfaces for adding comments, and both sites store all of the user-entered metadata in systems controlled by the site.*

GOALS OF SEMANTIC WEB

The Semantic Web, related with simple aspects, is divided between following goals:

(i) *The first goal is simple : get people to use more meta-data. The Semantic Web was one of the earliest efforts to rely on the idea of XML as a common interchange format for data.*

(ii) *An ontology seemed a logical next step : But the meta-data came into picture without needing the ontology.*

The Semantic Web imagines that completeness and correctness of data exposed on the web are the cardinal virtues, and that any amount of implementation complexity is acceptable in pursuit of those virtues. The systems that have succeeded at scale have made simple implementation the core virtue, up the stack from Ethernet over Token Ring to the web over gopher and WAIS. The URL regards semantics as a side conversation between consenting adults, and makes no requirements in this regard whatsoever.

The fact that a URL itself doesn't have to mean anything is essential. The Web succeeded in part because it does not try to make any assertions about the meaning of the documents it contained. The Semantic Web, with its neat ontologies and its syllogistic logic, requires too much coordination and too much energy to effect in the real world, where deductive logic is less effective and shared worldview is harder to create than we often want to admit. The amount of meta-data is increasing dramatically. The issues related with Semantic Web are discussed below:

(i) Aggregation : Systems (like Google) aggregate the many pages from the World Wide Web into a cohesive database that user can search. Developers are working on similar systems for RDF data, to create a sort of Semantic Google. There are two main approaches:

- *The centralized one, where all the data is collected onto one system;*
- *The decentralized one, where the data is organized across many computers, each taking responsibility for a different portion.*

One of the important parts of the aggregation process is keeping track of activities or statements. RDF databases can use this information to better answer queries.

(ii) Security : RDF builds a "Web of Trust". It takes into account who user trusts and how much he trusts them. Further it builds a Web that interconnects almost everyone. RDF also uses digital signatures for confirmation of the sources of triples.

(iii) Logic : Logic provides a way for to express rules that take in triples and output new ones in RDF. It has following feature:

- *Inference Engines are the tools that take in rules and data and process them, writing out the resulting RDF triples.*
- *Programming using rules is what's called declarative programming, and is often simpler*

than writing out code to do the work.

- *It also makes it easy for others to use user-specified rules, and since rules are just RDF, user can have rules that operate on rules. In the future, it's possible that there will be inference engines searching through the Web, looking for interesting inferences to make.*

SEMANTIC WEB APPLICATIONS

The Semantic Web activity demonstrates how RDF and Semantic Web technologies can be applied to the W3C Process to increase efficiency, reliability, etc. RDFWeb is a RDF database driven hypermedia blogspace. It is a site where all information is stored as RDF, and then that RDF used to render XHTML. Intelligent software agents automatically give a single, customized answer to a particular question without our having to search for information or pore through results.

There would be a common language for:

(i) *representing data that could be understood by all kinds of software agents; ontologies (sets of statements) that translate information from disparate databases into common terms;*

(ii) *and rules that allow software agents to reason about the information described in those terms.*

The data format, ontologies and reasoning software would operate like one big application on the World Wide Web. These are analyzing all the raw data stored in online databases as well as all the data about the text, images, video and communications the Web contained. Like the Web itself, the Semantic Web aided by working groups within the World Wide Web Consortium, which helps to advance the global medium. Semantic Web would not be too difficult for people to understand or exploit. Not so. The enabling technologies made the Semantic Web practical to use:

(i) Large companies have major projects under way that will greatly improve the efficiencies of in-house operations and of scientific research.

(ii) Other firms are using the Semantic Web to enhance business-to-business interactions and to build the hidden data-processing structures, or back ends, behind new consumer services.

The Semantic Web is not different from the World Wide Web. It is an enhancement that gives the Web far greater utility. It comes to life when people immersed in a certain field or vocation, whether it be genetic research or hip-hop music, agree on common schemes for representing information they care about. As more groups develop these taxonomies, Semantic Web tools allow them to link their schemes and translate their terms, gradually expanding the number of people and communities whose Web software can understand one another automatically. For example, British Telecom has built a prototype online service to help its many vendors more effectively develop new products together. Categorization is explained as below:

- *Various companies use the Semantic Web internally to more accurately and inexpensively generate geographic maps and few of them are improving the back-end operations of consumer services.*
- *Some companies are using Semantic Web software to manage the schedules and program guides that viewers use online.*
- *Consumers are also beginning to use the data language and ontologies directly.*
- *Companies are moving toward building a Semantic Web where relations can be established among any online pieces of information, whether an item is a document, photograph, tag, financial transaction, experiment result or abstract concept.*

- *Ontologies and other technologies are helping to create, query, classify and reason about those relations.*
- *Few of the companies are promoting open-source Semantic Web frameworks—common tools for crafting polished programs. For example, Oracle's flagship commercial database, 10g, used by thousands of corporations worldwide, already supports RDF, and the upgrade, 11g, adds further Semantic Web technology.*
- *Few smaller vendors offer Semantic Web database programs and ontology editors that are akin to the HTML browsers and editors that facilitated the Web's vibrant growth.*

The Semantic Web thus permits workers in different organizations to use their own data labels instead of trying to agree industry-wide on one rigid set. The Semantic Web enables the deployment of software programs that can discover relations among data sources. Semantic Web sites can now be built with virtually all of today's major computer programming languages, including Java, Perl and C++. Case studies of real systems built by these pioneers show how powerful the Semantic Web can be. Search engines on the World Wide Web cannot provide a single answer to a broad-ranging question. For example, a new Semantic Web engine called pediax can, by analyzing different concepts (top, in approximated form) found on Wikipedia's seven million online pages. Pediax, which grew from the DBpedia project to extract information from Wiki-pedia, provides a clean result (bottom) that merges text and images. The Semantic Web is about two things. It is about common formats for integration and combination of data drawn from diverse sources, where on the original Web mainly concentrated on the interchange of documents. It is also about language for recording how the data relates to real world objects.

ACTIVE GROUPS

1. Semantic Web Coordination Group

The Semantic Web Coordination Group is providing a forum for managing the interrelationships and interdependencies among groups focusing on standards and technologies that relate to the goals of the Semantic Web Activity. This group is designed to coordinate, facilitate and (where possible) help shape the efforts of other related groups to avoid duplication of effort and fragmentation of the Semantic Web by way of incompatible standards and technologies.

2. Rules Interchange Format Working Group

This Working Group is chartered to produce a core rule language plus extensions which together allow rules to be translated between rule languages and thus transferred between rule systems. In future, the Working Group will have to balance the needs of a community diverse including Business Rules and Semantic users Web specifying extensions for which it can articulate a consensus design and which are sufficiently motivated by use cases.

3. RDB2RDF Working Group

The mission of the RDB2RDF Working Group (part of the Semantic Web Activity) is to standardize a language for mapping relational data and relational database schemas into RDF and OWL, tentatively called the RDB2RDF Mapping Language, R2RML.

4. SPARQL Working Group

It was formerly known as RDF Data Access Working Group. It developed the SPARQL Query Language recommendation published in January 2008. The group is currently chartered to make small updates to the SPARQL specification that have been identified as users and implementers as feasible and useful extensions.

6. Semantic Web Interest Group

The Semantic Web Interest Group is a forum for W3C Members and non-Members to discuss innovative applications of the Semantic Web. The Interest Group also initiates discussion on potential future work items related to enabling technologies that support the Semantic Web, and the relationship of that work to other activities of W3C and to the broader social and legal context in which the Web is situated.

7. Semantic Web Health Care and Life Sciences Interest Group

The Semantic Web Health Care and Life Sciences Interest Group is designed to improve collaboration, research and development, and innovation adoption in the health care and life science industries. Aiding decision-making in clinical research, Semantic Web technologies will bridge many forms of biological and medical information across institutions.

COMPLETED GROUPS

The following groups have completed their deliverables:

1. OWL Working Group

The mission of the OWL Working Group was to produce a W3C Recommendation that refined and extended the 2004 version of OWL. The proposed extensions are a small set that: have been identified by users as widely needed, and have been identified by tool implementers as reasonable and feasible extensions to current tools.

PAST GROUPS

1. RDF Core Working Group

The RDF Core Working Group was chartered to

consider update to the RDF Model and Syntax Recommendation, and to a few revisions to the RDF Schema specification.

2. Web Ontology Working Group

The Web Ontology Working Group was chartered to build upon the RDF Core work a language for defining structured web based ontologies which will provide richer integration and interoperability of data among descriptive communities.

3. Semantic Web Best Practices and Deployment Working Group

The focus of the Semantic Web Best Practices and Deployment Working Group was to provide hands-on support for developers of Semantic Web applications.

4. Semantic Web Education and Outreach Interest Group

The Semantic Web Education and Outreach Interest Group (SWEO) was chartered to collect proof-of-concept business cases, demonstration prototypes, etc, based on successful implementations of Semantic Web technologies, collect user experiences, develop and facilitate community outreach strategies, training and educational resources.

5. POWDER Working Group

The mission of the Protocol for Web Description Resources (POWDER) Working Group is to develop a mechanism through which structured metadata ("Description Resources") can be authenticated and applied to groups of Web resources. This mechanism was intended to allow retrieval of the description resources without retrieval of the resources they described.

6. GRDDL Working Group

The mission of this Working Group was to complement

the concrete RDF/XML syntax with a mechanism to relate other XML syntaxes (especially XHTML dialects or "microformats") to the RDF abstract syntax via transformations identified by URIs.

THE SEMANTIC WEB GOES UP!

The Semantic Web is an extension of the current Web in which information is given well-defined meaning, enabling computers and people to work in better cooperation. The W3C Semantic Web Activity is tasked with defining standards and technologies that allow data on the Web to be defined and linked in a way that it can be used for more effective discovery, automation, integration, and reuse across applications. It is supposed to provide environment where data can be shared and processed by automated tools as well as by people. The raw information that may answer the routine questions may indeed be on the Web, but it's not in a machine-usable form. User still needs a person to discern the meaning of the information and its relevance to the needs. The Semantic Web addresses this problem in two ways.

- *(i) First, it tends to enable communities to expose their data so that a program doesn't have to strip the formatting, pictures and ads from a Web page to guess at the relevant bits of information.*
- *(ii) Secondly, it plans to allow people to write (or generate) files which explain - to a machine - the relationship between different sets of data.*

This will allow machines to follow links and facilitate the integration of data from many different sources. This notion of being able to semantically link various resources (documents, images, people, concepts, etc) is an important one. This can provide a platform to move from the current Web of simple hyperlinks to a more expressive semantically rich Web. This kind of web will allow expressing a whole new set of relationships among resources, making explicit the particular contextual relationships that are implicit in the current Web. This will open new doors for effective information integration, management and automated services.

FUNDAMENTAL STANDARDS

Uniform Resource Identifiers (URIs) are a fundamental component of the current Web and are a foundation of the Semantic Web. The Extensible Markup Language (XML) is also a fundamental component for supporting the Semantic Web. XML provides an interoperable syntactical foundation upon which the more important issue of representing relationships and meaning can be built. URIs provide the ability for uniquely identifying resources as well as relationships among resources. The RDF family of standards leverages URIs and XML to provide an stepwise set of functionality to represent these relationships and meaning. The base level of the RDF family of standards is a W3C Recommendation. Modification of the original RDF Model and Syntax Recommendation provides a simple yet powerful framework for representing information in the Web.

Simple data integration, aggregation and interoperability are enabled by these base level RDF standards. An increasing need for interoperability at a more expressive descriptive level is also desired. The Web Ontology Working Group is charted to build upon the RDF Core work a language for defining structured, Web-based ontologies. Ontologies can be used by automated tools to power advanced services such as more accurate Web search, intelligent software agents and knowledge management. Web portals, corporate website management, intelligent agents and ubiquitous computing are just some of the identified scenarios that helped shaped the requirements for this work.

SEMANTIC WEB ADVANCED DEVELOPMENT (SWAD)

The W3C Semantic Web Advanced Development (SWAD) initiatives are designed to work in collaboration with a large number of researchers and industrial partners and stimulate complementary areas of development that will help facilitate the deployment and future standards work associated with the Semantic Web.

1. SWAD DAML : The purpose of the SWAD DAML project is to contribute to the development of a vibrant, ubiquitous Semantic Web by building critical Semantic Web infrastructure and demonstrating how that infrastructure can be used by working, user-oriented applications. SWAD DAML is designed to build on the DARPA Agent Markup Language (DAML) infrastructure to provide an interchange between two or more different applications:

(i) The first involves structured information manipulation required to maintain the ongoing activities of an organization such as the W3C. These include access control, collaborative development, and meeting management.

(ii) The second application is focused on the informal and often heuristic processes involved in document management in a personalized information environment. Integrated into both environments will be tools to enable authors to control terms under which personal or sensitive information is used by others, a critical feature to encourage sharing of semantic content.

2. SWAD-Europe : SWAD-Europe is about practical examples of where real value can be added to the Web through Semantic Web technologies. The focus on this initiative is on providing practical demonstrations of how the Semantic Web can address problems in areas such as: site maps, news channel syndication, thesauri, classification, topic maps, calendaring, scheduling, collaboration, annotations, quality ratings, shared bookmarks, Dublin Core for simple resource discovery, Web service description and discovery, trust and rights management and how to effectively and efficiently integrate these technologies together.

SWAD PROJECTS

1. Project SWAD Simile : W3C has been additionally working with HP, MIT Libraries, and MIT's Lab for Computer Science on Simile, which seeks to enhance interoperability among digital assets, schemas, metadata, and services across distributed individual, community, and institutional stores and across value chains that provide useful end-user services by drawing upon the assets, schemas, and metadata held in such stores. The project also aims to implement a digital asset dissemination architecture based upon Web standards, enabling services to operate upon relevant assets, schemas, and metadata within distributed stores. Such an approach will lead to a powerful deployment channel through which the utility and readiness of Semantic Web tools and techniques can be compellingly demonstrated in a visible and global community.

2. SWAD Oxygen : The MIT/LCS Oxygen project was designed to enable pervasive, human-centered computing through a combination of specific user and system technologies. Oxygen's user technologies directly address human needs. Speech and vision technologies enable us to communicate with Oxygen as if user is interacting with another person, saving much time and effort. Automation, individualized knowledge access, and collaboration technologies help us perform a wide variety of tasks in the way developer/user likes to do them. In Oxygen, these technologies enable the formation of spontaneous collaborative regions that provide support for recording, archiving, and linking fragments of meeting records to issues, summaries, keywords, and annotations.

The Semantic Web is designed to foster similar collaborative environment and the W3C is working with project Oxygen to help support this goal. The ability for "anyone to say anything about anything" is an important characteristic of the current Web and is a fundamental principle of the Semantic Web. Knowing who is making these assertions is increasingly important in trusting these descriptions and enabling a 'Web of Trust'. The Annotea advanced development project provides the basis for asserting descriptive information, comments, notes, reviews, explanations, or other types of external remarks to any resource. Together with XML digital signatures, the Annotea project will provide a test-bed for 'Web-of-Trust' Semantic Web applications.

FEW CONSIDERATIONS

Many existing fields for knowledge representation and data management have typically made assumptions regarding a conceptually or physically centralized system, and as such their application to the Semantic Web is not straightforward. There are few questions, arising naturally:

(i) *Given a mass of rules relating data in different vocabularies, and an unbounded set of datasets in different vocabularies, what algorithms will efficiently resolve general queries?*

(ii) *What conventions for the storage of tips and pointers will allow data to be reused and converted automatically?*

(iii) *What techniques will allow a system to operate securely while processing very diverse data from untrusted agents?*

(iii) *How can one represent - and then implement - personal privacy in such a world?*

The Semantic Web starts as a simple circles-and-arrows diagram relating things, which slowly expands and coalesces to become global and vast. The Web of human-readable documents spawned a social revolution. The Semantic Web may in turn spawn a revolution in computing. In the near future, more RDF content and Semantic Web Services are likely to become available, along with interesting and novel ways to use them.

REFERENCES

1. http://semanticweb.org/index.php?title=Main_Page&action=edit
2. SOA Definitions - Semantic Web. http://searchsoa.techtarget.com/home/0,289692,sid26,00.html
3. http://searchsoa.techtarget.com/sDefinition/0,,sid26_gci213331,00.html
4. http://www.w3.org/
5. http://sweet.jpl.nasa.gov/guide.doc
6. Information Management: A Proposal, 1989. http://www.w3.org/History/1989/proposal.html
7. Business Plan for the Semantic Web, 2001. http://www.w3.org/DesignIssues/Business
8. http://www.ietf.org/rfc/rfc2396.txt
9. http://www.darpa.mil/
10. http://www.daml.org/
11. http://purl.org/swag/whatIsSW
12. http://www.opensource.org/
13. http://www.hpl.hp.com/semweb/
14. http://www.w3.org/TR/owl-features/
15. http://knoesis.wright.edu/
16. WSMF. http://www.swsi.org/resources/wsmf-paper.pdf
17. IRS-III. http://kmi.open.ac.uk/projects/irs/
18. METEOR-S. http://lsdis.cs.uga.edu/projects/meteor-s/
19. HALEY. http://denali.cs.uga.edu/haley
20. Belhajjame, K., Embury, S.M., Paton, N.W., Stevens, R. and Goble, A.C., (April 2008). "Automatic Annotations of Semantic Web Services Based on Workflow Definitions". ACM Transactions on the

Web 2 (2): 1–34. doi:10.1145/1346337.1346239. http://portal.acm.org/citation.cfm?doid=1346337.1346239.

21. *Sinuhe Arroyo et al. (2004). Semantic Aspects of Web Services in Practical Handbook of Internet Computing. Chapman Hall and CRC Press.*
22. *Cardoso, J., Sheth, Amit (Eds.), (2006). Semantic Web Services, Processes and Applications. Springer. ISBN 0-387-30239-5.*
23. *Zeng, Honglei; T.C. Son (March 2001). "Semantic Web Services" (PDF). Intelligent Systems (IEEE) 16: 46–53. http://ieeexplore.ieee.org/iel5/9670/19905/00920599.pdf.*
24. *Kuropka, D.; Tröger, P.; Staab, S.; Weske, M. (Eds.) (2008). Semantic Service Provisioning. Springer. http://www.springer.com/computer/database+management+&+information+retrieval/book/978-3-540-78616-0.*
25. *Information Management: A Proposal, 1989. http://www.w3.org/History/1989/proposal.html*
26. *Business Plan for the Semantic Web, 2001. http://www.w3.org/DesignIssues/Business*
27. *http://www.w3.org/People/Berners-Lee/Weaving/Overview.html*
28. *http://www.iana.org/*
29. *http://zooko.com/distnames.html*
30. *http://www.sciencemag.org/cgi/content/full/299/5606/520?ijkey=1BUgJQXW4nU7Q&keytype=ref&siteid=sci*
31. *http://www.ietf.org/rfc/rfc2396.txt*
32. *http://www.w3.org/Addressing/schemes*
33. *The Semantic Web in Action. Lee Feigenbaum, Ivan Herman, Tonya Hongsermeier, Eric Neumann and Susie Stephens (http://www.thefigtrees.net/lee/sw/sciam/semantic-web-in-action#authors.)*
34. *http://www.pearsonified.com/2007/04/definitive-guide-to-semantic-markup.php#comments*
35. *http://www.freebase.com/edit/topic/en/semantic_web*
36. *Semantic Web Tutorial. http://www.w3schools.com/semweb/default.asp*
37. *http://www.w3schools.com/semweb/semantic_example.asp*
38. *http://jena.sourceforge.net/index.html*
39. *http://www.ibm.com/developerworks/xml/library/x-*

plansemantic/#ibm-pcon

40. *Rob Crowther. Planning a Semantic Web site: Prepare the site for structured datahttp://www.ibm.com/developerworks/xml/library/x-plansemantic/#ibm-pcon*
41. *Life cycle. http://www.semanticfocus.com/blog/entry/title/semantic-web-service-life-cycle-and-service-modeling/*
42. *Semantic web 'ready to implement', by Cliff Saran. http://www.computerweekly.com/Articles/2006/05/30/216145/Semantic-web-39ready-to-implement39.htm?printerfriendly=true*
43. *Tim Berners-Lee. Semantic Web Road map http://www.w3.org/DesignIssues/Overview.html*
44. *What the Semantic Web is not http://www.w3.org/DesignIssues/RDFnot.html*
45. *The basic assertion model . RDF Model and Syntax Specification http://www.w3.org/TR/WD-rdf-syntax/*
46. *Semantic Web Services Initiative (SWSI). www.swsi.org*
47. *Joshua Allen. Making a Semantic Web. Ontology is Not A Requirement http://www.shirky.com/writings/semantic_syllogism.html#ontology_is_not_a_requirement*
48. *http://216.239.41.104/search?q=cache:fosg_EhEDo4J:aoir.org/members/papers4/rothenberg_aoir.pdf&hl=en&ie=UTF-8*
49. *Artificial Intelligence Reborn. http://www.shirky.com/writings/semantic_syllogism.html#artificial_intelligence_reborn*
50. *Worldviews Differ For Good Reasons. http://www.shirky.com/writings/semantic_syllogism.html#worldviews_differ_for_good_reasons*
51. *http://www.shirky.com/writings/semantic_syllogism.html#worse_is_better*
52. *http://www.w3.org/DesignIssues/Semantic.html*
53. *Semantic Web Applications. Circles and arrows diagrams using stylesheet rules, Dan Connolly. http://www.w3.org/2001/02pd/*
54. *Dan Brickley et al.'s RDFWeb. http://rdfweb.org/*
55. *http://www.thefigtrees.net/lee/sw/sciam/semantic-web-in-action#foaf*
56. *http://www.thefigtrees.net/lee/sw/sciam/semantic-web-in-action#to-combining-concepts*
57. *W3C Semantic Web Activity*
58. *http://www.w3.org/2001/sw/*

59. *The Semantic Web lifts off by Tim Berners-Lee and Eric Miller. Contents ERCIM News No. 51, October 2002 http://www.ercim.org/publication/Ercim_News/enw51/index.html*

60. *The Semantic Web in Education. Jason Ohler. The Semantic Web in Education. http://creativecommons.org/licenses/by/3.0/. EDUCAUSE Quarterly, vol. 31, no. 4 (October–December 2008)*

GLOSSARY

A

Adblock: Adblock allows users to prevent page elements, such as advertisements, from being downloaded and displayed. Ad blocking is removing or altering advertising content in a Web page. Advertising can exist in a variety of forms including pictures, animations, text, or pop-up windows.

Aggregation: It is the process of gathering and remixing content from blogs and other websites that provide RSS feeds. The results are displayed in an aggregator website like Bloglines or Google Reader.

Application Programming Interface (API): An API is a documented interface that allows one software application to interact with another application.

Archive : It is a list of previous blog posts, in chronological order. It is also to place files or blog posts in a safer place for longer-term or backup storage. An archive may refer to topics from an online discussion that has been closed but saved for later reference.

Asynchronous communications: These are independent of time or place, and messages go to and fro rather than appearing in one place at almost the same time (synchronous communication). Examples of asynchronous communication are email lists, bulletin boards and forums.

Atom: Atom is a simple way to read and write information on the web, allowing user to easily keep track of more sites in less time, and to seamlessly share words and ideas by publishing to the web. Atom is designed to be a universal publishing standard for personal content and weblogs.

Atom feed: A feed contains entries, which may be headlines, full-text articles, excerpts, summaries, and/or links to content on a website, along with various metadata.

AtomPub: Atom Publishing Protocol (AtomPub or APP) is a simple HTTP-based protocol for creating and updating web resources

Attribute: Attributes are used in an HTML tag to give an instruction to a Web browser.

Authenticity: It is the sense that something or someone is "real". Blogs enable people to publish content, and engage in conversations, that show their interests and values, and so help them develop an authentic voice online.

Avatars: These are graphical images representing people. User can build a visual character with the body, clothes, behaviors, gender and name of his choice. This may or may not be an authentic representation of user. An Avatar is an image or username that represents a person online within forums and social networks.

B

BackType: BackType is a social media analytics company that helps companies measuring their social engagement. Previously the service started as a blog comment search engine.

Back channel: These types of communications are private emails or other messages sent by the facilitator or between individuals during public conferencing. They can have a significant effect on the way that public conversations go.

BPEL: BPEL (Business Process Execution Language), short for Web Services Business Process Execution Language (WS-BPEL) is an OASIS standard executable language for specifying actions within business processes with web services. Processes in BPEL export and import information by using web service interfaces exclusively.

Bit.ly: Bit.ly is a free URL shortening service that provides statistics for the links users share online.

Block: It is a tool to stop all contact with a MySpace user. None can comment on the blog page or send user any message that user actually receive.

Blog: Basically it is a combination of the words Web and log. Bloggers (individuals, groups, or businesses) post a chronological log of information. Content is determined entirely by the author(s) of the blog; many are personal journals. These are websites with dated items of content in reverse chronological order, self-published by bloggers. Items – sometimes called posts - may have keyword tags associated with them, are usually available as feeds, and often allow commenting.

Blog Talk Radio: Blog Talk Radio is a free web application that allows users to host live online radio shows.

Blogger: Blogger is a free blogging platform owned by Google that allows individuals and companies to host and publish a blog typically on a subdomain. Example: itforpeace.blogspot.com

Blogosphere: It is the term used to describe the totality of blogs on the Internet, and the conversations taking place within that sphere.

Blog post: It is an entry in a blog, possibly containing text, images, and other media.

Blogroll: A Blogroll is a list of sites displayed in the sidebar of blog, showing who the blogger reads regularly.

Blogger: The author of a blog.

Blogging policy: The Blogging Policy refers to what others are allowed to post in a blog.

Blogging software: The blogging software enable user to blog.

Blogroll: A collection of links used or recommended by a blogger.

BoardReader: BoardReader is a free search engine that allows users to search for keywords only in posts and titles of online forums, a popular forum of social networking.

Bookmarking: By bookmarking, a user is saving the address of a website or item of content, either in user's brower, or on a social bookmarking site like del.icio.us. If user adds tags, others can easily use his research too, and the social bookmarking site becomes an emormous public library.

Boxee : Boxee is a social video application that allows users to watch online videos on their TVs and computers. Users can share and watch videos from a variety of online videos sources for free.

Bulletin boards : These were the early vehicles for online collaboration, where users are connected with a central computer to post and read email-like messages. They were the electronic equivalent of public notice boards. The term is still used for forums.

C

Categories: These are pre-specified ways to organize content - for example, a set of keywords that user can use but not add to when posting on a site. They form part of taxonomy.

CERN: CERN, the European Organization for Nuclear Research, is one of the world's largest and most respected centres for scientific research. The name is derived from the acronym for the French Conseil Européen pour la Recherche Nucléaire, or European Council for Nuclear Research, a provisional body founded in 1952 with the mandate of establishing a world-class fundamental physics research organization in Europe. At that time, pure physics research concentrated on understanding the inside of the atom, hence the word 'nuclear'. Its business is fundamental physics, finding out what the Universe is made of and how it works.

Champions: This is a group of enthusiasts willing and confident to get things moving by posting messages, responding, and helping others.

Chat: It is kind of text-based interaction on a web site at the same time. It differs from a forum as the conversations happen in "real time".

Collaboration: For collaboration, there are various social media tools such as email lists to virtual worlds. Low-risk activities like commenting, social bookmarking, chatting and blogging help develop the trust necessary for collaboration.

Collecta: Collecta is a real-time search engine that includes results from blogs, microblogs, news feeds and photo sharing services as they are published.

Collective Intelligence: Collective Intelligence is a shared or group intelligence that emerges from the collaboration and competition of many individuals and appears in consensus decision-making in social networks.

Comment: A piece of feedback left by a reader on a blog post, or to leave such a comment. Blogs may allow readers to add comments under items. It allows user keeping up with conversations without having to revisit the site to check whether anything has been added.

Community building: It is the process about network participants, helping them to find shared interests and goals, use the technology, and develop useful conversations.

Cookie: It is a short piece of computer code, stored on user's computer, that enables Web sites to remember certain settings and information the next time user visit that site.

Craigslist: It is a popular online commerce site in which users sell a variety of goods and services to other users.

CTSS: Control time-Sharing System (CTSS) and Multics Compatible Time Sharing System. This IBM 7094 timesharing operating system was created at MIT Project MAC and first demonstrated in 1961. It was used as the programming and debugging tool during initial Multics programming and bringup by Project MAC, GE CISL, and BTL personnel. In some sense the intellectual offspring of CTSS, Multics was conceived as the next step into the future of multiple-access computing. Many of the MIT Multics principals had worked on the earlier system.

CWM: Cwm (pronounced coom) is a general-purpose data processor for the semantic web, somewhat like sed, awk, etc. for text files or XSLT for XML. It is a forward chaining reasoner which can be used for querying, checking, transforming and filtering information. Its core language is RDF, extended to include rules, and it uses RDF/XML or RDF/N3 serializations as required. Cwm is written in python; it is part of SWAP (a Semantic Web Application Platform). It is open source under the W3C software license.

Cyberspace: It has been widely used as a general term for the Internet or World Wide Web. More recently blogosphere has emerged as a term for interconnected blogs.

D

DAML: DAML (DARPA Agent Markup Language) is a markup language for the Semantic Web. The goal of the DAML effort is to develop a language and tools to facilitate the concept of the Semantic Web.

DAML+OIL: DAML+OIL is a semantic markup

language for Web resources. OIL stands for Ontology Inference Layer or Ontology Interchange Language.

Dashboard: A kind of control panel in Blogger that shows user the blogs user's set up, giving user access posting, using help resources, or even creating another blog.

Delicious: Delicious is a free online bookmarking service.

Digg: Digg is a social news website that allows members to submit and vote for articles.

DocStoc: DocStoc is an online sharing service for documents. Users can view, upload, share and sell documents.

DTD: (DTD declaration) The <!DOCTYPE> declaration refers to a Document Type Definition (DTD). The DTD specifies the rules for the markup language, so that the browsers render the content correctly. The <!DOCTYPE> declaration is the very first thing in the HTML document, before the <html> tag. The <!DOCTYPE> declaration is not an HTML tag; it is an instruction to the web browser about what version of HTML the page is written in.

E

Entry: An single posting in a blog containing text, images, or other media, or any combination of those things.

ETags: Entity tags (ETags) are a mechanism that web servers and browsers use to determine whether the component in the browser's cache matches the one on the origin server. (An "entity" is another word a "component": images, scripts, stylesheets, etc.) ETags were added to provide a mechanism for validating entities that is more flexible than the last-modified date. An ETag is a string that uniquely identifies a specific version of a component. The only format constraints are that the string be quoted. An ETag, or entity tag, is part of HTTP, the protocol for the World

Wide Web. It is one of several mechanisms that HTTP provides for cache validation, and which allows a client to make conditional requests.

EventBrite: Eventbrite is a provider of online event management and ticketing services.

F

Facebook: It is a social-networking service that enables user to keep in contact with families and friends via the Web. Facebook is the largest social network in the world with more than 500 million users.

Feed URL: A feed URL is the Web address of a news feed, Javascript include or RDF metadata. The feed URL is made of three parts: the Base URL for the service is the part that points to the Metacentric Web site; unique Site ID identifies users' own Web site; and the relative Page URL specifies the source of the feed.

Feeds: Feeds are the means by which user can read, view or listen to items from blogs and other RSS-enabled sites without visiting the site, by subscribing and using an aggregator or newsreader. Feeds contain the content of an item and any associated tags without the design or structure of a web page.

Flash: Flash is a popular authoring software developed by Macromedia. It is used to create vector graphics-based animation programs with full-screen navigation. Flash can be used to create interactive rich media content (including text, photos, music, video, vector graphics, voiceover, and a wide variety of motion graphic. Adobe Flash (formerly Macromedia Flash) is a multimedia platform used to add animation, video, and interactivity to web pages.

Flash Mob: The term flash mob is generally applied only to gatherings organized via telecommunications, social media, or viral emails. A flash mob is a large group of people who assemble suddenly in a public place, perform an unusual and pointless act for a brief time, and then quickly disperse.

Flex: Flex (Adobe) is a software development kit (SDK) released by Adobe Systems for the development and deployment of cross-platform rich Internet applications. Adobe/Macromedia Flex takes to the next level of web application development with the concept of Rich Internet Applications (aka RIAs).

Flickr: Flickr is a social network based around online picture sharing. A Web site that allows user to share, organize, edit, and otherwise manage his photos. The service allows users to store photos online and then share them with others through profiles, groups, sets and other methods.

FOAF: FOAF (an acronym of Friend of a friend) is a machine-readable ontology describing persons, their activities and their relations to other people and objects.

Folksonomy: Folksonomies are the way folk create less structured ways of classifying by adding tags.

Forums: Forums are discussion areas on websites, where people can post messages or comment on existing messages asynchronously. Earlier the forums were the main means of conversing online.

Foursquare: Foursquare is a social network in which friends share their locations and connect with others in close physical proximity to each other.

Friends: These are contacts whose profile user link to in his profile.

Front-end usability: It is the user interface portion of a piece of software; the portion of the software that faces the user; opposite of back-end, the underlying functionality of the application.

G

GDrive: GDrive is a service by the Search Engine giant

Google that would enable users to access their personal computer from any internet connection making the desktop computer virtually redundant, predict technology experts. The GDrive System meant to Google's all existing web-based services to make them easier to use together. It was capable of storing the user's personal files and operating system on Google's own servers and accessed via the Internet. The GDrive would make it possible to access and update information like emails, photographs, music, documents and spreadsheets from any device with an Internet Connection. Currently it's called Google Docs. The Docs service to allow its users to upload files of any type to it, from .aac to .zip.

Google Buzz: Google Buzz is a social networking and messaging tool from Google.

Users can share links, photos, videos, status messages and comments organized in "conversations" and visible in the user's inbox.

Google Chrome: Google Chrome is a free web browser produced by Google that fully integrates into its online search system as well as other applications.

Google Documents: Google Documents is a group of web-based office applications that includes tools for word processing, presentations and spreadsheet analysis. All documents are stored and edited online and allow multiple people to collaborate on a document in real-time.

Google Wave: Google Wave is a collaboration tool developed by Google as a next-generation solution to e-mail communication. A wave is a live, shared space on the web where people can discuss and work together using richly formatted text, photos, videos, maps, and more.

Gowalla: Gowalla is a social network in which friends share their locations and connect with others.

Groups: It is basically the collections of individuals with some sense of unity through their activities, interests or values. A group may use a blog, and an email list may serve a network.

H

Hashtag: A hashtag is a tag used on the social network Twitter as a way to annotate a message. A hashtag is a word or phrase preceded by a "#".

hi5: hi5 is a social network platform.

HootSuite: HootSuite is a web-based Twitter client. With HootSuite, user can manage multiple Twitter profiles, pre-schedule tweets, and view metrics.

I

IANA: The Internet Assigned Numbers Authority (IANA) is responsible for the global coordination of the DNS Root, IP addressing, and other Internet protocol resources.

IMPS gateway: IMPS (Instant Messaging and Presence Service) clients used for Instant Messaging/Chatting and Presence services. User requires a IMPS server to connect to from his handset and he can start chatting with his mobile instant Messenger or update the mobile phone presence to "Free for chat" to start a conversation.

Inference Engines: An inference engine is a computer program that tries to derive answers from a knowledge base. It is the "brain" that expert systems use to reason about the information in the knowledge base for the ultimate purpose of formulating new conclusions.

Inferences: Inference is a word enabling to reach to a conclusion or judgement. It is the act or process of deriving logical conclusions from premises known or assumed to be true. It is also the act of reasoning from factual knowledge or evidence.

Information Retrieval: Information Retrieval is the study of systems for indexing, searching, and recalling data, particularly text or other unstructured forms. Information Retrieval is a field at the intersection of information science and computer science. The term was coined by Mooers in 1951, who advocated that it be applied to the intellectual aspects" of description of information and systems for its searching.

IRC: IRC is a text-based chat system that allows millions of people around the world to communicate in real time. IRC (original code was written by Jarkko Oikarinen) is a multi-user, multi-channel chatting network. It allows people all over the internet to talk to one another in real-time. It is a functional replacement and improvement to 'talk'; 'talk' is an old, primitive, atrocious, minimalist sort of keyboard/screen conversation tool, using a grotesque, machine- dependent protocol (blah!). IRC does everything 'talk' does, but with better protocol, allowing more than 2 users to talk at once, with access across the aggregate Internet, and providing a whole raft of other useful features. IRC is based on a client-server model.

IP address: An identifier for a computer or device on a TCP/IP network. Networks using the TCP/IP protocol route messages based on the IP address of the destination. The format of an IP address is a 32-bit numeric address written as four numbers separated by periods. Each number can be zero to 255. For example, 1.160.10.240 could be an IP address. Connecting a private network to the Internet requires using registered IP addresses (called Internet addresses) to avoid duplicates.

J

J2EE security: J2EE applications are made up of components that can be deployed into different containers. These components are used to build a multitier enterprise application. The goal of the J2EE security architecture is to achieve end-to-end security by securing each tier.

Java: Java is a programming language originally developed by James Gosling at Sun Microsystems (which has since merged into Oracle Corporation) and released in 1995 as a core component of Sun Microsystems' Java platform. The language derives much of its syntax from C and C++ but has a simpler object model and fewer low-level facilities. Java is currently one of the most popular programming languages in use, particularly for client-server web applications.

K

Kyte: Kyte is an online and mobile video application that provides video hosting and stream for both recorded and live video feeds.

L

LDAP provider: LDAP is often used by organizations as a central repository for user information and as an authentication service. There are many different scenarios for how an LDAP server may be configured so Spring Security's LDAP provider is fully configurable. It uses separate strategy interfaces for authentication and role retrieval and provides default implementations which can be configured to handle a wide range of situations. It can also be used to store the role information for application users.

Like: A "Like" is an action that can be made by a Facebook user. Instead of writing a comment for a message or a status update, a Facebook user can click the "Like" button as a quick way to show approval and share the message.

Link: It is a short term for hyperlink. It is a navigation tool that allows a user to go from one Web location to another by clicking. Links are typically underlined.

LinkedIn: LinkedIn is a business-oriented social networking site. It is mainly used for professional networking.

LiveJournal: LiveJournal is a vibrant global social media platform where users share common passions and interests. Pages no longer need to refresh after adding comments, which helps reduce load times. Keyboard shortcuts to ease navigation (Ctrl + enter for a new comment, Alt + left arrow/right arrow moves between pages, Ctrl + Alt + '+ / -' expands or collapses all comments on a page). Buttons for editing, tracking, adding to memories, etc. are now accessed by hovering over a comment, removing general clutter. New comments on pages are marked as such there's a new, more visual icon selection tool.

Logic: It is the science that investigates the principles governing correct or reliable inference. It is also a particular method of reasoning or argumentation. It can be said to be the system or principles of reasoning applicable to any branch of knowledge or study.

Lurker: A lurker online is a person who reads discussions on a message board, newsgroup, social network, or other interactive system, but rarely or never participates in the discussion. Lurkers are people who read but don't contribute or add comments to forums.

M

Malware: It is a destructive program that masquerades as a benign application.

Mashups: In Web development, a mashup is a Web page or application that uses and combines data, presentation or functionality from two or more sources to create new services. The term implies easy, fast integration, frequently using open APIs and data sources to produce enriched results that were not necessarily the original reason for producing the raw source data. A content mashup contains multiple types of media drawn from pre-existing sources to create a new work. Digital mashups allow individuals or businesses to create new pieces of content by combining multiple online content sources. Mashups are the smart mixes that techies do to combine several tools to create a new web services.

Micro-blogging platforms: Microblogging is a broadcast medium in the form of blogging. A microblog differs from a traditional blog in that its content is typically smaller in both actual and aggregate file size. Microblogs "allow users to exchange small elements of content such as short sentences, individual images, or video links".

Multics: Multiplexed Information and Computing Service.

MySpace: It is a social-networking service that enables user to keep in contact with families and friends via the Web. MySpace is a social networking website owned by News Corporation. MySpace became the most popular social networking site in the United States in June 2006 and was overtaken internationally by its main competitor, Facebook, in April 2008.

MySpace profile: User's MySpace identity. It can contain as much or as little information about user as he'd like.

MyPunchbowl: MyPunchbowl.com is a social network that facilitates party planning and provides members with ideas, invitations, favors, gift registries, photo/video sharing, and more.

N

.NET class library: The .NET Framework includes classes, interfaces, and value types that expedite and optimize the development process and provide access to system functionality. To facilitate interoperability between languages, the .NET Framework types are CLS-compliant

and can therefore be used from any programming language whose compiler conforms to the common language specification (CLS). The .NET Framework types are the foundation on which .NET applications, components, and controls are built. de GUI, and server-controlled, client-side GUI. The .NET Framework provides a rich set of interfaces, as well as abstract and concrete (non-abstract) classes.

N3: Notation 3 ("N3") (or the subset called Turtle) is a de facto standard for writing out RDF. It is not a W3C standard, but it is widely deployed, commonly used in email discussions between SemWeb developers, and the most important RDF notation to understand because it most clearly captures the abstract graph.

News aggregation: It is the ability to aggregate news by using RSS feeds. News aggregator allows user's site to pull in information from another blog.

Newsreader: It is a website or desktop tool that acts as an aggregator, gathering content from blogs and similar sites using RSS feeds so user can read the content in one place, instead of having to visit different sites. A news reader allows users to aggregate articles from multiple websites into one place using RSS feeds. The purpose of these aggregators is to allow for a faster and more efficient consumption of information.

Newsvine: Newsvine is a social news site similar to 'Digg'.

Nonhosted service: It is a kind of blog software that user set up on user's own Web server. It allows user to take on all responsibilities related to maintaining user's blog.

O

On-the-fly: On the fly means something created when needed. The phrase is used to mean something that was not planned ahead as well as the changes that are made during the execution of same activity. On-the-fly programming (or live coding) is a style of programming in which the programmer/performer/composer augments and modifies the program while it is running, without stopping or restarting, in order to assert expressive, programmable control for performance, composition, and experimentation at run-time.

Ontology: Ontology is an explicit specification of a conceptualization. The term is borrowed from philosophy, where Ontology is a systematic account of Existence. In computer science and information science, ontology formally represents knowledge as a set of concepts within a domain, and the relationships between those concepts. It can be used to reason about the entities within that domain and may be used to describe the domain. Ontology is about the exact description of things and their relationships. For the web, ontology is about the exact description of web information and relationships between web information.

Ontology Languages: The Web Ontology Language OWL extends RDF and RDFS. Its primary aim is to bring the expressive and reasoning power of description logic to the semantic web. Unfortunately, not everything from RDF can be expressed in DL. For example, the classes of classes are not permitted in the (chosen) DL, and some of the triple expressions would have no sense in DL.

Opera: Opera is an open-source web browser. While not as popular as Firefox, Opera is used as the default browser on some gaming systems and mobile devices.

Orkut: Orkut is a social networking website that is owned and operated by Google. The website is named after its creator, Google employee 'Orkut Büyükkökten'. It is one of the most visited websites in India and Brazil.

OWL: The Web Ontology Language (OWL) is a family of knowledge representation languages for authoring ontologies. The languages are characterised by formal semantics and RDF/XML-based serializations for the Semantic Web. OWL is endorsed by the World Wide Web Consortium (W3C) and has attracted academic, medical and commercial interest. OWL is a part of the "Semantic Web Vision"

OWL-S: Web Ontology Languages for Services. OWL-S (formerly DAML-S) is an ontology of services that makes the functionalities possible.

P

P2P technology: Stands for "Peer to Peer." In a P2P network, the "peers" are computer systems which are connected to each other via the Internet. Files can be shared directly between systems on the network without the need of a central server. In other words, each computer on a P2P network becomes a file server as well as a client.

Pandora: Pandora is a social online radio station. It allows users to create stations based on their favorite artists and types of music.

Parser module: In the parser module, each microsyntax is supported by a pair of classes: a parser and a handler. The parser is a class that implements the Parser interface, which has methods to parse values from a Reader or a String. The microsyntaxes supported by the parser module are: Angles, Clock values, Fragment identifiers, Lengths, Length lists, Numbers. Number lists, Path data, Points, Preserve aspect ratio values, Transform lists.

Parsing: [From the verb parse, from Latin pars/partis a part, abstracted from the phrase pars orationis part of speech].

1. *Analysing a SENTENCE into its constituents, identifying in greater or less detail the syntactic relations and parts of speech.*

2. *Describing a WORD in a sentence, identifying its part of speech, inflectional form, and syntactic function.*

Peer-to-peer: It refers to direct interaction between two people in a network. In that network, each peer will be connected to other peers, opening the opportunity for further sharing and learning.

Perl: Perl is a high-level programming language with an eclectic heritage written by Larry Wall and a cast of thousands. Perl's process, file, and text manipulation facilities make it particularly well-suited for tasks involving quick prototyping, system utilities, software tools, system management tasks, database access, graphical programming, networking, and web programming. Perl derives from the ubiquitous C programming language and to a lesser extent from sed, awk, the Unix shell, and many other tools and languages.

Permalink: A permalink is an address or URL of a particular post within a blog or website. It is the address (URL) of an item of content, for example a blog post, rather than the address of a web page with lots of different items. User will often find it at the end of a blog post.

Photosharing: It is about uploading user's images to a website like Flickr. User can add tags and offer people the opportunity to comment.

PHP: In early versions, PHP used to stand for Personal Home Page. It was renamed to 'PHP: Hypertext Preprocessor'. The expanded form contains the acronym itself, therefore it is a recursive acronym. PHP is a widely-used general-purpose scripting language that is especially suited for Web development and can be embedded into HTML. PHP is mainly focused on server-side scripting, so user can do anything any other CGI program can do, such as collect form data, generate dynamic page content, or send and receive cookies. PHP can be used on all major operating systems, including Linux, many Unix variants (including HP-UX, Solaris and OpenBSD), Microsoft Windows, Mac OS X, RISC OS, and probably others. PHP has also support for most of the web servers today. This includes Apache, IIS, and many others. And this includes any web server that can utilize the FastCGI PHP binary, like lighttpd and nginx. PHP works as either a module, or as a CGI processor.

Podcast: Podcast is audio or video content that can be downloaded automatically through a subscription to a website so user can view or listening offline. A podcast, or non-streamed webcast, is a series of digital media files, either audio or video, that are released episodically and often downloaded through an RSS feed.

Post: 1. (noun) A post is an item on a blog or forum. An entry in a blog containing text, images, other media, or any combination of these. 2. (verb) The act of creating and/ or uploading a blog entry.

Poison URLs: Search engine poisoning attacks use ranking algorithms to link and direct users to websites that host malware. The attacks can be hard to trace because hackers don't require control of the servers involved in the scheme, instead relying on knowledge of vulnerable URLs. Combining HTML code injection with cross site scripting (XSS) lets hackers insert a malicious script into browsers, tricking search engines into indexing dangerous links. When users follow these links, their computers are infected with malware. This has a negative impact on a site's accessibility via search engines. Companies can prevent sites from being abused by protecting web applications against XSS.; protection from malicious references returned as search results is also a responsibility of search engines. Current solutions that warn the user of malicious sites may be enhanced by studying the footprints of a SEP via XSS, allowing more accurate and timely notifications, as well as prudent indexing.

Posterous: Posterous is a blogging and content syndication platform that allows users to post content from any computer or mobile device by sending an e-mail.

PostRank: PostRank monitors and collects social engagement related to content around the web. Essentially it helps publishers understand which type of content promotes sharing on the social web.

Profiles: These are the information that user provides about himself when signing up for a social networking site that contains a picture and basic information.

Protocol: In information technology, a protocol is the special set of rules that end points in a telecommunication connection use when they communicate. Protocols specify interactions between the communicating entities. Protocols exist at several levels in a telecommunication connection. For example, there are protocols for the data interchange at the hardware device level and protocols for data interchange at the application program level. In the standard model known as Open Systems Interconnection (OSI), there are one or more protocols at each layer in the telecommunication exchange that both ends of the exchange must recognize and observe. Protocols are often described in an industry or international standard.

Q

Q-Link: Quantum Link (or Q-Link) was a U.S. and Canadian online service for Commodore 64 and 128 personal computers that operated from November 5, 1985 to November 1, 1995. In October 1991 the name was changed to America Online, which continues to operate the AOL service for the IBM PC and Apple Macintosh today. Q-Link was a modified version of the PlayNET system, which Control Video Corporation (CVC, later renamed Quantum Computer Services) licensed. Q-Link featured electronic mail, online chat (in its People Connection department), public domain file sharing libraries, online news, and instant messaging (using On Line Messages, or OLMs).

Qik: Qik is an online video streaming service that lets users to stream video live from their mobile phones to the web.

Quantcast: Quantcast provides website traffic and demographics for websites. The tool is primarily used by online advertisers looking to target specific demographics.

R

Reddit: Reddit is similar to Digg and Newsvine. It is a social news site that is built upon a community of users who share and comment on stories.

RFC: It is short for Request for Comments, a series of notes about the Internet, started in 1969 (when the Internet was the ARPANET). An Internet Document can be submitted to the IETF by anyone, but the IETF decides if the document becomes an RFC. Eventually, if it gains enough interest, it may evolve into an Internet standard. Each RFC is designated by an RFC number. Once published, an RFC never changes. Modifications to an original RFC are assigned a new RFC number.

Remixing: Social media offers the possibility of taking different items of content, identified by tags and published through feeds, and combining them in different ways. User can do this with other people's content if they add an appropriate copyright license.

Resource Description Framework: The Resource Description Framework (RDF) is an infrastructure that enables the encoding, exchange and reuse of structured metadata. RDF is an application of XML that imposes needed structural constraints to provide unambiguous methods of expressing semantics. RDF additionally provides a means for publishing both human-readable and machine-processable vocabularies designed to encourage the reuse and extension of metadata semantics among disparate information communities. The structural constraints RDF imposes to support the consistent encoding and exchange of standardized metadata provides for the interchangeability of separate packages of metadata defined by different resource description communities.

RIAs: A rich Internet application (RIA) is a Web application designed to deliver the same features and functions normally associated with deskop applications. RIAs generally split the processing across the Internet/ network divide by locating the user interface and related activity and capability on the client side, and the data manipulation and operation on the application server side.

RSS feed: Really Simple Syndication. An RSS feed is a computer-readable version of user's blog, standardized so that it can be displayed in newsreaders and on Web sites and blogs. This allows user to subscribe to content on blogs and other social media and have it delivered to user through a feed.

S

Second Life: Second Life is an online virtual world developed by Linden Lab that was launched on June 23, 2003. Users are called "residents" and they interact with each other through avatars. Residents can explore, meet other residents, socialize, participate in individual and group activities, create and trade virtual property and services with one another, and travel throughout the world.

Seesmic: Seesmic is a popular desktop and mobile social application. It allows users to share content on social networks such as Twitter.

Sidebar : It is a column to the right or left of the main content of a blog that contains navigational links, special highlighting graphics.

Semantic Web: The Semantic Web is a mesh of information linked up in such a way as to be easily processable by machines, on a global scale. It is an efficient way of representing data on the World Wide Web, or as a globally linked database.

Skype: Skype is a free program that allows for text, audio and video chats between users.

SMS gateway: An SMS gateway is a telecommunications network facility for sending or receiving Short Message Service (SMS) transmissions to or from a telecommunications network that supports SMS. Most messages are eventually routed into the mobile phone networks.

SOA: A SOA (service-oriented architecture) is essentially a collection of services. These services communicate with each other. The communication can involve either simple data passing or it could involve two or more services coordinating some activity. Some means of connecting services to each other is needed.

Social network: A service, such as Facebook or MySpace, that enables to keep in touch with people.

Social Media Monitoring: Social media monitoring is a process of monitoring and responding to mentions related to a business that occur in social media.

Solipsis: Solipsis is a pure peer-to-peer system for a massively shared virtual world. There is no server at all: it only relies on end-users machines. The shared virtual worlds of nowadays MMORPG strongly rely on privately owned servers.

SSO : SSO (Single Sign-On for authentication) is the feature that enables a user to receive a single challenge for credentials within a certain realm, and use the returned authentication token for access to other applications which require user authentication. The token is used to both uniquely identify and authenticate the user. When using SSO, the authentication token is provided by a user-authentication process running on the SSO server.

Startpage: A startpage- like Pageflakes, Netvibes or Google Personalised Home page - is web page that user can configure to pull in content from a range of web-based services including email, feeds from blogs and news services. It is a multi-purpose aggregator. Home pages used to be static affairs providing a sort of shop window for a site.

Syntax:

1. *The study of the rules for the formation of grammatical sentences in a language.*
2. *The study of the patterns of formation of sentences and phrases from words.*

T

Tag : It is a keyword assigned to a piece of information, such as an image, a blog entry, or a video clip or other item of content. Tags are usually chosen informally by the content creator or by the online community. They contribute the ease of searching. Tags can usually be freely chosen - and so form part of a folksonomy - while categories are predetermined and are part of a taxonomy.

Tag Cloud: A tag cloud is a visual depiction of user-generated tags, or simply the word content of a site. It is used to describe the content of web sites.

Taxonomy: It is an organized way of classifying content. It allows to add own keywords to endorse folksonomy.

TCO : Total Cost of Ownership (TCO) is a comprehensive assessment of information technology (IT) or other costs across enterprise boundaries over time. For IT, TCO includes hardware and software acquisition, management and support, communications, end-user expenses and the opportunity cost of downtime, training and other productivity losses.

Technorati: Technorati is a popular blog search engine. It provides categories and authority rankings for blogs.

Teleconferencing : It is holding a meeting without being in the same place, using a network connection and tools like Voice over IP, Instant Messaging, Video, and Whiteboards.

Terms of services : These are the basis on which user agrees to use a forum or other web-based place for creating or sharing content.

Threads : These are strands of conversation. On an email list or web forum they will be defined by messages that use the use the same subject.

TOGAF: TOGAF® (The Open Group Architecture Framework) is a registered trademark of The Open Group in the United States and other countries. It is a framework for enterprise architecture which provides a comprehensive approach for designing, planning, implementation, and governance of an enterprise information architecture.

Trackback: It is a technology that tracks references to a blog posting that occurs on other blogs. They allow bloggers to link to blog posts on related topics. Some blogs provide a facility for other bloggers to leave a calling card automatically, instead of commenting. The collection of comments and trackbacks on a site facilitates conversations.

Transparency : It is the way of enhancing searching, sharing, self-publish and commenting across networks makes it easier to find out what's going on in any situation where there is online activity.

Trojan horses: A Trojan horse, or Trojan, is software that is intended to perform desirable (documented or known) effect and a covert (undocumented or unexpected) effect. Trojan horses can make copies of themselves, (perhaps in addition to the expected function) steals information or harms the system. The term is derived from the Trojan Horse story in Greek mythology. Trojan may allow a hacker remote access to a target computer system. Once a Trojan has been installed on a target computer system, a hacker may have access to the computer remotely and perform various operations, limited by user privileges on the target computer system and the design of the Trojan.

TweetDeck: TweetDeck is an application that connects users with contacts across Twitter, Facebook, MySpace, LinkedIn and more.

Tweetup : A Tweetup is an organized or impromptu gathering of people that use Twitter.

Twitter: Twitter is a platform that allows users to share 140-character-long messages publicly.

Twitter Search: Twitter Search is a search engine operated by Twitter to search for Twitter messages and users in real-time.

Tumblr: Tumblr lets users share content in the form of a blog. Users can post text, photos, quotes, links, music, and videos from the browser, phone, desktop, or email.

U

Unconference: An unconference is a facilitated, participant-driven conference centered on a theme or purpose.

Unordered list: unordered list is a series of bulleted items.

URIs: Uniform Resource Identifiers

USTREAM: USTREAM is a live interactive broadcast platform that enables anyone with an Internet connection and a camera to engage to stream video online.

UUIDs: A UUID (Universal Unique Identifier) is a 128-bit number used to uniquely identify some object or entity on the Internet. UUIDs are intended to have a high likelihood of uniqueness over space and time and are computationally difficult to guess. UUID is an identifier standard used in software construction, standardized by the Open Software Foundation (OSF) as part of the Distributed Computing Environment (DCE). UUID is the same as GUID (Microsoft) and is part of the Distributed Computing Environment (DCE), standardized by the Open Software Foundation (OSF).

V

Video blog: A blog consisting of video files, or the practice of placing a video file in a blog post. A video blog is a blog the produces regular video content often around the same theme on a daily or weekly basis.

Viddler: Viddler is a popular video sharing site similar to YouTube and Vimeo in which users can upload videos to be hosted online and shared and watched by others.

Video-sharing service: A service, such as YouTube, that enables user to share video with others.

Vimeo: Vimeo is a popular video sharing service in which users can upload videos to be hosted online and shared and watched by others.

VOS: VOS is a virtual operating system that enables creating a virtual environment similar to Windows OS on the PC. On VOS, user can do everything as he does on Windows, installing and running applications, browse and bookmark the favorites etc. Virtual Object System projects goal is to develop a open platform for multi-user 3D virtual reality games, applications.

W

Web host: The Web server where user software, graphics, and other files live online.

Whitelist: It is a list of preselected users who are allowed to comment on the blog.

Widget: A widget is an element of a graphical user interface that displays an information arrangement changeable by the user, such as a window or text box.

Wiki: A wiki is a website that allows the easy creation and editing of any number of interlinked web pages via a web browser, allowing for collaboration between users.

Wikipedia: Wikipedia is a free, web-based, collaborative, multilingual encyclopedia project supported by the non-profit Wikimedia Foundation. The articles have been written and edited collaboratively by volunteers around the world.

Wizards: A Wizard is a tool to guide a user through the steps of a process or task by asking a series of questions or presenting options. A Wizard might help starting up a word processing document, install software, or create a database file for the first time.

WordPress: WordPress is a content management system. It contains blog publishing tools that allow users to host and publish blogs.

Worms: A computer worm is a self-replicating malware computer program, which uses a computer network to send copies of itself to other nodes (computers on the network) and it may do so without any user intervention. This is due to security shortcomings on the target computer. Unlike a computer virus, it does not need to attach itself to an existing program. Worms almost always cause at least some harm to the network, even if only by consuming bandwidth, whereas viruses almost always corrupt or modify files on a targeted computer.

WSMO: Web Service Modeling Ontology. It is an ontology called Web Service Modeling Ontology (WSMO) for describing various aspects related to Semantic Web Services.

Wuala: Wuala (derived from the French word) is a social distributed file-system-like online storage that allows Windows, Linux and Mac users to save files online. It is a file synchronization program which allows user to have as much online storage as user gives to other wuala users. Wuala is a new way of storing, sharing, and publishing files on the internet. It's a free desktop application for Windows, Mac, Linux, iOS and Android.

X

XFN: XFN™ (XHTML Friends Network) is a simple way to represent human relationships using hyperlinks. Recently blogs and blogrolls have become the fastest growing area of the Web. XFN enables web authors to indicate their relationship(s) to the people in their blogrolls simply by adding a 'rel' attribute to their <a href> tags.

XFN puts a human face on linking. As more people have come online and begun to form social networks, services such as Technorati and Feedster have arisen in an attempt to show how the various nodes are connected.

XSLT: (Extensible Stylesheet Language Transformations). It is a language for transforming XML documents into other XML documents (available in modern Web browsers). It is a powerful XML based functional language.

Y

Yammer: Yammer is a business communication tool. It operates as an internal messaging system for employees within an organization. It is used to provide real-time communication.

Yelp: Yelp is a social network and local search website that provides users with a platform to review, rate and discuss local businesses. Over 31 million people access Yelp's website each month, putting it in the top 150 U.S. Internet websites.

YouTube: A video-sharing service.

Z

Zachman Framework: The Zachman Framework is an Enterprise Architecture framework. The Framework is named after its creator John Zachman, who first developed the concept in the 1980s at IBM. It has been updated several times since. It provides a formal and highly structured way of viewing and defining an enterprise. It consists of a two dimensional classification matrix based on the intersection of six communication questions (What, Where, When, Why, Who and How) with six rows according to reification transformation. The Zachman "Framework" is a schema for organizing architectural artifacts (in other words, design documents, specifications, and models) that takes into account both whom the artifact targets (for example, business owner and builder) and what particular issue (for example, data and functionality) is being addressed.

Zooko's Law: a theory of the qualities of naming systems

ACKNOWLEDGEMENTS

Many sources were consulted for the creation of this glossary:

- *ISBD – International standard bibliographic description: consolidated edition. – Munich: Saur, 2007. (IFLA Series on Bibliographic Control, v. 31)*
- *Lanzi, Elisa. Introduction to vocabularies: enhancing access to cultural heritage information. Los Angeles: Getty Information Institute, 1998. Updated by Patricia Harpring. http://www.getty.edu/research/institute/vocabulary/introvocabs/*
- *http://www.dummies.com/how-to/content/blogging-social-networking-glossary.html*

- *Moen, William. An Overview of Z39.50, Supplemented by a Case Study of Implementing the Zebra Server Under the Linux Operating System http://www.unt.edu/wmoen/Z3950/GIZMO/appendix_d.htm*
- *http://blog.hubspot.com/*
- *RDA: Resource description and access. Glossary draft. 5JSC/Chair/11/Rev (Jan. 2008, Table Available online at: http://www.collectionscanada.gc.ca/jsc/rda.html#drafts*
- *Smith, Allison. Terms commonly used in authority control and thesaurus construction. Word document provided to DC-general listserv.*
- *http://socialmedia.wikispaces.com/A-Z+of+social+media*

INDEX

M

N

R

S

T

U

V

W

X

Y

Z